Dearest Doris

A Chaplain's Letters Home

to Dan & Linda,
with many singing memories

Gerald Fletcher Miller
Chaplain (Captain) U.S. Army
1943-1945

Edited, with commentary, by
Anthony Gerald Miller

Tony M.

Scribblers Press
Summerfield, Florida

Published in the United States of America in 2022 by
SCRIBBLERS PRESS
9741 SE 174th Place Road, Summerfield, FL 34491
www.scribblersweb.com

ISBN: 978-1-950308-39-2

1. Biography and autobiography – Military
2. Biography and autobiography – Personal memoir

Library of Congress Control Number: 2022908376

Introduction

In 1943, Reverend Gerald Fletcher Miller put his life on hold, as so many Americans did, and went to war. His weapons were Bible, hymnal and communion vessels; he brought to battle his faith, compassion, and skill in counseling. He left a parish ministry in East Arlington, Vermont, to serve a congregation of soldiers, doctors and nurses, returning at war's end to a parish in North Waterford, Maine. He left his wife and three children, and returned two years later to his wife and four children. I am that fourth child, conceived in Cambridge, Mass., during Mother's visit to him early in his chaplaincy training, and born shortly before Dad went overseas. He was hoping for a second girl and had the name Alice all picked out; hence he referred to me as Alice until I was born and Mother had to choose a boy's name.

Letters to and from home are the soldier's emotional lifeline—both for the soldier who goes to the fighting front, and for the loving and beloved soldier in civilian dress who "keeps the home fires burning." That was so for me in Vietnam in 1967-68 as much as for Dad in 1943-45. Letters from the absent loved one are read, reread and treasured. Presumably Dad could not keep Mother's letters with him as he moved about Europe, but Mother preserved nearly all his letters home. The earliest ones we have are from his training period in Texas; the latest was written just before he boarded a ship for home.

Reading and editing these letters from my past has been a joy and a privilege. Through them I have gotten re-acquainted with the father I was fortunate to know, and learned much about a part of his life and work I knew little about. Dad's love for his wife and family, his sense of humor and wordplay, and his faith and dedication to duty all shine through. Dad was a good writer, but not a good speller. I have corrected many of his misspellings, but not all. I thought "Missoury Synod" was charming, and things like "autobaun" instead of "Autobahn" add flavor. I have omitted and abridged redundant passages, and added explanations and comments. Dad wrote so well, however, most of the time I've only had to stand aside and let him tell the story.

This selection from our father's letters is dedicated to my siblings: Kenneth, who was nine years old in September, 1943; Priscilla, then seven; Bruce, four; and Paul, born in 1956 when I was twelve. I first compiled, typed, and printed the letters to hand out at a family reunion in 2004; Bruce and Kenneth have since died. I now offer this revised edition, with expanded comments and explanations, in hopes of widening knowledge of my father and his war experiences. A chaplain's work went far beyond planning and holding worship services. He wrote letters for all comers and found ways to fill many needs not met by regular military channels. He provided counsel and comfort for men and women of all faiths, or of no faith. And for those who died in his hospital unit, or never made it to the hospital, he saw to their last needs and final rest.

I owe thanks to Bruce for having the idea; to my wonderful wife Anne Marie for supporting my trip to Vermont to look at the letters; to Priscilla for her hospitality to the letters and to me; to her and Kenneth for valuable comments, and to Anne Marie and our son Douglas for typing and proofreading help. My insertions and comments are in sans-serif type; Gerald's own words are in Times New Roman if typewritten or printed, *italics* if hand-written.

Anthony Gerald Miller
Athens, Georgia, 2022

Below is Private Lieberman's map showing the many places the 111th Evacuation Hospital operated during its time in Europe, 1944-45. This is a scanned copy of a postcard-sized photograph of the original wall-sized map.

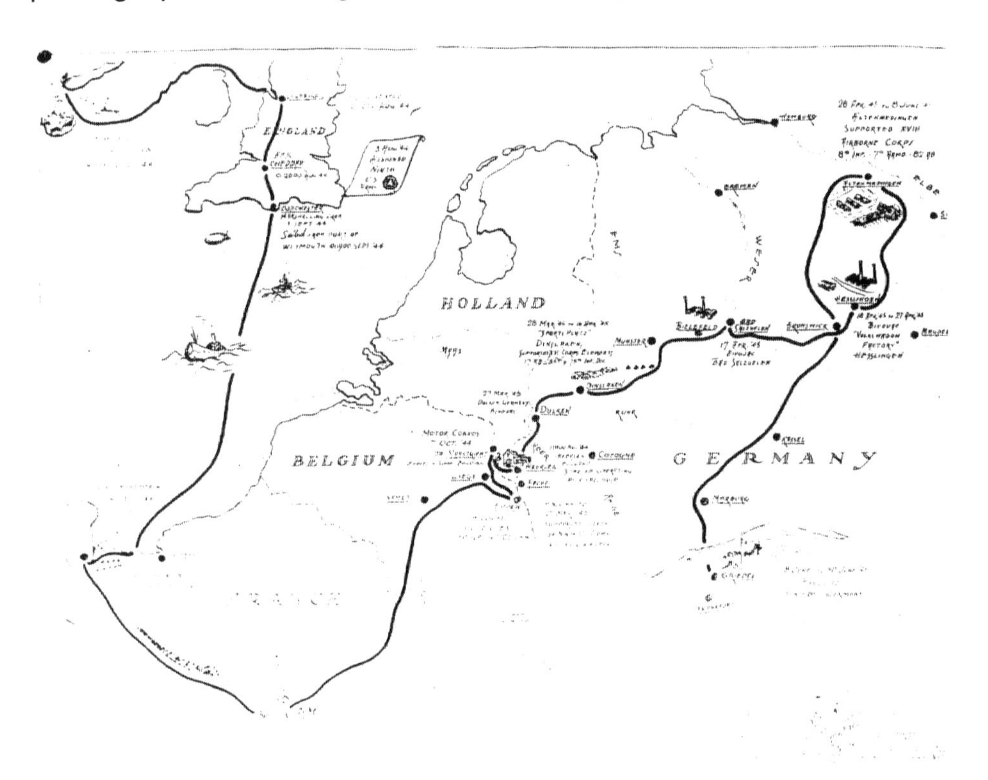

Contents

Illustrations

Texas

Gerald Miller was 41 years old in 1943, an ordained and experienced pastor of the Congregational Christian Church, having served as pastor in

Enosburg Center, Vermont	1928-1932
Westfield, Vt.	1932-1935
Berlin Corner, Vt.	1935-1938
East Arlington, Vt.	1938-1943.

Gerald wanted to help the war effort and volunteered to be a chaplain in the U.S. Army. Already a graduate of Bangor (Maine) Theological Seminary and Middlebury College, he took training for military chaplaincy first at Harvard University in Cambridge, Massachusetts, and then in Texas. His wife, Doris, was able to be with him for at least part of the time in Cambridge, but when he went to Texas, Doris had to stay behind in Vermont.

In this first letter he refers to Doris coming to Enosburgh, Vermont, to live. She and the children (Kenneth, Priscilla, and Bruce) must have moved from East Arlington, Vt., the last parish Gerald served before joining the Army, to stay with her parents, Carroll and Ruth Leach, on the farm in the town of Enosburgh, where she was born and grew up.

Chaplain Gerald Miller
85th Chemical Battalion
Fort D. A. Russell, Texas

September 26, 1943

Dearest Sweet Doris:

I've decided to spend this afternoon writing to the people I care most about. Naturally I start with you. Yesterday I received a

letter from your mother and another from your father and I was very pleased to get them. So I know they aren't mad. Your mother said she enjoyed having the family there this summer. She didn't say so, but I gathered she enjoyed it about as a football player enjoys a game in which he is carried out in the last quarter. She said she was looking forward to your coming up to Enosburg to live.... I am wonderfully relieved that you are going up there to live....

I am working hard now to get things ready for next Sunday which is World-wide Communion Sunday. I have one problem that I can't handle. Of all the close communion sects the Lutherans of the Missouri Synod cannot be served. There is no local church for them here and they won't take communion from my unconsecrated hands. If any one of these boys were dying of thirst and I poured out a cup of cool, pure water, he would be glad to take it from my hands and live.... But the handling of the element by me interferes with what they call the "real presence" of Jesus Christ. You see, Jesus belonged to the Missoury Synod. Judas did, too. He held the bag. Apparently they expect me to.

Anything like that makes me mad.

...I'm enclosing an air mail stamp. Won't you please write me just a page or so as soon as you get to Enosburg Falls. I want to know that you are safely there, how you feel, and that you are comfortable for the day and night....

Please remember I am thinking of you often and that every thought is one of love. I am wishing for you and every wish is for your health and comfort. I haven't heard much nor said much about the children. I am loving you entirely so that they will know what a fine mother they have and love you more. I am trusting you.

Your lover always,
Jerry

This next letter shows Gerald's concern for Doris's sister Edna, who was living and working in New York City. She apparently had a boyfriend named Les, but this is the only mention of him.
Gerald also demonstrates how much he admired his wife. My

parents' happiness with each other and their abiding love were the bedrock of my happy childhood. While Gerald was completely committed to his own marriage, this letter shows how compassionate he could be toward those who were not so happily mated.

September 29, 1943

...I am mighty sorry about Edna. Her first letter to me here was so full of feeling and when she told about Les going A.W.O.L. to her I did some investigating here to find out what would happen to him. When she wrote again I was really excited about what the letter might contain but when I opened it and read it I felt as if I had trustingly sat down on a chair that wasn't there.... I wonder, Doris, if we couldn't gang up on her and do some praying for her. I mean for us each to pray, not just for her happiness in general, but to be shown exactly how we can help her or to be told just why she misses the happiness that she should get. She talks about this major and that captain that throws himself at her and she stands aside. Is she thinking of herself? I think she will do well to study herself and see if she can find out what is dragging.

I have done a lot of thinking about the children and I look at the pictures I have of them a great deal. I have been proud of them but when I think of how well they do and how nice they look I realize it is due mostly to their mother. She's the jewel of the family. Honestly, I think Kenneth and Priscilla and Bruce have the best mother I know anywhere. Mighty fortunate kids. And are you interested to know the different reasons why?

1. Their mother is young and lovely. [Doris was 30 years old when he wrote this, eleven years younger than Gerald.] *When Kenneth shows his mother off a few years later at high school or college graduation he is going to notice how favorably she compares with the mothers of the other boys.... And when Priscilla begins to bring home young people she's going to discover that they will fall in love with you and want to come again and again.*

2. You have always been so careful to send them out looking their best whether they were sweet smelling babies or kids ready for school. Nothing has taken precedence over them.

3. You have been so careful to explain the reasons for everything so that, though you have been the queen, you have not been a despot. They come to you for explanations of everything and consequently they will keep coming.

4. You have spent so much time reading to them what they wanted. Dishes could wait and did. House could wait and did. The natural inference was that they were more important than dishes and housework. And I think they are.

5. No lying, no sneaking away. When we went out they knew it. They didn't wake up calling for Mother when she wasn't there.

6. You always looked so nice yourself. Do children notice that? If they did they could see how their mother always looked good enough to kiss and good enough to enjoy a hug from.

...I was in conference with the commander of Co. B about this chap I wrote you about who wants to get a divorce from one girl so he can marry another girl who is already 3½ months along with his baby. We are trying to arrange so he can get enough time off to make a personal appeal to his wife. Tough situation!

...Tell the children I'll write to them again soon and tell them how much I appreciate their helping their mother....

Be good to yourself and don't forget to pray for me that I may be equal to this big task. Pray that nothing will happen to prevent your coming down. Pray that you will find me as lovable to you as I hope to be. And don't forget to write and tell me that you love me even if you are too tired for anything else. When you finish a letter like this one it gives me a great big lift. Don't let me down like your sister does. Let me know what is in your heart.

Mine is pounding for you.

Your loving sweetheart
Jerry

Here Gerald is planning for Doris to visit him in Texas. The army paid him better than the small-town churches he served before and after the war, but making the money stretch to cover needs was still a constant concern. Meanwhile, supplying the chapel in wartime had its challenges.

October 4, 1943

Dearest Doris:

I've been working hard for you today. First of all I went down town and reserved the room at the hotel. A room with a double bed. Boy! When I can spend the night with you there'll be room. And when I can't spend the night with you it's conceivable we might use that bed together for a while, huh? And you'll have all those days living in a hotel. All the time you're here, if you like it. Gee! I'm excited over it. Your mention of a trousseau makes me think I'm getting married again. It seems more thrilling to me than our first wedding. Twenty-two more days and then I'll have you.

...I [went] to the Red Cross officer and borrowed the top amount he could let me have, seventy-five dollars... I don't believe this will be enough for the complete fare and reservations. Perhaps if you ask for an upper berth it will. How are you fixed for dough? ...If there is no other way you can ride part way by day coach...and after you get here you'll have weeks to lie down and rest with an adoring husband to love you and caress you, and ask you, "shall I put on a rubber overcoat?" ["Rubber overcoat" must be a euphemism for condom. Mother told me decades later that when they first married, their doctor advised them to put off having a baby by using condoms for birth control. He gave Dad a note to take to the pharmacist. Very different times from today, when condoms are out on the open shelf in every drugstore! At this time, though, Mother was already pregnant with me, so why would they bother?]

I certainly had my ups and downs last week. On Thursday I was so elated I was ready to sing and dance (as well as I could). I went out on the rifle range with about sixteen other officers to shoot for record once more. I wanted so badly to qualify as expert.... On the last two shots I had to get a five and a four to make it. I got two fives! Was I happy! I had made expert and one point over. That's forty points better than what the enlisted men are required to do. Here, at least, I am up to officer's standard.

On Friday I had my downs. I had put a great deal of work into publicizing World Wide Communion Sunday.... Friday I went to mess and checked with the matron on the grape juice supply. I had spoken for a bottle of grape juice the Sunday before. She told me she had commandeered it all for her punch to be served on Sunday afternoon, another floorsweeping affair.... And she gave me the encouraging news, "And I don't think you can buy any down town." That made me feel bad, not so much because of the lack of the grape juice as to think that my speaking for something for a religious purpose had so little weight. So I went over to the P.Ex. bar and ordered six bottles of Delaware Punch, a soft drink with grape flavor and color. Then I went to the hospital and tried to see Sergeant Roberts to see if he would play for me. I was a little worried over that, too, because he is Jewish and I didn't know how he would feel about playing for the Communion service. But when I got there I discovered that he was in the hospital as a patient. Well, I was blue. No wine, no music. And after all this advertizing. Whew!

I remembered the old song, "Take it to the Lord in prayer?" So I did. On Saturday I got up with that do or die spirit... First I went to the Commissary. No grapejuice there. But I saw a captain and a lieutenant there and got points to buy it if I could find it. It helped me to see how anxious they were to help me even though the captain was a Catholic. Armed with the [ration] coupon book and the moral support they gave me...I went into four grocery stores and in the last I found an imitation that smelled so much like it that I bought it, and without points. I went to the editor's office and asked there for the names of persons who might play for me and the editor's wife said she would. When I came back to dinner the matron asked me what luck I had and when I said I hadn't found any grape juice (I didn't tell her about the imitation or the Delaware Punch) she said, "I'll let you have a bottle." So in that short morning I went from darkness to light. We had 107 out for chapel Sunday morning and fifty stayed for communion afterwards. And Mrs. Jacobs, the editor's wife, turned out to be just about as good a pianist as Dorothy Lawrence.

...You know, I was mighty proud and happy to take you as my own back there in 1932. But, if it is possible, I'm looking forward to this even more.... I think we had to be separated for me to know how much I can miss you and how much I can love you....

Yours with love,
Jerry

Doris rented a second-floor apartment in Enosburg Falls, the shopping and population center of the town of Enosburgh. (I've seen these different spellings on the town website.) "The Falls" are six miles from the Leach farm by road—mostly gravel roads in the 1940's.

Sunday
October 10 [1943]

Dearest Doris,

How do you like your new home? Is it home yet? I am looking eagerly for a letter from you which tells me, I hope, that you have arrived, are comfortable and not too tired and that everything came all right. I am wondering if you got enough help to carry the piano up stairs...and most of all I wonder about you. How you are and what you are thinking about....

I expect the children have received my letter by this time.... I do hope they get along in school as well at the Falls as they did in Arlington. I expect all three are excited about moving and find a great deal in interesting things to do. Tell Priscilla I was seven when I experienced our first move from Natick, R.I. to Danielson, Connecticut. While I was still seven we moved again from Danielson, Connecticut to Fall River, Mass. I had my eighth birthday in Fall River but before school started in the fall we were off again to Newtonville, Mass. I had my ninth birthday at 14 Clarendon Ave. in Newtonville, my tenth at 94 Bowers St. where we could sit on the fence and see the trains go by, and my eleventh, twelfth and thirteenth birthday at 28 Churchill St. Think of what all these moves meant to my mother.

...Well, sweetheart, remember I love you. There's a heart here in Texas that beats for you. When you come here and see me you just listen and you'll hear it saying "Doris, Doris, Doris, Doris,"

seventy-five times a minute. I have two arms here that will find their way around you just as naturally as if they belonged there. I have two lips here that will gravitate towards yours and want to stay there. I have two hands that are going to be mighty hard to control when you're within their reach. See what I mean?

October 14, 1943

Dearest Doris:

Your letter arrived this morning and it did me more good than any letter I have ever received.... When I read that last paragraph a wave of emotion gripped me so strongly I gave myself away to tears. It means so much for you to love me! More than anything else I know of.

I am immensely relieved to know you are safely delivered. How magnificent of your brother and Wilbur to help you out so. [Doris's younger brother, Carroll Leach Jr., lived on the farm with his wife, Virginia. Wilbur Wright was a cousin.] And your dad and mother, too.... I am mighty glad you took meadows [the dog] along. About the time Alice [the name Gerald had selected for their second daughter, now (he hoped) in Doris's womb] makes her appearance I'm going to ask for my first leave so I can be right on hand to comfort you and get in the way of the nurse.

...Do you remember the man I wrote you about who wanted so much to get a divorce so he could marry the girl who is now carrying around within her his son or daughter? I have been working might hard for him. We managed to get him a furlough and he went home, obtained the divorce and has brought the girl down here with him. I have been working mighty hard to find a place for her to work for her lodging and after trying three possibles and found them blanks I got a call last night from a major's wife offering just the thing if she can qualify. If it goes through I honestly think I have taken part in saving a life. And if it does work out well I believe more thoroughly than ever in prayer....

In his first interview with me this man told me something that opened my eyes a little. In explaining how he happened to get married in the first place he told of having a stepmother with whom he could never get along. He also said his father never paid any attention to him. He would have liked nothing better, as a boy, than to go fishing or hunting or to a game with his father, but he would have none of it. A little more friendliness on the part of his father might have made a great difference in his life. I listened and took note and made resolutions.

...I am certainly looking forward to your coming and I can hardly realize it is only twelve days more. I don't know how long you are planning to stay but the longer the better for me. Perhaps I can give you some idea of how much I love you while you are here.

Yours with all my love,

Jerry

P.S. Since I concluded this letter the Colonel called up and said I have been transferred to Fort Swift in Bastrop, Texas.... I'm going to leave on next Monday.

I still want you to come down but I suggest you make it about three days later. Start on Monday, the 25th... I'll have all the more to show you.

Jerry

October 15, 1943

Dearest Doris:

Your second letter arrived today and I can see that you are worried about money. Poor Doris! It's no fun worrying about money when you need it so badly. But don't let the lack of money stop you! [Discusses possible arrangements for a loan.]

People who have been there say Camp Swift is a swell place. Perhaps our arrangements will be such that I can't have you there so long as I could here, but I know we'll have at least two glorious weeks together. <u>Let Nothing Hinder You</u>. I want you!

[hand-written above printed Fort Russell address:]

111th Evacuation Hospital
Camp Swift, Texas

October 19, 1943

Dearest Doris:

Here I am at Camp Swift at last. What a big place it is and what a lot is going on all the time! We are about forty miles from Austin and about seven miles from Bastrop and about five hundred miles nearer Vermont than we were in Marfa....

My address is the 111th Evacuation Hospital. It is just being formed. In fact, it is not really being activated until tomorrow. I have met my commanding officer, Colonel O'Brian, and a few of the other officers. We are associated with the 110th Evacuation Hospital here now and I suppose their chaplain and I will share the same chapel and work together somewhat. This is going to be so different from what I am used to that I shall spend much of my time trying to find my way around....

One of the first things I did when I got in to Austin yesterday morning was to go to the Austin Hotel and reserve a room for you. I think, after your long trip you will appreciate a day of complete rest. I am quite sure I can make arrangements to stay with you every night while you're there....

P.S. I'm expecting you on Wed. afternoon Oct 27 in Austin. I'll be there to meet you. Telegraph me if your plans are otherwise.

Jerry

Doris arranged for Kenneth and Priscilla to stay with our Great-Aunt Helen Maynard, Grandma Leach's sister, who lived on Church Street, Enosburg Falls. Bruce went to stay with our grandparents on the Leach farm. Thus the children were cared for while Doris traveled by train to Texas alone.

Naturally Gerald wrote no letters during Doris's 2½-week visit. What bliss it must have been to Gerald can be seen from his first letter afterwards, written while she was still on the way home.

111th Evac. Hosp.
Camp Swift, Texas
Nov. 19, 1943

Dearest Doris:

...I was mighty glad no one came along and spoke to me just after your train pulled out last Tuesday. There was an empty feeling that took hold of me and I'm sure tokens of that empty feeling would have been noticed in my eyes and in my voice. It is hard to believe that one small engine and one short train could take so much away from me. But I console myself that another set of trains and a couple of buses can carry me to you next year.

Doris routed her train trip home to take her by New Orleans to visit a cousin.

November 20

Your card and letter came in this morning. I was glad you could see New Orleans and meet your relative. Your mother will be very pleased to know you could do both.

This is Saturday afternoon and I am reading "One Foot in Heaven" by Hartzell Spence. He's the one who wrote "Get Thee Behind Me." He's a major in the U.S. Army and the editor of "Yank," the army paper. I'm enjoying the book as much as the movie.

As usual, most of our officers are leaving for the week-end. I'm staying in because of three reasons all of which are, I haven't much money. If I go to Austin I am sure to see something I want to get for you. If I get it I won't have the money to buy a ticket back. If I don't get it I'll wonder, "How can I tell Doris I love her when I never give her anything but bad advice?" So I'm staying in until I get ready to take a long journey.

November 22, 1943

...We had a little visitor in chapel yesterday morning. A very little visitor. He weighed perhaps nine pounds. He did not have any

G.I. uniform but was clothed with a black and white coat and, since the temperature was about fifty outside, no pants. He came in before chapel started and, not being properly attired he was carried out. Again he entered and was quite curious about the texture of the carpeting before the alter. He scrutinized it with both his eyes and his nose. He wanted to know whether it was from either Persia or Angora, in either case he would be ready to chase it up a tree. About then he was once more picked up and ushered out, and the door was closed in his face. After service started and we were singing about the cross of Jesus being like the shadow of a great rock within a weary land he entered again. Apparently he didn't like the attitude of Chaplain Morford because he looked at him down, or rather, up his nose and then barked at him. Several grins from various people including Chaplain Miller. Again he was taken out. That was too much. He'll go back home later on and look over every church in town and say, "I've been thrown out of better places than this."

...I went over to Wake Island with [Chaplain Morford] ...a new outfit has moved into that area and it has two chaplains. One is a stout man from the Episcopal church and the other a small man from the Catholic. The former is a captain and takes charge. He and Morford had a long chat about what they were doing with emphasis upon the Episcopal part of it while I just listened. I felt that they considered the getting of a few men ready for confirmation the climax of their ministry here. They talked about a visit of a bishop to Camp Polk and, being a typical Episcopal bishop he was broad of girth rather than broad of mind. He got into a tank and he was so long getting out of it that he was almost late for his next appointment. Then and there I discovered the difference between a medium tank and a heavy tank. A medium tank becomes a heavy tank when an Episcopal bishop gets into it....

November 23, 1943

Dearest Doris:

...It's still a mystery who sent that gorgeous box of cookies.

Gee it's good!... I've been for the mail and there is no clue yet as to who the sender may be. And there's no word from you either, darn it. One of these days when other things have gone bad and I'm discouraged and I don't hear from you on top of it all I'm going to do some wondering that won't be at all good for my morale. I wish you'd get on to yourself as a correspondent. As a sweetheart in one's own home and in his own town and in his own arms you leave nothing to be desired. But as a sweetheart two thousand miles away you are enough to make a chaplain want to see the chaplain.

November 26, 1943

Dearest Doris:

I have been very unjust. Please forgive me. Your card mailed Saturday arrived today. Probably there is a letter in the mail from you. I am glad to know you got there [New York City] *all right and that Edna was on hand to meet you....*

... I've been a model chaplain since your departure. Only once have I left the post and that was with Morford in a jeep.... I saw a dart game I would like to get for Kenneth so I could play with it when I came home. But I guess I won't get it because I don't believe you have any walls you would like to have peppered full of holes. Have you. I think instead I'll get Kenneth a pincushion, Priscilla a Greek grammar and Bruce a year's subscription to "The Nation's Business."

December 1, 1943

Dearest Doris:

Your air mail letter and the other letter arrived yesterday. I was so glad to get them that I sat down and read them both the same day.

I find myself asking a lot of questions that no one seems to be able to answer. The Colonel can't answer them. None of the Lt. Colonels can answer them. The major can't and not one of the three captains can. So you will have to. Here they are:

1. How did the ninety dollars hold out? How much have you left? Did you have to skimp and go without things you needed?

2. How do you feel after your long trip? How does Alice behave?

3. How are the children? Has Kenneth received his present yet?

I look upon our seventeen days together as the seventeen most perfect days of my life. I have come to the conclusion that the best gift this world has to offer me is your presence.

I didn't have a very large range of choice in picking out Kenneth's present. It was either that or something to wear. If it were something to wear it would have to be earrings or bracelets or lockets or a pin. I knew if I got a pin for Kenneth I would be expected to get one for Priscilla and Bruce and Alice so I decided against that. Besides, Kenneth has always wanted a billfold. At least for the last ten years. So I thought, if he had a billfold he would save up his allowance money long enough to have a few dollar bills to put into it.

...I am to give a Current Events talk this afternoon. I am also to tell the men not to bring their wives. And to give the reasons for it. I don't know how these men will react to this but I feel it is my duty to give them all the facts and help them face them.

...Yours with love from one who would like to hold his own right now.

Your lover forever
Jerry

Dec. 5, 1943

Dearest Doris:

Here I am sitting at Chaplain Morford's desk, sitting in Chaplain Morford's chair, using Chaplain Morford's pen. Perhaps I am Chaplain Morford. I hope not. Chaplain Morford is a fine fellow but I like Chaplain Miller's wife better than Chaplain Morford's wife. I like Chaplain Miller's children better than I do Chaplain Morford's children. I like Chaplain Miller's church better than I like Chaplain Morford's church and I like Chaplain Miller better than I like Chaplain Morford. So I hope I'm the former & not the latter. Gee! When I think of all the things I done to, with and for Chaplain Miller's lovely wife I hope I'm the former! Gosh!

...Now we are at the beginning of our third week of our M.T.P (Military training period) and all in a position to know seem to think everything is going on fine. We've had two marches of about four miles each and I gave a lecture on current events. I was quite thrilled after I started to notice the Colonel standing to one side listening to what I had to say. He didn't stay long but he made no move to interrupt me so I took it that what I said was all right.

The Bennington *Banner* ran a story about Gerald's three children welcoming him home in uniform. The news photographer took this picture on the steps of the East Arlington church. Left to right: Doris, Bruce, Priscilla, Kenneth, Meadows.

...Your letter was very interesting and sweet, too. I often think how proud I am about my wife and family. I love you, Doris, and I

am not forgetting how lucky I am to have you.... I bet they [children] *were glad to get you back! If you have any more pictures of them please send me some. I look at the one with you all saluting until it is almost worn out. And I wonder a lot about how you are feeling and about the little life within you. "You are always in my heart."*

Dec. 7, 1943

Hello Sweet Thing!

...This morning I answered [East Arlington friend] *Ruth Grout's letter by writing one to Joyce & Dorothy. I put a lot of foolishness in it, purposely getting Mrs. O'Brian mixed up with Noah's ark, the officers here with Haman's sons and made a few wise cracks, 75% original. I suggested that I might be losing my mind but I didn't expect to miss it much. They'll agree to that after they read the letter. I hope they have as much fun reading it as I have writing it.*

...I went to the hospital today and called on five men from the 85th who caught cold coming over from Marfa. They made the trip 480 miles by jeep and slept on the ground one night. Out of 850 men only 12 were subjects for the hospital. I called on one of our men who wanted me to see what I could do about getting him a furlough. Poor chap! He's been in since Nov. 11. His outfit was already to go to parts unknown when he wrenched his knee. He wants so much to go home for Christmas. His father is a traveling man and will be home for a week at that time. His girl will be there for college and he hopes to see her and make her his fiancée. His girl joins the church on New Year's Sunday and he wants to be there to serve her her first communion. But it's just no go. The more good reasons a man has for going home the less chance he has to get there. How is the Chaplain going to keep a man from feeling bitter? The hospital has dozens of men who feel that being there has cheated them out of a furlough.

...Well, be good my dear. In other words just act natural. As long as you are just Doris you're the girl for me.

Good-bye sweetheart

Dec. 13, 1943

...I took your advice about opening up the box from the Olivet Church and found six maple sugar cakes. I've already eaten five. They were excellent. If you wish to give me something nice for Christmas see if you can make some of the maple pull candy. That and your love, of course. If I can't have both send your love. That means more to me than candy.

December 14, 1943

Dear Doris:

You may be interested to know that my weekend was brightened up by a letter I received from a lovely lady on Saturday. It told about the birthday of her ten-year-old son [Kenneth] *and the parties that were held on that day. Such a letter is a real gift of love and I treasure it above all other communications.*

We had another Sunday. Morford did the preaching and I conducted the service. We had 37 out. I went to the Post Chapel for the eleven o'clock service and the whole attendance consisted of Chaplain Collier, who directed the service, three enlisted men, Chaplain Gurtner and his wife, the organist, a soloist and your adoring husband. Understand, it is you he adores, not any of the persons present at the service. I'd want to be promoted to Captain if I had to preach to such a small congregation Sunday after Sunday.

...I suppose Edna is up there now.... I was intrigued by your quoting her as saying, "I'd like to have a chance to fix Doris the way I want to. I think I could make her look real pretty." If she can make you look prettier than you can make yourself look in that black dress she's a genuine artist. And if she still has the yen to try her hand on you let her try. But get a statement in writing that she won't do you any permanent injury.... The Doris whom I took to our Mess Hall on those two Sundays you were there with me is just about the loveliest

creature I know anywhere. She's sweet.

...It certainly is thrilling to know there is a home waiting for me and a sweetheart to come into my arms. And I am mighty anxious to see that home and the children in it. You'll have a hard time getting me out of it as long as you're in it. The time is so short I'd like to spend it all with you.

December 16, 1943

Dearest Doris:

Another day, another dollar—gone.

Yesterday was cold and windy. A Norther, as the Texans call it. It made me:

1. Put on my winter underwear.

2. Decide to buy an overcoat.

3. Write you a letter filled with grief because if I bought an overcoat I would have to:

a. Take the money from the $150 I plan to send you or

b. Not come home to see you in January.

But I didn't mail the letter. I was plumb discouraged yesterday. Our outfit was in a field problem and every officer had an assignment but me. I came down to my office convinced that I was a poor relation in my unit and I asked God to transfer me to some place where I can be of some use. I felt bad. I was very sorry for me. I was even willing to exchange my chance for a leave for a position of usefulness.

What do you think of me, Doris? I'm up to my old tricks again of making promises and not keeping them. I promised you $150 per month. You've doubtless planned on that and made your budget accordingly. But yesterday convinced me that I can't get along here without an overcoat.... That will cost $40. I'll only be able to send you $110. Will you still love me or would you rather have a husband 2300 miles away who keeps his promises than one in your arms who doesn't? I leave it for you to decide.

...I suppose you have now made up your mind about where

Alice is to be born. So far none of our children have been born in the same place and I suppose that will be true of Alice. Which will it be, Richford or St. Albans? I suppose next month he who runs can read the story that Alice is on her way. Put in a good store of rubbing alcohol because when I come my primary interest will be you and being good to you all the time I'm there.

Please be sure to have in stock some beans for baking and a bottle of ketchup.... Also please put in an order for oysters for oyster stew while I'm there.

With love,
Jerry.

December 20, 1943

...Today...a man from the 110th came in to see Morford for counsel. I told him this was Morford's day off so he told me his story.... See if you think I advised him right.

[Long story of the young soldier's problems with his wife and the advice Gerald gave him, asking if Doris thought the advice was sound.]

Now Morford has arrived and they are talking it over. I'm going to find out later what his point of view is. It's darn interesting to compare notes like that. Like a consultation of doctors.

So you can see that I'm reasonably content this morning because I've had a little of the kind of work I like. There's no doubt about it, counseling is going to be my field of study. There are some books in the library which I think I'll study on the subject of marriage, for most of my counseling problems resolve themselves into either man & woman relationships, financial difficulty or physical inability to carry the load. The latter I can only refer to the medical officers but the other two I can really sympathize with.

Christmas Eve
1 9 4 3

Dear, Dearer, Dearest Doris:

Christmas Eve and you 2300+ miles away. Oh me, oh mi. So sorry you can't be with me. But your lovely letter arrived....

Shake the envelope and a check will fall out, I hope. It is for $100.00. When I come to you in January I'll leave all the money I have except ten dollars. So I hope this check will last until the middle of next month. After that I think I can give you $150.00 regularly. Now, remember, as boss of our financial affairs, it's up to you to chart our course through the fog of debt, by the ice bergs of extravagance, past the shallow waters of want and into the channel of systematic saving....

We went on our bivouac and had a fine day for it. We marched about three miles and rested. Then we marched three miles more. This time we had two files, one on each side of the road. The men were supposed to keep twenty paces apart. That was to make our losses from machine-gun fire or bombs or gas as light as possible. When we got to the bivouac area we were ordered to keep under cover. At night we went on patrols. Not at all like what I told Kenneth it would be. We were sent out a squad at a time. Each squad had its instructions and a squad leader. We started out at about nine at night and we were to scout until 10:30. The weather was just about like we have in May. Our squad was called the N. squad. We went out quietly. Whenever we saw anyone someone was to challenge him with the word "Roosevelt." If he answered, "Casablanca," we were to allow him to proceed in peace. If not, he was our prisoner if one of us tagged him. We had to be careful lest we find the enemy after he found us because a tag from him and we would be prisoners. So we went cautiously and quietly, drawing closer and closer until ... the enemy was saved by the bell. We had orders to quit at 10:30. We did, like the workman, with the hammer in the air. But going back wasn't all peace. Just about that time we'd hear a "pop." In about two seconds an amber colored flare would appear and light the country for quite an area. We were then supposed to blend in with the ground so we couldn't be seen. This would happen at inconvenient times such as when I'd be over a sand bur bush. I got lots of prickers in my hands. We soon caught on. As soon as we heard that pop we'd fall flat. By the time the flare appeared we were part of the scenery. But the flares were so pretty we wanted to look at them. There were three amber flares about three minutes apart, then three green flares, then a red one. Like fireworks at Max Grout's [in East Arlington]. *When we got in from the patrolling we were allowed to turn in. Like Elijah, I slept under a juniper tree (is that what you call a cedar with blue berries) and slept quite well. We came back the next morning at 12:30. Just in time to miss the swell turkey dinner for the chaplains.*

January 1, 1944

Dearest Doris:

Just a few words to assure you that:

1. I love you and think of you very often.

2. Let you know your presents arrived. I am writing with your pen.

3. My leave has been granted.

4. I love you.

[Discussion of planned travel schedule] *That will give me plenty of time to connect with the bus for St. Albans and the one from St. Albans to Enosburg Falls. So, if I'm lucky I'll be "holding my own" again on Thursday evening January 14, 1944. Oh Boy!*

Tell the children I'll write to them tomorrow.

With love,
Yours
Jerry.

Gerald was able to get home for his January leave. Priscilla remembers looking out the window of their second-floor apartment and seeing her daddy walking up the street from where the bus left him off. This was on Main Street in Enosburg Falls. The next letter shows him back in Texas.

January 30, 1944

...Last Friday I went out to training area no. 5 where our hospital had its tents set up. Gee, what an outfit this is! It looked like a little city. I got an inkling of what my job will be. There will be from thirty to forty ward tents with ten or more patients in each one. My job will be to visit every one of those tents and speak to every one of those patients every day. If not a one of them asks for any service, just the physical effort of visiting four hundred a day will be something. And when this one asks me to do one thing and the next another I can see that I shall be plenty busy.

A movie based on the life and work of Marie and Pierre Curie, the discoverers of radium, reminded Gerald of his own marriage.

February 7, 1944

...On Friday night I went to see Madam Curie, a wonderful picture.... What impressed me most about that marvelous production was not the great discovery but the perfect teamwork between Madam and Pierre Curie. They worked together perfectly, they had supreme respect for each other and their devotion and love for each other, according to that story, was a sacred thing. It brings tears to my eyes even now. It is just the way I feel about you. Perhaps that is why I enjoyed the picture so much.

...I suggest you subscribe for the [Burlington] Free Press or some other paper. A Chaplain's wife ought to keep posted. Perhaps you may even see my picture in it some day over the caption, "Chaplain gets perfect-attendance-at-mess-medal" or, "Chaplain preaches patient to sleep when ether supply is exhausted,"... I've another request for you. The Bible I have been using for the last eleven years is a Christmas present from you, but you never wrote in it. I'm sending it home for you to write your name in. That Bible is going around the world with me and it will be helpful to turn to your name in it when I feel the need of a little comfort. And please dig through the books out back and send the Abingdon Commentary....There is so little of the Bible in the preaching of these army Chaplains and so much of what there is ain't so that I feel the need of correcting that and keeping myself thoroughly grounded on the facts about the different Bible books....

Did you get your Valentine?... I'm going to visit the commissary tomorrow and see if there is any more of Whitmans chocolates there. Lt. Balsley, our WAC organist had one which she brought to our choir rehearsal on Saturday and passed around. Gee! They're good. The lieutenant is about your age and about Edna's size and has come down to help us with our music. She is the kind of girl who doesn't care for dancing and boisterous entertainment à la G.I. and appreciates contact with persons interested in deeper things. She's Episcopalian so Morford appropriates her. However, she is low church instead of high church and she has a brother whose wife is a Quaker, just the other extreme. Morford and I went with her to the movies after choir rehearsal and I found that she is a little more open to 20th century sense than he is.

Lt. Balsley and Gerald's meeting of minds was a consolation to both, as later letters show. She took a great interest in our family and maintained contact with us after the war. I remember her annual gift of fine mail-order pears at Christmas.

Around this time, Doris became aware she would have to move from the apartment on Main Street.

February 13, 1944

...I am as sorry about the moving as you are. I, too, had hoped you would be able to stay there until I could be back to help. But I hope you can find a good place to live in. You certainly are not in any condition to do much moving now. Perhaps, if you wait until after April 15 you may have a boy, although I hope not, and he may be able to help you. Please keep me informed about what you are doing.

...Did Priscilla get her skates all right?

This last week we nailed down some more essentials of our training.... On Thursday we had a "County Fair," a demonstration of what we can do. A patient was brought in and one M.C. (medical corps officer) showed us exactly how a transfusion of blood was done. Then we went to the admission tent and we saw how the E.M.T. (enlisted man's tag) is filled out. We went to the X-ray tent and they had the X-ray machine right there and demonstrated how it works. We went into the operation tent and they demonstrated how an operation is performed. And so, step by step we were educated as to the function of our unit....

This week I expect I shall be called upon to give a talk on "The Post War World." I have been reading up about it quite extensively. The P. & T. officer likes to have me to fall back upon when they have a rainy day. Usually a rainy day upsets the outdoor events scheduled so, when I am ready with a talk or a discussion, they like it....

Today Lt. Balsley, our Wac. organist, invited me to dinner, so I went. Chaplain McKeith, who uses her at the organ in his 11 o'clock service, drove us up there. We ate at the hospital officers' mess where nurses, M.C.s, Wacs, Red Cross workers and civilian workers in the Station Hospital eat. She introduced me to other Wacs and when dinner was over, drove me back here to the chapel. It's refreshing to talk with her because she is a college girl, she is a preacher's daughter and she does a little thinking of her own.

I like the snap-shot I sent to Caroline, and which was returned in her letter, the best of all because it is the very best picture of you I have. Do you remember it? You are standing behind Bruce and looking down at him. I can see your left arm up to the elbow. There is a good view of your face and a slight smile on your mouth. I can see the cheek I have kissed so many times. Your hair is long and only part of your left ear peeks out. You look mighty good in that picture! Just as kissable and hugable as ever. You look like the Doris I know and love. My Doris!

Valentine's Day

Dear Sweetheart:

I'm a tired little man.... But I'm not too tired to answer your letter. Nor is my memory too tired to remember the only other time we were not within a two hour walk of each other on Valentine's Day. On that other occasion I sent you a box of candy, too. Remember? Perhaps on the next one I can send you a pearl plucked right out of the South Seas by a diver at my behest. Until then you'll have to be my pearl of great price.

The next big event will be Bruce's birthday. Wish him a happy one for me. I would like very much to read a story to him. I hope he likes the little books I sent him and I expect Kenneth and Priscilla, both, can read them when you haven't the time.

...How does you mother feel about another move when the last one wasn't paid for yet? I hope you do succeed in staying there until six weeks after Alice is born. You see, I'm figuring since July Fourth just as in Priscilla's case. And I'm basing the new one's sunny disposition to be like Priscilla's for the same reason. Two perfectly blissful Fourths. One when we went bathing together in our birthday suits and afterwards gave ourselves entirely up to each other in love's sublime embrace. That resulted in Priscilla. The other when we were together in quiet on a noisy street and enjoyed what we thought might be our last one for a long, long while. If the real happiness of the first had anything to do with our beautiful Priscilla, Alice ought to be very much like her.

February 20, 1944

Dear Bruce!

Just think. By the time I get this letter to you I shall have lost my 4 year old boy and in his place there will be a five-year old boy. What do you know about that? Are five-year-old boys as good as four-year-old boys? Do they eat all their cereal in the mornings? Do they eat some of all the vegetables their mother gives them? Do they pick up their toys when they get through with them? And do they help their mother as much as they can? After you've been five for a little while I wish you would tell me.

...I'll bet you & Kenneth and Priscilla would like to have been

with me last Thursday afternoon. I went out with Chaplain Morford and we went to the place where they fly airplanes by radio. When we got there we saw four airplanes on the ground and one on the catapult. Kenneth will explain to you what a catapult is. These little airplanes are about eight feet long and have about a 12' wingspread. They have the motor in the nose and a double propeller. One propeller goes one way and the other the other way. When they get ready someone winds up the catapult which draws the plane back. The plane's engine is started and then away it goes. It is controlled on the ground by radio. The man at the radio set makes it climb, bank, dive and loop...and while it was in a position where it was safe to shoot there was a man with a machine gun to shoot at it. After shooting at it 750 bullets he hit it and shut off the gas supply so the motor stopped. Then the man at the radio did something and a parachute jumped out of the plane and the plane floated down as gently as you please. Quite a sight.

I got Mother's last letter this afternoon and I'm going to answer it now. I hope you had a happy, happy, happy, happy, happy birthday. Now I am only eight times as old as you. On your next birthday I shall be only seven times as old. Ask Kenneth to figure out for you how many times as old I was when you were four.

Yours truly
Daddy

February 29, 1944

Bivouacs are usually a great bore for me because I have so little to do, but they are becoming less and less so. I know more about ropes and the use of a sledge hammer than most of the men so I wander from group to group helping where they are short. I helped raise and pitch seven ward tents yesterday. A ward tent is 51' x 15' and 13' at the peak. It weighs 350 pounds. Eight men and a sergeant are supposed to pitch a tent but often they are short a man so I help. It's much better than hanging around as still life.

There's a new major around here who is helping me make a

first class hypocrite out of myself. He offers again and again to give me pointers about military life. That's all right. But he rags the sergeants that probably know more about their job than he'll ever know. I always act pleased to see him and act appreciative of his suggestions. He's even trying to get me interested in his church, the Roman Catholic. Well, I know too much about the history of that church and the practical results of its work in Catholic countries and communities to care a damn about its forms or ceremonies. He gave me a book called, "The Faith of Millions," to read. I put it on the shelf, let it stay there a week and then returned it...

Well, this bud got to discussing birth-control with me. "Does your church believe in the use of contraceptives?" I explained to him that with us it was an individual matter. "But don't you believe that a man ought to have sexual intercourse with his wife alone?" I admitted that we did. "Don't you look upon the reproduction of children as a gift of God?" I said we did. Then I pointed out that it was grossly unfair to a woman to make her have a baby every year, as he does his wife. I pointed out that the denial of that instinct usually led to unbalance on one hand, and the having of a large family with a small means was not fair to the children. I also pointed out that, with our advance in medicine it was not necessary to have twenty children in order to have five grow up as was true in Mexico. He was called away then so our discussion terminated. It is just as well for in time I would let him know what I thought of his priest-ridden mind and what I thought of him in the bargain. I hope he or I get transferred elsewhere before that time comes.

I asked Morford how he broke the news of his promotion to his family. He said his wife noticed it before he got out of the car and screamed so loudly his mother thought there was an accident. "She was more thrilled over it than I was." I guess she's pretty proud of her man now.

I'm might glad you are reassured about your health. I hope you won't hesitate to tell me all about your worries and problems. I am more interested in you than anybody in the whole world. About this time next month I shall be anxiously waiting from day to day to find out about the great event.

I'm going to close this letter now. I'll write again soon.

Your lover,
Jerry

March 5, 1944

...Our Wac Lt. who plays the organ in Chapel 4 was in for a while last night to see my office and complain about the petty tyrannies of the army. I was hoping she would be in again to complain some more. I could lead the conversation from Cabbages and Kings [a novel by O. Henry] *to books and discussion of literature or Bible criticism, subjects I so seldom have a chance to talk about. Sometimes I feel the need of a bath for my soul which is always associating itself with army life and discussion. How I long for you to talk to and to be with. I sure will be glad when the time comes that you will be within the sound of my voice twelve hours of every day! Well, that is ahead of me, I hope, and not too far away, either.*

The package with my Bible and other books arrived yesterday. And the cookies. They were very good and I ate them all up this morning. The cookies, I mean. It was so nice of you to send them that I love you all the more. I would like to kiss the hands that made them. I would like to rub my nose against the nose that first smelled them cooking. I would like to look into the eyes that first saw them. And I'd like to kiss the lips that belong to the person whose hands, nose and eyes I mention above. (Gosh! wouldn't it be awful if someone else made them!)

March 12, 1944

From what you say about yourself the big day must be nearing. I am glad your good mother has cooperated so well in providing things for you. I'm beginning to expect and think, "by this time next month I'll know whether I have another girl or another boy." I wish I could be near you this time as before to give you all the moral support I can. I'm praying for you, dear girl, and sending to you all the spiritual force my love for you can produce. I hope it will be a girl with the name of Alice written on it. But if it's a boy I hope Alice will not be written on it for that will have to be changed. I'm leaving the naming up to you in case it's a boy. Anything you like will meet with my approval.

I am beginning to discover among our officers a few very good friends. Col. King is a source of great comfort to me. He is second in rank in our unit and a Methodist. With the exception of the two Sundays his wife was here he has been out to service here at Chapel 2 every Sunday. Very occasionally he gives me a friendly word and a little helpful advice. Major Lewis is another who has been very good, too. He never calls me chaplain but always Boy or Young feller. On bivouac I always find a friendly welcome in his tent. I have also occasional boosts from Captain Lyons, one of our dental officers. It's a big help. And when I stopped to think how much their friendliness means to me I became aware how insecure my position is. Almost unique in this army. A Protestant Chaplain in a Unit which has among its men only 30% Protestants and among its officers 40% Protestants finds it mighty difficult to reach his men.

Another source of comfort is the occasional conversations I have with Lt. Balsley, our Wac organist. She dropped in on Saturday evening a week ago after playing for an hour or more on the organ. We began to talk about many things of mutual interest. When she mentioned several composers of musical productions I was very quickly out of my depth. But when the conversation swung around to different theories of worship and Bible criticism and history I was right in my element. She presented the only opportunity I have to talk about those things. I think I wrote you that she invited me to have dinner with her at the hospital and that I invited her over to our mess hall in return. I had her to dinner again yesterday and at supper the men had lots of fun kidding me about it. When the Colonel hears about it he's going to take me for a long ride. Just about all he ever says to me is in the jocular mood. Out on bivouac last Monday he was true to form. We had just set up the operating tent and Sergeant Tisa, who was the non-com in charge said, "Do you suppose I can get the Chaplain to steal some gas for me?" Colonel O'Brian said, "He won't steal it for you but if you steal it he will pray like hell for you afterwards." So, I can see that he'll have some crack about me leading a double life. How do you feel about it, dearest? I will be entirely guided by you.

I'm gaining a reputation as a preacher down here. Chaplains, as a whole, seem to be notoriously poor preachers. Morford says he likes to have me preach for him. I still help him with the nine o'clock service at Chapel 4 and preach there every other Sunday. I use the same sermon up here at Chapel 2. I am using a Jewish man, one of our own men, as organist. He told me yesterday evening that he enjoyed very much the sermon I preached. It was on Philippians 4:8. "Think on these things." I pointed out how Philippians was Paul's best letter to his favorite church. I compared it to the letter each of us writes to his very best friend, whether that friend be wife, mother, father, brother, sister, buddy or what not. This man said he mentioned it to his wife and he became particularly interested in Philippians. Well, a few compliments are as grateful to me now as ever.

I certainly hope all things work together for good for you, my dear. Each day I am going to get more anxious for you. I am glad for you that moving won't come until you have gone through with your great effort and have taken many steps towards recovery. And I thank you for your last paragraph. I quote, "Oh my dearest, how I love you." It is a great comfort to read it. I want to be where I can hear you say it and see you say it and kiss your lovely lips at every word.

To Doris's father, Carroll Leach, Sr.:

March 14, 1944

Dear Carroll:

...I am making out a check for $5.15. The $5 is to get some flowers for Doris while she is in Richford recovering from the big

event about to take place. The 15¢ is to cover the collection charge which, I expect, will be the cost of cashing this check. Please see to it that some nice flowers such as roses or carnations or something lovely that Doris would like get to her bedside as soon as she can enjoy them. Have them put this new shoulder patch in as my card.

Doris writes that she expects the new arrival will make its appearance in a couple of weeks. I shall be more and more anxious each day until I hear that the new Miller is safely ushered in and that Doris is not in any danger at all.

And this naturally leads me to the subject which is a very tender one with me. It is the wonderful care you and Mother Leach have taken of Doris and our little family. Not only now, but all through our married life you have both been their guardian angels. I have been in a position before to help Doris a little when she was going through the trying time before, but now I have to leave it all to you.

The Leach farmhouse in the 1940's

March 15, 1944

Dear Mother Leach:

...Let me give you a peek at today's schedules. At ten o'clock Chaplain Morford is going to stop by for me and offer to give me a ride to a Chaplains' meeting. The chaplains of the 23rd Corps, of the 102nd Division, of the Fourth Army Special troops and of the Station Compliment will be there, perhaps. This will include about twenty-five chaplains, but I shall be surprised if more than ten get there. Chaplains, like ministers, like to have meetings for some else to attend. Most of them resemble David Harum who decided to go to church regularly, every Thanksgiving day, but he missed the second and lost interest. But I'll be there if for the same reason that the man who sat on the varander went to the cemetery, just for the ride. This afternoon we are going to have a demonstration of how our hospital handles casualties from the receiving tent to the finish. Of the forty or so one is going to die. I'll be ushered into the picture and asked to bury him. I have to take his dog tags off, wrap one in a piece of cloth and put it on his body and the other I have to tack on the grave peg. I have to search his clothes and make a list of all his belongings. I have to wrap them and label them and if he is the kind of a boy who has pictures he wouldn't want his mother to see I'm supposed to burn them up. Then I make a map of the area where he is buried and mark his grave so that it can be easily found by those who come later to exhume him and put him in a permanent cemetery. Then I have to have a suitable ceremony so that the gates that swing outward ever won't close in his face. This evening from eight till twelve we have a practical problem in map reading. We'll wander hither and yon in search of the golden fleece or the end of the rainbow on the basis of a map made from an aerial photograph. We won't be so lucky as last week because there is no moon. And then to bed. So, you can see what I mean by hinting that I might not finish this letter today.

Now that I have moved up to Chapel 2 I am having a much more interesting time of it. Back there at Chapel 4 we were at the dead end of the street and almost no one ever came in. Besides most who did come in stopped at the first office, that of Chaplain Morford. From October 20 until February first I had exactly eight interviews in my office at Chapel 4. In four weeks up here at Chapel 2 I have contacted ten different men, some of them several times. And, believe me, some of those men have problems that challenge the ability of Solomon. I don't know what good I'm doing in this army but the army is certainly increasing my experience and enriching my small fund of knowledge about human nature. Remember how Mrs. Rosewall of Sandgate used to come over and whine out her troubles to me? Well we have a lot of soldiers, so called that do the same. Some I get pretty sick of, others I feel genuinely sorry for. But I have to try to help them all.

One man who comes in makes a visit of about an hour and a half each time. I write a letter for him and read the ones he gets. He receives about four letters a week from a girl who is the sister of his fiancée, now two months deceased. He assures me there is no romance connected with it, but he certainly encloses plenty of love and kisses and affectionate terms. Judging others by myself, as I always do, I can't quite understand how he can be so promiscuous with his devotion and not mean anything about it. For me there is only one person of whom I think of terms of love and kisses. She gets all my kisses and she's the only one whose letters I conclude with, "Yours with love." So I feel funny taking dictation from an unromantic young man as if I were Anthony writing to Cleopatra. But I guess the letters have the desired effect because they are enjoyed. I'm afraid we're a little hypocritical about them because they don't represent his thoughts entirely and they certainly are not couched in his English. Letter writing is my talent and I use it. I think up stories for him to include. I prompt him about the things he ought to write about, and by using the typewriter we get said a lot more than really seems. But I'm not the only one. They tell us that when Plato reported the dialogues of Socrates it is mighty hard to divide Plato from his teacher. And they say that in the Gospel of John you have mostly John and very little of Jesus. Certainly for anyone who isn't "book bound" like a wrestler is sometimes muscle bound, any comparison between the Christ of John and the Christ of the other three Gospels gives a picture of an altogether different person. So, I hope I'm not leading my friend into something that he'll have to explain away later. I guess not. He punctuates about every third sentence with "Say Irene," or "Well Irene," or "Now Irene," and his phrases such as "I didn't do too good," and "And I want to tell you," are distinctly Scanlon and not Miller. And what impresses me is how pathetically grateful he is for what little I do. He said "Chaplain, please think of something I can do for you." He brings me a couple of candy bars every time he comes. Perhaps it isn't just the reading of his mail and the writing of his letters he likes, but the leisurely way we do it. It gives him a chance to talk and in mentioning certain things in the letters we read and write he explains who this person or that is and it is a little like a short visit home. Although very low in literacy he is as good in his line, that of mechanics and machinery as I am in mine. So we have basis for mutual respect.

Edna paid me the compliment of asking me to advise her about marriage and did what I knew she would do, made up her mind to do what she was going to anyway. However, I think she is much to be admired in her determination to stand by her guns as far as entering the portals of Rome is concerned. She is to be admired. I hope she doesn't get married too soon. I want time enough to save the money necessary to provide a worthy wedding present for her. My heart isn't very big and what little room there is in it is taken up almost entirely by her sister, but she has a very special place in it just the same.

March 18, 1944

Dearest Doris:

Before I get deep in this letter let me ask a few questions.

1. Have you managed to get a telephone yet? If so, what is your number?

2. Of course our next child will be a little girl but supposing she were not. What would his name be? Or is that a secret.

3. Supposing Alice comes as expected. Will she have a middle name? [As I recall the story, Priscilla was not given a middle name until after the birth certificate was filed. Then Grandma Leach's name Ruth was chosen as her middle name, but since the birth certificate did not show this, Priscilla never had an official middle name. Later, Priscilla decided she liked not having one.]

...A letter came from Mr. Warner [in East Arlington?]*... Ralph Nesbit has joined the army in order to get a little peace. Although he thought he got a good wife when he married Agnes he discovered that he got the world's worst mother-in-law, too. Although he considered himself one of the family Mrs. McDonald didn't and poor Ralph had to eat in the kitchen with a boarder (and you know the kind of people Mrs. McDonald has for boarders) and didn't allow him to sleep with his wife. Gosh! What a dame. The more I see of mothers-in-law the more I appreciate how lucky I am. I got one of the few good ones, don't you think?*

The shadow of things to come is beginning to fall upon us. Lt. Col. Kidder has been transferred to Camp Livingston to start a new evacuation hospital. We are also sending out a cadre of about forty non-coms and one captain to a camp in Mississippi to help out with another. Col King says he thinks we shall be on maneuvers in Louisiana by April first. So there! Certainly we are ready for maneuvers or Europe or Asia or Greenland's icy mountains or the perfumes of Arabia. Let it come.

...You can imagine, can't you, with what interest I read everything you write about yourself and the new baby. Of course I am not forgetting that I have three other children, either. In your last letter when you suggest that you may have your baby in two weeks you surprise me. Can it possibly be so soon? I hope so for your sake as I know you are carrying a heavy load on your mind and elsewhere. Gee! But I'm anxious to know how you are every minute. And I talk about you a lot, too. To whom? To God. I have made new arrangements for my devotions....

Yes, my scope is broadening out, all right. Besides Scanlon, for whom I have written and read several letters I have other more or less regular callers. One man came to me with tears because his barracks was quarantined for measles and his wife was due to arrive the next morning. So I helped him arrange to have his wife met and then gave them the use of my office that evening. I saw him and his wife together this afternoon (Sunday now), both radiantly happy....

All chaplains are now authorized a jeep and trailer. My assistant is to be the driver so he has to spend some time each week learning how to take care of it. The idea is that there are so many small units in the army that don't have a chaplain that, on maneuvers I shall have to move from place to place to have services on Sunday and personal interviews at other times....

Well, my dear I'll conclude with this thought. I love you, I admire you, I am very proud of you and I trust God to take care of you.

Yours with love
Jerry

March 23, 1944

...I take it that you expect Alice to be really visible and audible about next Wednesday. Dear Doris, I am hoping for you and praying for you that you may be well and everything will be as you wish. I am vastly comforted by the thought that you have such a good helper in your mother. I feel that you are in better hands than you would be even if I were there. If Alice arrives before next Thursday telegraph me here at Camp Swift. If later than that telegraph me at my new A.P.O. which I will give you as soon as it is known.

And this leads me to the big news. It is now official that we are to arrive at the maneuver area on Sunday, April second. That means we shall probably leave Camp Swift on Saturday, April first. That is why it would be useless to telegraph me here later than Thursday. Probably after that time you had better just write by air mail, or have Mother Leach write. I think we shall be given our A.P.O. by Saturday if not by tomorrow. I'll forward it to you as soon as I can. Mail will be delivered to us daily out there. Where are we going? Somewhere near Shreveport, Louisiana.

I am glad you are so reasonable about Lt. Balsley. I think she is pretty reasonable. Although very nice and very helpful in the service, and very much an influence for more stimulating conversation she is very careful not to let me get within arm's length. I think she realizes what a man away from his wife is up against and how easy it might be to get too friendly. I am Chaplain Miller to her and she is Lt. Balsley to me. But I suspect that she finds my companionship as interesting as I do hers. And it is mighty sweet of you not to cut off the one softening influence there is in my life down here. It will be cut off soon enough. I'll have just one more service here.

Have I told you about my assistant? His name is Louis Figlioli. He is a Catholic boy but not thoroughly indoctrinated with all the hocus pocus of that medieval institution. He has been giving me a lot of soft soap which I really don't know whether he believes himself, or not. Such as "I wish you would help me with my letters some time. You're a master at that sort of thing." "How do you know?" "Because of the way you speak." Now what would you do, hand him a quarter or throw the vase of flowers at him? He has been talking to the Catholic boys about me, trying to convince them that I would be mighty glad to help them with their problems. So far none have come up. Personally I could have picked others whom I would rather have but they are of the caliber that wouldn't long be satisfied with the rank a Chaplain's assistant rates. So I could do a lot worse. Figlioli was to have graduated from engineering school had he not been inducted. So he is educated and talented.

Did you know I am supposed to have a jeep? And a quarter ton trailer, too. Boy, will I be popular! Figlioli has been given instruction about taking care of said Jeep and trailer. Probably I shall have several small units to visit and do pastoral work for. That's the reason for the jeep. I haven't seen it yet but when it is officially delivered I'm going to put your name on the side. Mind? If I can get that done I'll get permission to have its picture taken and then you can see for yourself.

...Your description of your sickness was quite graphic. I could just see you making your periodic trips to the bathroom and getting weaker all the time, and I could see Kenneth and Priscilla standing by to be helpful if they could. Are they excited about this new baby as well as you? I know you have so skillfully prepared their minds for this new sister that there won't be a shade of jealousy when she does come and requires so much attention. I'll bet Priscilla's just as happy as she can be over it all. Am I right?

March 28, 1944

Dearest Doris:

The wisecrack of Major McGuire relative to "the only thing you are sure of in the army is your last meal," has much truth in it. Last Friday we had it officially that we were going on maneuvers, to be in the proper area by April 2. Yesterday we were called in for an officers' meeting and the Colonel told us officially that we are not going on maneuvers.... Now our next rumor meat is this. We have, by a Fourth Army rule to spend at least three weeks in the field. Well, that will be a maneuver after a fashion. I heard two officers in a small bull session Sunday evening. Said one, "He starts a rumor and when it gets back to him a half hour later he believes it himself." Some of the fatalists like to quote the Biblical passage, "There shall be wars and rumors of wars." Perhaps, if Jesus had been a soldier he would have said, "rumors in wars." Oh hum....

March 29

Your letter came today. A fine, sweet letter from a fine, sweet girl. Thanks for answering the questions. And I like Alice Ann for a name. Now I'll answer a few for you.

Louis Figlioli, I think I mentioned in my last letter, is my assistant. He does seem to admire me a lot and I don't know why unless it's because I don't allow my rank to impress the men. Out on bivouac I pitch right in with the tent pitching, loading and unloading, and when I can I get in the mess line instead of barging right into the mess tent like the other officers do. He says the men like me very much. I hope so, but he may be judging others by himself.

March 31, 1944

...I played with the officers in a game of softball with the enlisted men. After that I packed the case my communion set came in full of things I want to send home..... I've something in it for everybody. I'll ask you to be arbiter of the possession of all those things except the present for Priscilla. That is marked.... I suggest that the scissors go to Bruce. You mentioned that Bruce would like some like mine. These I bought in the P. Ex. for 32¢. And you can tell which child will like the pictures of dogs and wild life best. Probably Kenneth will want the cartoons and the steel pennies and I know Alice will want the Brillo to use as a teething ring....

April 3, 1944

Dearest of the Dear Doris:

I've about a half hour to snap off a letter to you before the activities of a busy day start.... We are planning an Easter sunrise service for seven next Sunday. The sun will come up about seven-ten and it really is an experience seeing it rise. We're going to have an army band, two soloists, and a chance for a few chaplains to take part but I tell everyone that God has the greatest part to play for the rising of the sun is more impressive and glorious than anything we can produce....

Major Lewis asks me just about every time he sees me, "Have you received that telegram yet?" He's very sympathetic and interested. I told him what you said about Virginia being there with you in the sanatorium and dropped the remark that you might visit each other. [Aunt Virginia had my cousin Allen on April 1 in Richford, Vt., in the same nursing home, as Mother called it, where

I was born nine days later.] He said, “A woman ought not to get up except to go the bath room, for the first three weeks.” And after she is sent home she ought to spend twenty hours out of the twenty-four laying down, especially on her stomach. So, stay there as long as you can, won’t you sweetheart. Don’t drop a single hint to anyone that you are in the least bit of a hurry. You have those that love you there, let them have a chance to express that love by helping you all they can. I want you to recover from this with record speed and comfort. Don’t spare any money that can buy you the rest and comfort you need.

Well, I hope by now everything is well under control. Please keep me well informed. I decoded Kenneth’s letter and I am very glad that both he and Priscilla are so well prepared to meet the April Showers.

April 3, 1944

Dearest Doris:

Day is ending and perhaps I’ll have a little time to write you my daily note.... I went on a convoy trip with the unit and this time I drove the first truck. What fun! We had another soft ball game with the E. M. This time I umpired. That was fun, too. This evening I expect at least two men in for help. Perhaps more. Tomorrow will be a busy day, too. I’m going to a meeting of the Division Chaplains and hear about the work of the chaplain in hospitals, both here and in combat....

While I was out on Sunday p.m. along came John Scanlon and left a box of cookies from his girl, Irene, two candy rolls and this stationary. Apparently he likes me.... Figliola showed me the letter you wrote him about the candy. It seemed strange to see your nice, friendly writing on an envelope addressed to someone else.

I’m still waiting to hear from you that Alice has made her advent.... Each day brings us closer to it and I’m eager to know. If you wish me to direct my mail to Richford give me the address. Probably you shall have frequent visitors who will bring my letters to you.

I am getting a book for Priscilla in addition to the present in the suitcase. It will come from the Pilgrim Press.

[The Pilgrim Press is the publishing arm of the Congregational Church, and Gerald evidently used their retail and mail order service to buy a lot of his books.]

April 4, 1944

Dear Kids:

I have received the letters you wrote. It was so nice of you to enclose Mother's letter with them. Thanks.

Would you like to know what we didn't do on April Fool's day? Well several men were walking up the street we live on and they saw the flower of Texas blooming loudly about in the grass between the road and the sidewalk and do you know what they didn't do? When the flowers were nodding their blue bonnets at the soldiers the soldiers didn't take off their garrison caps and put on these blue bonnets. They didn't do that.

...I've just been down to see Captain Weinberg, the Detachment Commander and do you know what he gave me? Guess. No it wasn't a red, white and blue helmet. And it wasn't a cat with a white stripe down its back. No, it wasn't a picture of the man in the moon showing him returning with porrage crumbs all round his mouth. Wrong every time. It was one hundred dollars! Whew! What would you daddy do with one hundred dollars? Buy his sweetheart a watch? He'd like to. Buy Kenneth some switches for his electric train? He'd like to. Buy a real big baby carriage with an electric motor for Priscilla's doll? He'd like to. Buy a machine that would make ice cream without any ice or milk or cream or sugar for Bruce? He'd like to. No, he isn't to spend the money for that. He is supposed to go to the P. Ex. Warehouse and buy $100 worth of candy, cigarettes, and razor blades to sell to the soldiers while we are on the field problem next three weeks. Can you guess who's liable to be Daddy's best customer for two of these items? You guessed right that time.

Has your little sister arrived yet. If so, do you like her? Can she sing? Can she knit?... Now you will all help out, won't you. I want Bruce to go right down and mow the lawn. I want Priscilla to bring in the ice and I want Kenneth to be ready to do everything that whoever keeps house for you wants him to do before she knows she wants him to do it. Be all the help you can. When I hear from Mother I want her to say that she has three such fine children, three such helpful children, three such good children that she won't need a fourth so she'll just leave it in Richford for the next mother whose children aren't any good.

Well, I'll say good-bye until the next time. Tell Mother I'll write to her tomorrow.

Daddy.

[On Easter card enclosed with April 4 letter to Doris] *Lt. Balsley suggests that our girl might arrive on Easter. "Then she'll be an Easter Bunny," says she.*

April 7, 1944

...It seems that I don't write to the right people for the ones I do write to, with the exception of you and Edna, take a mighty long time to reply. Ruth Grout, the Montgomerys, the Webbs and some other East Arlington people just don't know what a letter means to a soldier. Marilla Grout is the very best correspondent I have in Arlington. She writes splendid letters. I have been much surprised about her. I always considered her pretty cold towards me while I was there until I inaugurated the Cub movement. Now she writes the best letters, next to yours, of all I get....

In closing let me tell you that I am very much in love with a certain minister's wife. She's so very lovable that I have made her the object of my devotion for thirteen years. She's nice to look at. She's nice to be with. She's nice to talk to. She is a wonderful mother to fine children. But when she's in my arms. Boy, that's something. It gives life interest and beauty and purpose to be in love with her. Be good to her, won't you. Remember when you said to me, "You've cut my sweetheart"? I do. Well you have it in your power to be good to my sweetheart.

Write when you can and tell me a lot about that sweetheart of mine.

Your lover,
Jerry

I was born around 1 a.m. on Monday, April 10. Gerald received a telegram saying that I was, alas for his hopes, a boy.

April 11, 1944

Dearest Doris:

Well, now, what kind of a trick is this? Another boy! Just like any dad, I'm not sorry. But poor Priscilla. Did she cry? I'll bet she was mightily disappointed. Poor girl. Now she is really outnumbered, but I suppose it will have its compensations for by still being the only granddaughter in both families, unless Gladys [his sister] has a girl, she'll still be quite a favorite. She'll be my favorite daughter, anyway. Tell her that. And how about you. Are you greatly disappointed? I remember your saying that no matter what you had you would love it just the same.

...So Gladys has a girl. [This was my cousin Sally Craven, born April 2. Gerald must have received a letter announcing her birth after starting this letter.] How nice. I'll bet she's pleased. And I'll bet you're pleased with your new boy. Now I have the largest family of any of the officers in this outfit and, so far as I know, of any of the men, too. But it isn't for me to strut. You are the one who deserves all the glory.

...Colonel O'Brian has visited our tent twice and is quite impressed by our display. Figliola is talented at this sort of thing and has made the tent look might inviting. He has the candy and other merchandise attractively displayed and has also the books laid out so anyone who likes to read will be irresistibly drawn to them. I have my chaplains flag flying out in front so we are really in the running.

Lt. Colonel King told me that Colonel O'Brian is well satisfied with my work as chaplain. You can imagine what a boost of my spirits that provided. It is nice to know you have the approval of the C.O. I hope I can continue to keep it.

...Tell Kenneth this P.Ex. business gives me a grand time to accumulate steel pennies. If he is still interested in them let me know. I have 33 of them already and before this job is finished I shall probably have nearly 100.

Yours with all my love, Dearest,

Jerry

Figliola wants me to forward his congratulations to you.

April 12, 1944

...By now our little girl has had her birthday. [Not quite true: Priscilla's birthday is April 15.] *I wonder how she will make out. Have my presents for her arrived yet? I suppose someone is there to see that she doesn't feel neglected. I don't know as she will speak to you for a while, having a boy instead of a girl....*

April 13, 1944

...I have been wondering a lot about how you are and little questions about whether you run your own dairy or have to depend upon Albert Perly's guernseys. And I have been wondering if the little fellow has blue eyes like mine or nice, brown ones like yours. And I wonder how big he is and whether he has any hair. And I'm hoping very much that everything is as it should be.

April 14

...Last night we had a big business at our P. Ex. Every time someone came in Fig would say, "Here comes my favorite customer." He has a lot of favorites. They come in, get a few candy bars, or some cigars, or some Brillo, or some razor blades or some

stationary. Then they stay around and talk. They love that. It gives them all the social value men back home enjoy hanging around the post office waiting for the mail.

Tomorrow our favorite daughter will be eight years old. I hope she has a pleasant day. I suppose by now she has seen the new baby and knows his name, which is more than I know about him. If you get a chance wish her a happy birthday for me.

April 16, 1944

...Your mother wrote a short letter telling me that you seemed to be getting along all right and that you were pleased with the flowers she brought from me. She said you were mystified at first that I could get them to you so quickly, but that she solved the mystery for you very quickly. I hope you like them and that they conveyed a message of love from your devoted lover down here in Texas. I think your mother said she got roses for you. I knew her selection would be good.

You can well believe that I am very anxiously awaiting some word from you that tells me:

a. That you are well and gaining fast.
b. That you have a name for our boy that he approves of.
c. That the three children we already have have seen the new member of the family and vote to keep him.
d. That you still love me.

111th Evacuation Hospital
Camp Swift, Texas
Way Down Yonder in the
Peanut Field
April 18, 1944

...I was very pleased with your letter which told about Anthony and you. It was so good [to] get a word directly from you. It seems that each child comes a little easier than the last. I am mighty

thankful for you. I suppose you will be home to take charge of things by the time this letter gets to you.

We are now in our second week in the field. We are going to move tonight. We'll begin after dark to take down tents. We have to move, set up again and be ready for business. We don't get to sleep again until 7 tomorrow morning. I move my P. Ex and tent and Chaplain's equipment in the first truck. I am the second assistant commander of the first echelon of the convoy. My job is to see that my truck keeps the right speed. My experience as leader in a funeral procession serves me well in this.

I was greatly surprised at the name you chose for our progeny. Should I consider it a compliment that you wished to include my name in his or was it that you liked the sound of it? [He's referring here to my middle name, Gerald] *I tried to guess what name you would use and about the only name that occurred to me was Robert. If I had guessed 150 times I wouldn't have thought of Anthony. It's a good name, however. Major Elias who handles our operating tent has that name. I told him you had named our little boy that and he said, "That's good. He'll grow up to be a great man."* Kenneth recalls (and Mother told me a similar story) that an older male relative, perhaps our great-grandfather Fergus Wright, objected to the name Tony for me: "That's a name for a *horse*!" Mother replied, "No, his name is Anthony, a fine old English name." Nevertheless, Dad and all the family have called me Tony for as long as I can remember.

April 23, 1944

...Two weeks of bivouac have passed and next Saturday we come in for good.... I am getting much better acquainted with many of the men and they are getting much better acquainted with me. Tomorrow we move again, this time in two echelons.... The purpose of the two different places is to give us practice in being in two places at once. We do not dismantle the second echelon until the first one is already set up in the forward area and receiving patients.

Then, after the last patient is evacuated from the second echelon, that moves forward and joins the first. My job is to be with both. "How are you going to do it?" asks the Colonel. "You know I'm supposed to have a jeep," I said. "You'll need more than that. You'll need wings." I've settled it that I shall stay with the second echelon until the first is ready to receive patients and then I'll make my way up to the first.

Edna writes that she's making plans to get married, probably in June. I have a crazy idea as to what I'd like to do in the way of a wedding present. I'd like to get a nice, crisp fifty dollar bill and put it in an envelope and send it to her. In order to do that you'll have to consent because thirty of that fifty dollars would come from you. Edna's the kind of a girl that likes to pick out what she wants rather than have it thrust upon her. Let me know what you think about it.

She seems to be all steamed up about this Al of hers. She sent me a picture of him and if she hadn't told me he was French I would guess he was Irish. Oh hum! I'm afraid the girl is letting herself in for a lot of unhappiness in years to come..... [Aunt Edna married Alphonse Paré, of French-Canadian background. Gerald shows here that he was opposed to Edna marrying a Catholic, but his relations with Uncle Al were always friendly. Al remained Catholic, Edna stayed loyal to the Congregational Church, and they raised their children in both faiths. I remember their son Edmond, about five years younger than I, making sure he had a rosary to attend mass with his father during a visit to us in Hinsdale, NH, about 1960.]

April 25, 1944

There is a special reason why I am writing to you just now. I wonder if you have already guessed why. If you haven't just look this letter over carefully inside and out and you will see....

April 26, 1944

...I suppose my screwy letter of yesterday has arrived by now. Did you guess before opening it up what it was all about?... If I were going to bet on it I would bet that you knew of my promotion before you opened the letter. You usually notice things quickly.

...Yesterday afternoon a very official looking envelope was in my mail and it was from the War Department. It was addressed to me in this way:

Chaplain (Captain) Gerald Fletcher Miller, C522096, AUS

...One of the medical officers lent me one set of bars so I could show my rank.

...My base pay will be $2400 yearly instead of $2000 and the rental allowance will be $90 instead of $75. This month's check won't be any different, but next month's will. Besides that, if we go overseas we get ten per cent more. So it almost looks as if you married into money at last. Well, dear girl, you deserve it. And I think I will arrange to get a fifty dollar war bond each month instead of the twenty-five dollar one....

Well, I guess I'll stop now. Nothing I write from now on will make any sense until I get used to the "railroad tracks" as the twin bars are called by some.

Yours with great love,
Jerry

Doris suffered from arthritis throughout her adult life; in fact, their marriage in 1932 had to be postponed because of it. She was very sick and lame with arthritis after I was born. She had to walk with crutches part of the time, and both Kenneth and Priscilla helped by carrying me when she couldn't. Gerald's constant concern for his wife's health crops up often in the letters that follow.

Since Doris was living near her parents, they were able to help her get through this period while her husband was away. Here Gerald expresses eloquently how grateful he is to have Carroll and Ruth Leach on the scene to see his beloved through a difficult time.

April 30, 1944

Dear Mother Leach:

...Doris says you have been wonderful to her all during the crisis necessary to bring another life into the world. Of course she knew you would be, but that doesn't mean we shouldn't be grateful and mention it. I'm getting so that I'm impressed by all the miracles that are expected to happen just as much as by those that aren't. I feel that it is a miracle that you should be so good to us over so many years, and just because we knew it would happen makes it none the less wonderful for me. I don't know whether I shall get a chance to go home again or not, but if I don't I shall feel that Doris is in perfectly safe hands and that will mean much more to me than anything that can happen to me in the army. I hope you get acquainted with the new boy and like him for I expect Doris and the children are beginning to like him already. What his relationship to me will be I don't know but I hope he will have an opportunity to get acquainted sometime. And if he grows up near enough to your farm I expect he and little Allen Leach will be brought together and become almost as a pair of twins....

My cousin Allen grew up on the farm with his older brother Robert, and we played together during our visits there several times a year. We are far from twins. Allen was a husky, sturdy, active boy; I was scrawny and bookish. Now in 2022, he runs the farm with his son, Billy, and their wives.

May 2, 1944

...On our bulletin board yesterday afternoon was a notice that officers could apply for leave. So I put in my application this morning. I asked for 14 days starting on or about June 7.... [The leave evidently was granted for the middle of May instead, for the next letter discusses the train ride back via Troy, NY, where Gerald's father and brother lived. This was my father's last time with Mother, and his only time to meet me, the new baby, before he returned at the end of the war late in 1945.]

May 21, 1944

...I got here as per schedule on Friday evening. It was a long trip in crowded trains but I was fortunate enough to get into comfortable seats for the whole journey. I didn't realize the Rutland Railroad had such good coaches as the one I rode in. I went out to Father's as his card suggested and discovered he didn't expect me at all. You can imagine how my stepmother sputtered. [Gerald's mother died when he was still young. His father, John Miller, remarried a woman with a peppery personality.] *But they let me stay the night so I did. True to form he got me to help him in the garden and to mow the lawn. I bought some things in Troy...and then went out to Charles'. They were very good to me and Florence put me up a lunch so that I didn't eat in the diner all the way back.* [Charles was Gerald's older brother. His wife, Florence, died within a few years after this. I never met her.]

...We received thirty nurses this morning, although we shall not have anything to do with them for a while. But you know what that means. Colonel King says we are boiling hot. That means that our departure date is not distant. He is taking his leave right after the bivouac. Exciting!

...You gave me a lovely visit, Doris, and I hope you enjoyed having me around. Of course, what I liked best was the moments with you. I didn't try to do so much with the children because my stay was too short to be able to finish anything I started. I hope I can get back for good before they grow entirely away from me. But I guess I shall have to reconcile myself to leaving them to your care mostly until this big job is finished.

In the meanwhile I'll write to the children as frequently as I can so as to keep them "on the ball," as they say in the army.

Good-by, sweet wife. I'll write again soon.

With love,
Jerry

May 26, 1944

...We're getting all ready to go somewhere because we had "showdown" inspection today.... One significant thing on the list was that each man was supposed to have only one suit of summers and two suits of winter O.D.s. [Olive Drab uniforms] He was supposed to have two pair of summer underwear and three of winter underwear. It looks as if we were going to be sent where it was cold. Perhaps Iceland or Norway, if it is reconquered....

Doris, I'm going to make a suggestion about this letter writing that I would like you to consider a request. I'm asking you to write twice a week. But that isn't the hard part. I'm going to ask you to take an hour out of the best part of the day, two days a week, to do it. It won't be long before your letters are going to mean more to me than anything else in this world. I know how it will be if you leave it to the end of the day when you are all tired out. You will look upon it as a burden and more often than not the letter won't get written. If I leave my letter writing until evening I find that the letters I write are not really expressive of me at all. So I'm asking you to give me A-1 priority two days a week. Of course I don't expect you to try to write while Anthony is demanding his refreshment. But I am audacious enough to ask that if you have to choose between writing to me on a certain day and giving him his bath that you'll give me the break. Do you love me enough for that? Somehow my requests have always been shoved down to the bottom of the boot and more often than not you never get around to carry them out. It was so on my last leave. And I felt it. I guess I'm getting childish to be offended over things like that, but war makes kids out of men sometimes as well as making men out of kids. So, Dear Girl, if this is hard to do, do it just the same. The harder it is the more it shows you love me. Can I depend upon you?

Lt. Balsley walked out of my life last night. She is being transferred to Camp Bryan, about eighty miles away. She's recruiting Wacs. Our paths may cross again and they may not. She has done a lot for me in unloading her troubles on my shoulders in exchange for my troubles unloaded on hers. She has been so vitally interested in you and our children that she may write to you just in an attempt to get better acquainted. I hope we can meet after the war so I can show her my lovely Lady and our fine children....

Doris moved from the apartment to a small rented house on Church Street, Enosburg Falls. Gerald must have had some acquaintance with that house, since he tells Kenneth he knows where the rooms are.

May 29, 1944

Dear Kenneth:

Thanks for writing me a line. Being sick does something to you, doesn't it? I like to have you write to me but I don't wish you to be sick in order to think of it. We have a rule in the army that all correspondence will be answered within twenty-four hours. It's a good rule to follow at home, too. Lots of friends are lost because their letters are not answered.

So you are moving. Tell mother there is one big item of consolation for her in this moving business. It is the low rent that she will have to pay at Enosburg Falls. Mrs. Gurtner (she will know who that is) told me yesterday that she and Chaplain Gurtner are moving into a furnished apartment consisting of three rooms and bath. It's a made-over two car garage. How much do you suppose they are paying for that mansion? Fifty bucks a month! Whew! I hope you are well enough to help her now and that you help just as much as you can. They say three moves are worse than a fire because there is so much work cleaning up and settling. But just think of it. When I was ten years old our family had moved four times. First when I was seven, again while I was seven, the third time when I was eight and the fourth when I was nine. Believe me, they made me help. And if mother is wise she'll just be the first sergeant and boss you kids around. It really is fun getting settled in a new place if you take the right attitude. I am so glad you have that new house and I'll bet that you have lots of fun putting your things where they belong. Please tell me just who has what room because I remember just where the rooms are. I hope you are all living there when I come back from the war.

As I told Mother in my last letter, I sent the check for repairing your air rifle... I hope it will work well when you get it. Try it out and then tell me about it. It will probably get to you sometime late in June.

While I was home I talked to mother about you and Bruce. You are both getting older and bigger and a little hard to handle. Mother has so much to do she can't stand over you boys with a hairbrush and give you a whack every time you need one. If I were home all the time I could work out a program of things we could do together or I could see about starting up the cubs or something else to keep you occupied. But I can't. So mother and I thought it might be a good idea to pretend that there at home we had a little army consisting of a captain and four soldiers. Mother would be the captain and you four kids would be the soldiers. We would work out a system of things to do and of promotions. If any of you did those things well she would recommend promotion. Right now you are all privates. But as you caught on you would be advanced. First corporal, then buck sergeant, then staff sergeant, then technical sergeant and finally master sergeant. We thought we would make the allowance correspond, too. Right now you are getting fifty cents a week. So does a private get fifty dollars a month. A corporal gets sixty-six dollars a month, so when you make corporal you will get sixty-six cents per week. The sergeant gets seventy-eight dollars a month and so, when you make sergeant, you'll get seventy-eight cents a week. Staff sergeant gets $96, technical sergeant $114 and master sergeant $138. So there you are.

Now the things that bring promotion to a soldier are these. First comes the appearance. Neatness, shoes shined, hands clean, teeth brushed without being told, clothes all there with all buttons buttoned that need to be, and all equipment in good order. His room and his bed have to pass inspection. One way they inspect a soldier's bed is to see if there are any wrinkles on it. If there are it's K.P. for him. Another way is to throw a half dollar on the bed. If it bounces the bedmaking job passes. If not, make it over. Clothes have to be hung up in a certain way and all things picked up and in order. Inspection usually happens once a week but if the first sergeant has had a bad breakfast and wants to gig somebody he may happen in to the barracks any time and if he sees a bed with wrinkles or shoes not in order or clothes out of place, "Extra detail for that yardbird!" Another thing that counts very much in the army is promptness. Be exactly on time. If you are told you are wanted home at five, be there at five. Making people wait for you is a very sure way not to be promoted in the army, and if you happen to have a rating, to lose it. And another thing that counts is to do right off what you are told to do. If an officer tells a soldier to fix up the bulletin board the soldier doesn't just continue what he is doing until he gets ready to obey that order. He gets right up and obeys that order. That was one thing I noticed about you children. You would be asked to do something and you would just sit and continue to read your comic book or do what you were doing as if no one had said anything. To be a good soldier you would immediately stop what you were doing and do what you were asked. That is most important.

This is enough to give you an idea. I suggest that you three older, privates have a conference with mother, draw up a chart for each week with places for marks on cleanliness, promptness, efficiency in the work you do, and obedience, so that when your rating for the week is up to ninety you consider you have passed for that week, and mother can decide how many passing weeks are necessary for promotion. How about it? Does that sound good to you?

I hope that by now your throat is all better and you are feeling very well. Did you get the baseball I sent you from Troy? I think I shall write to Priscilla tomorrow and if I do I am going to send some cute pictures I found in a magazine. I think you will all like them.

Yours sincerely,

Daddy

May 30, 1944

Dear Bruce,

Yesterday I wrote Priscilla a letter and, poor little girl, I told her to ask mother so many things I am sure I am keeping her out of school to do it all. So rather than do that I'm going to ask you to ask her something. After you've been a very good boy for fifteen minutes and mother feels rested up because of it will you ask her to send me ten dollars when she gets her next allotment check. I'll explain when I write to her tomorrow why I am short even though I am getting more pay.

I had a good time reading to you while I was home. I didn't do it half enough, though. I'm a funny daddy. While I'm down here I say, "I would love to be home so Brucie could sit side of me or on my lap and I could read to him." But when I am home I don't read to him hardly any. What a bum daddy! But someday I shall be home and I shall read to you again. And it won't be just for a little while for a few days but every day. When Kenneth was like you are now I used to stop at five o'clock and read to him. I'd read and when it came time to turn the page I would whistle and he would turn the page. After reading a while he would say, "Daddy, fool with me." So I would take off my glasses and we'd have a fooling match in which Priscilla would sometimes join. One summer we had a tire hung up from a limb of the tree right in front of the big front door. Priscilla, when she was three years old would sit in that tire and hang on for dear life while I pushed her so hard the tire and Priscilla were almost level with the branch it was hitched to. But she would hold on and I couldn't push her so high she would be afraid. Ask her if she remembers that.

I am going into Austin Saturday to see if I can find Johnny Crow's Garden and the Happy books. If I can I will send them. Then you can have a nice, fresh Johnny Crow to look at. [Johnny Crow's Garden, Johnny Crow's Party, and Johnny Crow's New Garden, all by L. Leslie Brooke, comprise a delightful children's series, full of droll cartoon drawings of the crow's bird and animal guests, and clever rhymes on the animals' names. I remember reading the first two books over and over when I was in 1st and 2nd grade.] I am sending some pictures in this letter I thought were cute and I think you will like them. Especially the Chinese baby. I told the lieutenants that live in the next room to me that it was a pin up girl for my little boy.

How do you like your new house? And how does the Doodle-bug Handcar work? Or does it?

And so, goodnight.

Yours sincerely,
Daddy

June 1, 1944

I expect we shall have two more weeks here at Camp Swift, maybe more. If we do well these two days out here and convince the inspectors that we are ready we may be off soon. Much depends upon the need. I hope there may be a possibility that, if we embark from New York I may see you again. I'm not planning on it in the least but if it should so happen I hope it can be arranged. But keep it secret because I would wish to have every minute with you and I wouldn't care to have dinner with anyone else while you were there.

I love you, dearest. Keep a good, big place in your heart for me, won't you. Mine beats for you.

Yours with love,
Jerry

June 5, 1944 [continued June 6]

Dearest Doris:

I received your letter this morning and was very glad to get it. Please forgive me if I seemed ungrateful for the magnificent work you are doing. But just keep the letters coming. I can only imagine how much you love me by the hard work you are doing, but nice, long letters from you, twice a week, full of you require no imagination. They offer proof that you think of me. I don't believe I can express myself forcefully enough to let you know how much I love or how much it would mean to hear from you often. Writing is a little thing and bringing up a family like ours is a big thing. Please don't get mad at me for being silly but I like to have attention. And if and when there is anything I can do for you that will bring you happiness and assure you of my love, please tell me about it.

The moving must have been some job. Were you sensible about Anthony? I certainly hope you were. You didn't say anything about it in your last letter but your phrase to the effect that with all you had to do usually the extra work of moving was very hard. Just how hard it was seemed to penetrate into the letter. There was nothing of your usual buoyancy in it, nothing of the spirit that I usually find and which makes me wonder if you didn't try to carry everything including the care of the baby.

June 6

I've read the first part of your letter over again and I feel more like a heel than ever. I guess it is because my head has cleared a little because I took...the first day off since I came back. I signed out this morning at seven-fifteen and missed the seven-thirty bus by a minute. It was a nice bus, too. So I went back and when I returned to the bus station I was picked up by one of our lieutenants who was going to San Antonio. He gave me a ride in our command car as far as Austin so I got there at about ten. And here's how I spent the day.

First of all I wandered around from street to street just to get the feel of city streets under my shoes again. Finally I decided it was time to spend some money so I walked into a store where military goods were sold and bought a couple of sterling silver crosses. Two bucks! The money began to go. Then I went to that store where they sell toys. How I wish you could have been with me! First of all I looked up Johnny Crow's Garden. They didn't have that but they had two other books by Johnny Crow. So I bought them, one for a dollar and the other for a dollar and a quarter. So Bruce was taken care of. Then I began to look around and remembered I have a very little boy. What could I get for him? I found a little set for his fun and development so I bought that. It's a regular little gym set and I'd like to be around when he begins to notice it and experiment... Now what to get for Kenneth... I saw lots of things he would have liked but they cost so darned much in that store... Finally I saw a lovely kaleidoscope, with such entrancing designs and so clear that I bought it. I know Kenneth will like that. I like it myself. I bought another with different colors and designs for Priscilla. I hope they come all right. When the package does come please give Kenneth first choice of the kaleidoscopes and Priscilla must be content with the other. Personally I think they are equally good. So I had the children taken care of, but what about you, sweet wife?...

...Finally I saw myself in front of a store with a very queer and unusual name, Sears. I entered with a very vague idea that I would find something. I saw some stockings but the clerk, when I asked, "Are these your best stockings?" sensed that I was after something for a very special person and gave me to understand that I could get much better stockings at a shoe store. Treasonable to Mr. Sears. Then I asked her about slips. She said, "How big is she?" About your height but bigger around I informed her. She weighs about 130. Said she "I take size thirty four but I used to weigh 130 once and then I took thirty-six." Buying clothes for someone else is a little like detective work I discovered. So I got you a slip for a present. I would like to have gotten a real fancy one, and thrown in a nice nightie, too. But I didn't dare to go the limit without knowing just what size. This one, the salesgirl said, is a good one although it isn't nearly as dainty looking as you deserve. Please accept it with my sincerest admiration and don't judge my affection by the lowliness of the gift. This is pioneering for me...

It was mighty fine of your brother to help you with the moving. How I wish I could have been around or it could have happened while I was there. Do you still have the telephone and if so please tell me the number. I hope you like your new home very much and that you keep well. It was tough having Kenneth sick just at that time. I am praying for you, dear girl, and oh, how I wish I could help you some!

Yesterday we officers had our shots, tetanus, typhoid, and the small pox vaccination. At the P.O.E. we shall receive the typhus shot. We have received about eight new captains and three new lieutenants as additional medical officers so I guess it won't be long. I'm praying for a chance for a good bye kiss and hug before we go but I am aware that that prayer may be answered with a no, but still I'm praying for it. Do what you can from your end, will you. Just suppose they get us over there and we are about to finish up Germany in three months and then they send us to China. I won't be seeing you for a long time. So far I've been able to see you every five months anyway. Who can tell?

This is quite a long letter isn't it. It can't begin to tell you how much I love you. You're a swell kid, Doris. Don't forget your picture. I want one before you [sic] go across. I want it badly like that letter twice a week. I had mine taken Sunday and when they are done I'll send you one. I'm only getting three.

Good bye, sweetheart. I hope you like the presents, humble as they are.

With great love,
Jerry
Your lover

June 6 was D-Day, the great invasion of Continental Europe by Allied forces. President Roosevelt announced the invasion to the nation on the radio and prayed for the troops. No A.C.L.U. to object then!

June 7, 1944

Dear Bruce,

What's the idea not answering my letter? Are you really becoming a flubdubjustlikeiusedtocallyou? Unless you reply real soon I'll recommend that you be reduced to the rank of yard bird which is only one rank above civilian. Now you get to work pronto and write me a long letter of at least five words telling me how you are, what you are doing and which way the wind is blowing. Get busy now or that recommendation will be coming though quicker than quick.

...I am enclosing my will. Will you please, if you will, give my will, willingly to your mother. It is all made, signed, sealed and delivered so that if your Daddy doesn't get back no one will come and lock up the piano and the sewing machine and the refrigerator and the chairs and the beds and say, "You can't use these until the estate is settled." So here it is. Please deliver it to Mother with my compliments and the hope that we shall not have to refer to it for a long time.

How are you getting along in the Miller army? Any sign of a promotion yet? Or are you bucking for a C.D.D.? I had a guard house service again last Sunday and five of the men wanted to see me afterwards. One of them had been discharged but he was so dumb that he kept wearing his uniform without a tie and with a civilian hat. So a sheriff picked him up and brought him into camp and received twenty-five dollars for it. So, it pays to be careful. I hope you will like the army as well as I do and that you will do whatever Mother says willingly. That's the way to get along.

Do you have any playmates in your new neighborhood? I hope you do and that you get along well together. When I was five years old we lived in a double house. People by the name of Watson lived on the other side of the house. My two sisters found a hole in the wall and they talked through it to the Watson girls, Marjorie and Doris. Marjorie was about my sister Caroline's age, somewhat of a grownup lady, about fourteen years old. Doris was only about six months older than I, but very much smarter. She started school when I did, but was she content to stay in the first grade two years like I did? I guess not. She was in the second grade before she got used to the temperature of the first. And how she used to boss me around. I never liked her because she was so smart and superior and bossy. Across the street there was a boy about my age named Jerry Iought. His name sounded like that. Up street two houses was another boy called Clarence Barry. Whenever I had any swearing I needed done I always got Clarence to do it for me. That is why I never have been much of a hand to swear myself. My little friends used to do it for me....

Playmates are lots of fun if they behave and I hope you have some as nice as Ruth Main was and not bossy like Doris Watson or the swearing kind like Clarence Barry. But if you have let the bossy one do all the bossing. It is the only way you can get along with them, and let the swearing kind do all the swearing. It dirtys you up inside when you do the swearing yourself.

This preaching will cost you one dollar.

I hope you are the same.

Your loving
DADDY

Here is the first mention of Lieberman, the Jewish enlisted man who continued to play for chapel services in Europe, and who made the map reproduced in the front of the book. With a Jewish organist and a Catholic assistant, this very Protestant chaplain had a three-man ecumenical team.

June 9, 1944

Next Sunday we are making a special effort to get as many of the 111th men out to chapel as possible. I am to be the preacher and I'm going to try to get Lieberman who used to play for me at Chapel to work up a male quartet for special music. My men have been most lax about attending chapel but I'm going to make a person to person canvas beginning Monday and invite every Protestant man personally to come. Pray for me, Doris, that this will be a success.

Mrs. Gurtner was in yesterday, looking as if she had just stepped out of a band box (a very big one) as usual. She was close to tears over this invasion because their son has been transferred from the air corps to the anti-tank section of a division. That means he will see service where the action is hottest when his division is sent overseas. Poor woman, but does she want other mothers' boys to die instead of hers? Probably so. How would you feel about it, or can you tell?

Good-bye for now dear one. Please write as often as you can

because your letters mean everything to me. Remember I love you.

With love,
Jerry

June 12, 1944

Dearest Doris:

Know what this is? My first anniversary in the army. Remember June 12 last year? Our trip to Rutland and the shopping excursion? I remember the sinking feeling I experienced when you and the children left me and got on the train for Arlington. What a day!

...I'd like to apologize here and now for my sappy letter I wrote about two weeks ago and rescind the request that you write twice a week. I'd like you to write often but busy as you are I realize that I must be grateful for any letters I do get. So it's "as you were." Write when you can and feel like it and try to forget how unreasonable I was.

I was talking with someone yesterday about you and the children. I think it was Mrs. Gurtner. She asked if the children had a yard to take care of and a garden. Then we happened to talk about how useful children can be on a farm.... See if Kenneth is interested in getting a job doing the kind of work he can do. He ought to be worth 50¢ a day of any man's money. If you like the idea consider whether he ought to apply for a job to his grandfather or someone else. That is if he likes the idea, too. Maybe when he really discovers that he is helping in a genuine way he will like it. Many a boy of ten is doing half a man's work. Mrs. Gurtner suggested both Kenneth and Priscilla raise something like a calf or some chickens. I don't like that idea so well because it really means just so much more responsibility for you. Everyone knows that you have plenty to do without that.

When you can write again tell me about yourself and the children. I would like to know how you came out with your hairdo. Did you decide to have your picture taken? I guess we shall be here until July first. In that case we'll have another pay day here. So don't let finances keep you from having a picture taken as it did before. Tell me about Anthony, too. Did those little bunches you thought you felt mean anything bad? And has he come to the stage when he notices that he has hand and fingers? How does he like the present I sent him or ___________

Since writing the last paragraph I received your letter so I know. I find it hard to imagine how you get by at all with the sickness and Bruce's [i.e. Anthony's] *hernia. How I wish I could help you!* [I was born with a hernia, which was repaired about a year later. Today it would be fixed right away, but 1940's medical practice was to wait until I was bigger. I assume Dad wrote "Bruce" out of habit—Bruce had been the "baby" for five years, after all.]

...I was mighty grateful for your letter.... You don't know how much good your little phrase, "yours with loads of love," meant to me.

And to think that you were sick, too. Poor Doris! Are you better now? And was there anyone to take care of you? With Bruce [i.e. Anthony] *eating at 6, 9, 12, 3, 6 & 10 I can see that you don't have any time to do much writing. And I remember what you read down here about the neurotic effect to an infant of leaving him on his back with the bottle propped up with a pillow. I know that Anthony's future is somewhat influenced by whether you hold him while you feed him or not. I know how nice your bosom is. It's nice to kiss, it's nice to touch and it's nice to lay my head on. I know how nice your arms are. I'm sorry little Anthony has his hernia but if I were he and had it I would rather have your loving care than anyone else's in the whole world. Anthony with a hernia is luckier than any other little child I know without one because he has such a sweet and beautiful mother. God take care of you, dear Doris. You mean so much to me and four other little Millers.*

June 13 was the date of the first V-1 rockets sent by Germany against London.

June 19, 1944

I'm awfully sorry, dear girl, about your sickness.... I find myself wondering if I did right in allowing you to accept another baby from me. Regrets don't do any good and I have never heard you complain but if you do feel, deep in your heart, that I have thrust a heavy burden upon you and then run away from bearing my share, I am willing to hear you say it and to read it if you wish to write it. I feel bad about it, dear. Bad enough to do anything I can that will help you.

...It is good and encouraging to read that you will come down to New York and see me if the opportunity arises. Colonel King says it is very possible, but not possible enough to plan on. You mother is a noble lady to make that wonderful offer [to keep the children?] and you may as well let her know that you may take it up. It is so simple to go to St. Albans and get on a train for New York. And remember, if the time comes, keep it secret. Just you and me. I'm selfish that way.

...Ruth and Max Grout sent me a birthday card and asked if I remembered the time we had a birthday party at Willis' for Jimmy, Leroy, Iva's husband and me. Of course. What swell times we used to have!

June 15, 1944

Dear Priscilla,

Here I am still in Texas but I am thinking about some people who are not in Texas. I am thinking of a girl with nice brown eyes, nice brown hair, nice brown complexion and who likes nice, brown maple sugar on her cereal, when the cereal is Maltex....

Mother writes me that she is very busy. Very busy, indeed. She says that Anthony isn't satisfied with coming to the table like the rest of you and eating three times a day but that he has to have a meal every three hours. That makes a lot of work for Mother, doesn't it? Don't you think she ought to have all the help she possibly can get? I have a few suggestions to make.

1. Wash the dishes twenty-one times each Saturday. You can see how helpful that would be. I always thought dishes should be washed every meal. So if you have 3 meals a day 7 days a week that makes 21 meals & 21 times to wash the dishes.

2. Dust each thing seven times every Saturday.

3. Play sweet music on the piano while Mother is giving Bruce [i.e. Anthony] *his dinner, breakfast, mid-morning snack, afternoon tea, and just-before-bed-luncheon.*

4. Read to Bruce often so that he won't have quite so many times to say, "Mother, I wish you'd tell me what would be fun to do."

5. Talk over with Kenneth the idea of having a little worship service once or twice a week. Fix up an altar, have candles, work out your service and invite Mother and Anthony to attend. Like the idea? I'm beginning to feel bad that we have so seldom invited God into our home. Of course you will find a place for Bruce in the service, too.

6. Mother and I both love you and your three brothers very much. And because we love you we both wish you to have the very best things life has to offer. Mother would not be satisfied to give you rotten oranges when she could give you good, fresh ones.... Well it is that way with the things Mother gives you to read. So I think I'm going to ask you and Kenneth to spend two minutes reading or listening to the good stories in your new books for every one minute you spend on the poor stuff you find in the comics. Mother and I wish you to feed your mind with good food as well as your bodies.

...How are you and Anthony getting along now? I suppose he does lots of singing, especially at night. Does he keep you awake? [Priscilla says I was fussy and fretful with the pain the hernia caused, so didn't sleep well.] *I am sorry he isn't very well but with a nice Mother like he has I think he will be all right....*

Yours with love,
Daddy

June 26, 1944

Dearest Doris:

There is a half an hour before bus time so I'll use it to start a letter to you. I came to Austin this morning for the purpose of getting you a birthday present. That purpose has been accomplished. I will hold the present until we get ready to leave and then send it. If it comes a week or two too soon please don't open it until the 21st. The package will be about 15"x8"x1½". So, if it comes too soon you will recognize it. [This was a large set of knitting needles in a beautiful, ribbon-decorated case. I remember looking at that set with fascination when I was little. Priscilla has it now.]

When you get your next check will you please send me $30 from the tything money. My venture into money lending was disastrous. The man I lent the money to has been court marshaled, given a month in the stockade and fined one month's pay for going AWOL and disobeying a non-com. I heard the sergeant-major mention it over the telephone and I expressed alarm. "There goes my $30," I said. I kissed my hand to an imaginary $30 flying away. The Colonel heard me and called me in to talk to me like a Dutch uncle about lending money. The result of the discussion was an order from him not to lend any more money. An order from the C.O. must be obeyed. So I won't do it any more. But my integrity is at stake now so I've got to pay up that money. Please send me the $30 if the fund has that much. It won't happen again.

I enjoyed your writing about Anthony. I'll bet he's beginning to be interesting now. Write me plenty about him, won't you because I'm very interested. Tell me lots about all the children. No telling when I shall see them again...

Well, it's 9:30 p.m. It was a dandy letter you wrote. I am going to enclose a couple of pictures of me. I don't like them much but I suppose that's what I look like. I'm going to enclose a piece of paper with directions on it about what to do if I don't come back. Read it carefully and then put it in a safe place. I want to know that you are taken care of.

Good night sweetheart.
I love you with all my heart.
Jerry

July 3, 1944

Dearest Sweetheart:

I remember one year ago at this time. I was in the North Station in Boston waiting for you. I saw one train unload all its people and you were not on it. I feared you were not coming. Then another train came in and unloaded its people, and there you were! Gee! How good you looked, your hair down to your shoulders attractively dressed and sweet from top to toe. Was I thrilled! I'll say I was. And we had a wonderful time, didn't we?

Well, dear one, our time has come. We have been given our departure date and we know what camp is to be our designation. Before long you will receive a change of address card with an A.P.O. so don't send any more mail down here.

We are all glad that the period of doing nothing is almost over. May and June of this year were some different from May and June of the two previous years.

This is a short letter. As soon as I hear from you again I will answer your letter right off.

Yours with great love,
Jerry

July 8, 1944

We are already to go and before you get this we shall be well on our way. It's going to be a long train. I have purchased $64 of candy to sell on the train, not at a profit, so the personnel will be able to buy some. Figlioli will be train boy and sell his wares from car to car with all his usual gusto. He is 75% clown anyway and we won't need any better entertainment than seeing him come. It will *break his heart, however, not to be able to make a profit on each transaction. If possible, I will call you as soon as we reach the staging area and know whether we shall be able to take some time out. Will Bruce's* [Tony's?] *condition make it impossible for you to come down if I were able to get a day off? I shall be satisfied to be guided entirely by your judgment in this case.*

Tuesday afternoon I was very much surprised to see Lt. Balsley at Camp Swift again. In previous talks she has done me a lot of good. I told her I hoped we would meet again after the war. She said she would like to write to you and I said I knew you would enjoy a letter from her. So you may hear from her.

I knew, when almost two weeks elapsed between letters that you must be in trouble. It was a mighty long wait, the longest yet. Your mother helped some with her letter of a week ago. Can't you get Kenneth to help out some? I don't want him to be a lazy boy when there is so much to do. It seems that now he is through the fifth grade he could write from your dictation. It would mean a lot if I could hear at least once a week. Soon my letters will be getting farther apart.

Soon our anniversary will be here. Twelve years! How have they been, sweetheart? For myself I can always say that I have always been happy in your presence. Living with you has been an experience of deep content. Never, during the fourteen years I have been in love with you have I ever wished I had someone else as a partner or a date. Love as lasting as ours is something very precious, don't you think?...

Is Bruce's [Tony's?] *urgent condition going to make it impossible for you to get your picture taken, too? Oh, I hope not. I wish so much for that before the boat sails. But here again I shall be guided entirely by your judgment. I won't be childish again and take offense. I'll just know it couldn't be done.*

Well, sweet girl, pray for me. Pray that I may be useful and helpful in this big job ahead. And pray that I may be worthy of my sweet and beautiful little wife. Please tell Kenneth I shall write to him when we are allowed to and I'll tell him about our long ride in our long train.

Goodbye now my loved one,
Jerry

July 21, 1944

Happy birthday, Sweetheart!

Rather late? No. I can wish you one even if you don't hear me.

I've been to New York twice. Once on that Tuesday evening when I hoped so much you would be there! It wasn't your fault, of course but if Edna hadn't been there to take me in hand I fear for my sanity. I wanted so much to see you! Edna was very nice to me. She took me to her apartment and gave me a good supper and kept me talking until midnight. Swell girl. If she hadn't been there I should have gone back to camp and sulked.

Believe me, my dear, I was might sorry to hear that you are sick again! It is nothing that you can't handle by plenty of rest and proper food, is it. Edna suggested that you were much sicker than your letter of a month ago indicated and you were trying to keep it from me. Now I don't want that. Please let me know all about it, sweetheart. I can stand it. I don't want to have you feel that you need to make life easy for me. If you are in any kind of trouble I want to know. Perhaps I can suffer with you.

I shall not forget our anniversary but I'm afraid you will have to take that on trust.

And remember that wherever I am you have a man who loves you.

Your
Jerry

Later, in a letter dated August 9, 1944, Gerald told his sister Gladys how his hopes to see Doris once more before sailing for Europe had been frustrated.

I hoped, when we got settled in our new camp I could get off long enough to see Doris so I sent her a telegram asking her to meet me at the Prince George Hotel. We did get passes that allowed us to spend a short time in New York but when I went to the Prince George no Doris appeared. Edna, her sister, came and told me that Doris received the telegram, but she was in bed with arthritis and couldn't come. Her mother called Edna, who lives in New York, and Edna came and told me. She invited me to her apartment for supper with her and her husband. While she was getting supper ready I put through a call to Enosburg Falls and talked with Doris. Poor girl! She's having a pretty tough time.

The 111th Evacuation Hospital, according to the map Lieberman, the Jewish organist, made later (see p. v), sailed from New York July 26 and arrived Liverpool August 1. The date of the following letter is partially unreadable.

July 2_, 1944

Dearest Doris:

Your V-mail letter arrived and I was very glad to get it. I hadn't thought of crutches in connection with your sickness. I wonder if it was as bad as it was 12 years ago. I am glad it is better and hope by the time this letter gets to you all traces of it will have disappeared.

We are now on a fine ship and have had a pleasant voyage so far. Morford is in charge of our activities as chaplains and we have six other Protestant chaplains and six Catholic chaplains. We have divided our chaplains into two teams of four each and each afternoon one team holds a service on the officers' deck. We alternate with this service. After that our team has a service for the E.M. forward and the other team has a service for the E.M. aft.

These services are hard on our neural resources. One of the medical officers said "While the chaplain was trying to run a song service I heard one man say 'I just played that ace.'"...

It's funny about chaplains. Often times a chaplain may be

swell with his men because he has got acquainted with them and they like him, and yet he may be a rotten preacher. But in a service on board where officers and men of several different units are present a poor, rambling and long winded sermon can give the cause of religion rather a bad blow and discredit the chaplaincy with those who would like to be its friends.

I hope, when our anniversary comes up you will marshal some of the many memories that are our common treasures. Here are some I'm going to bring up.

1. I'm going to think of the time we went to the 4-H round-up at St. Albans and I drove Genevieve I [his car] *well filled with the girls of your club. You rode right next to me on the front seat and I liked it. You said, "It's hard for me to realize that you're a minister." Somehow, coming from you I considered that high praise. Right then I made up my mind that you were the girl I was going after.*

...4. I'm going to think of the time we went from Worcester to Gladys' and I gave you your ring. And I shall remember how I drove down to Worcester for you and we came through the Notch [Smuggler's Notch, between Stowe and Jeffersonville, Vt.] *just at sunrise and how surprised your folks were to see you.*

5. I'm going to think of our wedding trip and the first night at the St. Johnsbury House. How nice you were in your silk pajamas

I'm going to think of lots more that I'll write about later.

Love, Jerry

England

The 111th Evacuation Hospital shipped across the Atlantic and set up for further training. Because letters were censored to conceal troop movements from the enemy, Gerald wasn't allowed to say where they were, but Lieberman's wall map shows them landing in Liverpool and spending time in Cheddar. It also states, "3 August '44 assigned Ninth US Army."

August 4, 1944

Dearest Doris:

Here we are somewhere in England. And what a country! We had a train ride from the disembarking port that showed us some of the English countryside. How beautiful it is! And there were so very many interesting things to see and do. There were the English trains, for instance made up of cars that opened on the side, of small engines and of still smaller freight cars. Those freight cars are about sixteen feet long and hold about ten tons and they are coupled by chains instead of the automatic couplers we are used to. And each car has four wheels instead of the eight we are used to.

The English countryside is beautiful. The scenery is similar to what we are used to in Vermont. But the English villages are very lovely. I can understand Miss Anderson's remark, "After being in England, America looks like one big junk pile." Even the stations are beautified. At one place I noticed a building of churchly appearance and wondered why a church should be so close to the railway. When we passed the end I saw it was just a freight house but it looked to be better built than 90% of America's churches. Almost all the buildings are of stone. And most of them have tile roofs. And most of them sit right close to the street. But unlike the houses in American cities that are so close together, they don't look badly at all. I noticed one village where there was a solid block of tenements and the roof of each tenement was sloping down from one side to the other. One could get on the roof of the first house and walk up and down, up and down on the roofs from the first house to the last. From a distance the roofs appeared to be like the teeth of a rip saw.

The village where we are now is no exception to the rule that all English villages are pretty. It, too, has stone houses. Almost every house has a garden and at least half of the garden is reserved for flowers. They use hillsides as steep as the last pitch up Hazen's Notch in Vermont to grow their food. This is a great place for bicycles. Almost everybody rides one. And that goes for old women in their seventies and little kids like Bruce. We see lots of tandems here. We've even seen one with a side-car. It was quite a sight to see mama and papa riding by with papa in front, mama behind and little feller about 1½ years old nicely tucked into his side-car. What fun!

Naturally I am very much interested in the English people, especially the children. The first words we heard said to us were "Got any gum?" That has been the constant chant ever since we arrived. I took a walk yesterday and saw two boys about seven years old. One said, "Have you any gum?" I had four chicklets. So I said I had. Before I could deliver those chicklets there were seven boys right there. Talk about the loaves and the fishes! Well I gave each a piece of candy and four of them a chicklet each. I have yet about nine Hershey bars. These children are allowed through rationing 12 oz of candy a month. An American with American candy and American cigarettes finds himself with some powerful bargaining power.

A propos to this I wish you would send me some candy. You are allowed to send a five pound package. So now you can reverse the process. Instead of my sending candy to you, which you should not eat, you send me a box which I shall use to gladden the heart of some English child or adult whom I am liable to wish to help. These people have carried on so wonderfully that it is a privilege to be able to bring some small measure of happiness to them.

I went to town on the bus today and returned in the afternoon. The bus was so full they had to leave some passengers behind. Here they have a practice of having a man driver who does nothing but drive, and a woman conductor who takes fares and tries to keep everybody happy. This one on the return trip reminded me of Gladys with her cheerful chatter and affectionate way with everyone. She had to squeeze though and take fares from the 54 original passengers, see that people got off and on safely and that no one went dead-head. One person offered her a piece of candy and she remarked she was very hungry, probably because the schedule made her go without her dinner. So, when we arrived I went over to my room, which is across from the bus terminal, dug out two chocolate bars, the orange I didn't eat for breakfast, and the small package of cigarettes we get in our K rations and offered them to her. How pleased she was! Most English people haven't seen an orange for years!

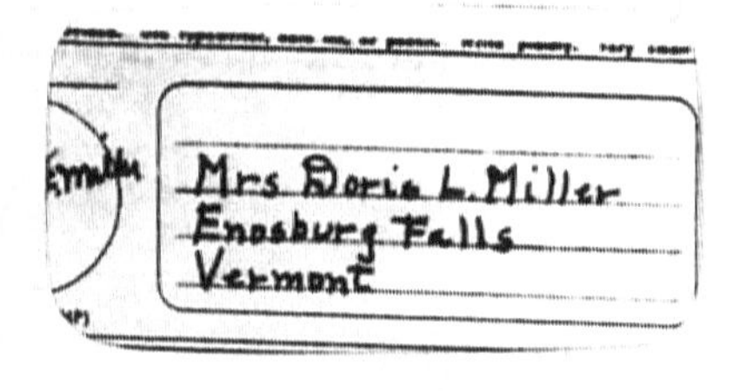

V-mail was developed to save space and weight on mail flights. A brief letter was written on a form with space for the address at top. The letter was microfilmed with thousands of others and the film flown across the ocean. There it was printed at reduced size, folded in thirds to fit in a window envelope (shown above in actual size), and delivered by regular mail. Gerald's V-mail message of April 8, 1945 is shown on p. 174.

I'll write again soon and tell you what I am doing. Please don't neglect to get your picture taken when you are well enough, and send it with the candy. And write by air mail after this. It gets here faster than V-mail and you can say much more.

I haven't seen anyone over here yet that looks as nice as you. How I would love to have you with me! And I hope we can be together before too long. Tell me all about everybody when you write and what you are doing. Tell me how you are, dearest, even if you aren't well. I hope you are better and that everything is all right with you.

I love you, sweetheart!

Your Jerry

The first line of this letter quotes a popular song. The mention of Westfield and Lowell further along refers to how he had served two churches in neighboring villages in Vermont, holding an early Sunday morning service in the smaller church and an 11:00 am service in the larger.

August 8, 1944

Dearest Doris:

How's the Lady today? Her lover who is far, far away is all right but having a cold. It's only about the second cold I've had since I joined the army but it's a real one.... Of course I hope you have by now completely recovered from the last attack of arthritis and that everything at home is well in hand.

We have been here a week now and I am beginning to feel quite at home. I have my office in the bank building right up against the sidewalk and people going by can see right in my window. Figliola has made a sign out of cardboard with the single word Chaplain in capital letters two inches high. It seems that everyone who goes by notices that sign. Some read it aloud and then look in the window at me as if to see the lion and hear him roar. Today a woman about your mother's age looked in and waved at me.

...In the evening I went to the Methodist church and after that service Col. King and I went in and had a two hour visit with the vicar and his family. He happened to have his daughter down from a nearby city and her husband was with her. The six of us had a fine time conversing together. They served us tea along with sandwiches, tarts and a fruit dessert, the whole of which must have cut somewhat into their rations. The next morning I took over four oranges, three I had saved from Friday, Saturday and Sunday's breakfast and one of Col. King's. Oranges have been off the market here for more than 4 years. I wish I had taken over 4 Hershey bars, too.

We are beginning to get very much attached to our village here. One evening after the movies I went to the pub with Col. King and three majors... After they talked quite a while and surveyed Englishmen who came in and were surveyed in return, we were invited to play a game of skittles. This is a bowling game of nine pins. The alley is wider than our alleys and the pins are placed right behind each other instead of alternately like ours. Here's the way the pins in skittles are set up: Look at that and you can see how easy it is to miss the whole business by sending the ball between the rows. That's what I did, time after time. Eight of us played and I got a very low score. I can see why they say the pub is the poor man's club. Lots and lots of people come out, drink their beer and play games.

We are looking forward to a treat on Thursday evening. The officers and nurses are going to our neighboring metropolis to hear the London Philharmonic Symphony Orchestra....

Your V-mail letter arrived after I wrote the last letter to you and I was thankful for the assurance it gave. I have written Edna one of my long letters and thanked her for all she did to help me through that difficult night. Did you have anyone to help you through? It is the worst part of the army for me to be able to do so little for you.

Our mess officer is getting after us in great shape about eating all our food. American officers are especially bad about that. The Methodist vicar said that along the first the preceding unit threw away so much stuff that the farmers who picked up the garbage were delighted. In one case whole hams were thrown away because they were a little mouldy. The farmers cut off the mould and were already to save a month's meat ration coupons. But you can bet that didn't last long. A general of supply made an inspection of one mess in England. He issued orders that if an officer left anything that should be eaten and threw it away, it was to be saved for him and eaten later. He went to a garbage can, delved down into its depths, found a whole pork chop that had been thrown away. He took it out, looked at it, took a bite out of it and then made the mess sergeant finish it. I have noticed a drastic change already in our officers. Most of the plates are clean when they are through. Well, they may as well. There's no place to go for food if they're hungry....

I went to our sectional HQ last week. I was given orders by the Post Chaplain in the Staging Area to report to the area chaplain as soon as I got here. So I went in and found the chief chaplain gone but the second in rank, a profane major of the corps, was there and he gave me the information. He told me I was going to be issued a bicycle. That'll be a help. I can get around much better. There may be other troops around here without a chaplain so he told me not to get so deeply involved in civilian affairs that I couldn't leave at short notice for some place else. I can see myself peddling about the countryside having a service at post 1 at nine, one at post 2 at 10:30, at post 3 at noon and at post 4 at 7. Shades of Westfield and Lowell! These English villages are so close together that one can take distances in easy stages.

There is a little old woman who lives right tight against the place where we are billeted. She does my washing and that of the other men in that building with me. Her name is Mrs. Scrouse. She is a source of so many things. The men below me were fitted out with a table, table cloth, two chairs, a pillow for their cot and she told them where they could get coal for their fireplace. She's always inviting us in for a cup of tea. That's bad because she's limited to a half pound of tea a month. I wonder, when you make up my box, will you put in some ¼ lb. packages of tea and a pound box of lump granulated sugar. That will help repay some hostess who has been kind to lonely Americans so far from home.

This next letter is to Gerald's sister, Gladys Miller Craven, whose daughter Sarah (Sally) was born April 2, 1944. Percy was Gladys's husband, Joe and John their two sons who were around 20 years old. Mikey, with a long *i*, was Gladys's nickname for Gerald. No one else ever called him that.

August 9, 1944

Dear Gladys:

...I suppose you hear regularly from John. And I suppose you hear regularly from Sarah Ann. Is that her name? Right now I hear a child crying and it sounds exactly like an American child crying although adults here talk somewhat differently. It's surprising how many English people there are over here. They're almost all English. It's a good place just the same. The only failing I've detected so far is their coffee. It's all it's cracked up to be and even worse. Fortunately we have our own mess personnel and they know how to make G.I. coffee that can be enjoyed. So we haven't anything to gripe about yet. And so far I like it fine.

Remember me to Percy and Joe, if he's there.

Yours sincerely
Mikey

August 13, 1944

Dear, sweet Doris:

Say, you're doing real well with your letter writing. I've already received three V-mail letters from you since we arrived. Your last one, written August 4 got here on Aug. 11. Thanks, dearest. They mean a great deal to me.

We are more or less settled by now. Our baggage has come and we have all we want. They did a good thing for me by putting my office where they did. It's right here on the main street. Up stairs is the dispensary so Major Lewis comes by my door and stops in frequently. I go up there occasionally and have a chat with the non-coms in charge there. Everything's handy. I have a library here so people come in for books and stop to talk and look over my religious display.

Had our P. Ex. got started when I wrote you last? Well, it's under way now and we find ourselves strictly on the ration system. Three candy bars a week, a package of gum a week, a package of cookies a week, two bottles of coke a week, a package of cigarettes a day, peanuts once in two weeks, a package of razor blades, a cake of soap, a package of laundry soap once in two weeks... I got my candy and gum last week and put it into our picnic with the Baptist minister's family. We used six candy bars that way. I gave my gum away yesterday to four children walking home from the show. So, you can see that the war has done something to these people.

I haven't fallen in love with any English girl yet. In fact I haven't even found a person to take Lt. Balsley's place. I hope to get well acquainted with our head nurse but she is of the old maid type, very business like and right to the point. The girls are a little bit in awe of her and she lays the law down in no uncertain terms. However, inside I think she is a fine girl. I imagine a friendship with her is something that will take quite a long time. One would have to prove himself before she would accept him. I have discovered a girl who lives across the street from us. I would like to cultivate her affection. I'm afraid the enlisted men will get farther with her than I will, however. They do more interesting things. She is nine.

August 15, 1944

It's very early to think about it but I want to get your advice about Christmas presents to the children. It seems that we are allowed to send things home provided they are not foodstuffs, rationed goods or battlefield curiosities. I've asked the schoolmaster what I could send and, true to form, he suggested books. How do you think the children would feel about receiving some English books from their daddy? Or would they like something else. I think I shall go to a city on Friday and look carefully about for something. I won't buy now but I'll look for ideas. And about your sweet self? What would please you?

At last I've purchased a bicycle. It was picked up by one of the Jewish men, Rosenbaum. I asked the Baptist minister about it and he said it was a good bike. It is a pre-war make which means that it is made of better materials than bicycles of today. It has three speeds which is a great help in this hilly country. It has brakes on both front and back wheels, hand brakes. Figlioli is quite interested in it and offers to clean it up for me. I'm going to give a real workout before the week is over.

August 21, 1944

My work is going well except that I'm bothered because I don't get any of the enlisted men out to my services. So far not more than ten of them have attended any of the three services. Last Sunday only one was out. However, before going to the Colonel about it I'm going to have a talk with the men. I'll squeeze it into my session next Thursday on knot tying. The prospects for having a good choir seem to be real good. One of our young medical officers, who is a first class organist, is directing the choir and so far we've had eleven nurses and five men out to rehearsals. So, things are looking up in that direction.

Joining the army hasn't deprived me of becoming a handy man. Now that we are in England lots of the men and the nurses, too, find it difficult to get the things they want. Now I have two watches to take in when I go to town again. A nurse came in this morning and told how there was a fireplace in her room but nothing to burn in it. So I said I would get her some coal if she would get permission to use the grate. If I succeed in supplying her I have visions of going into the coal business. We have nurses in more than a dozen different homes. Can you see me with my jeep and a two wheeled cart like Mr. Mc Donald's in East Arlington, running up one street and down another calling "Any coal today?" That would look good on my monthly Chaplain's report, "Delivered 200 lbs of coal to twenty people fifteen times." Whew. And now my office is being fixed up so well more and more are coming into it. Two nurses came in this morning and said, "We heard a rumor that you were serving coffee here." They had missed breakfast and were very hungry. Well my assistant has just been out and got a teakettle which we can put on this gas heater. We'll get our ration of Nescafe, buy some cups, and the next time we'll be prepared. I don't know where we are going to get the milk. But you know how much I like to have people come in and enjoy themselves. And I think the nurses deserve a special break because the work in an Evacuation Hospital in the field is no joke, especially for nurses.

I plan to take a bicycle trip each week. There's a very interesting city about twenty-five miles away which I think I shall tackle soon. But I think I shall wait and see what the Baptist minister has planned for this week. He said something about a bicycle trip and I hope it materializes. I want to get some of the value out of that wheel before I turn it in or give it away. There are many interesting places to go to and I always hunt out the book store and see what they display. So far I have not been impressed.

I'm looking anxiously for another letter from you and I hope, when it comes, that it will say you are all well again. I am praying for you, my sweetheart.

Yours with love,
Jerry

On August 23, 1944, the French 2nd Armored Division under General Jacques-Philippe Leclerc advanced on Paris from the north, while the U.S. 4th Infantry Division approached from the south. German General Choltitz defied Hitler's order to destroy the city's bridges and monuments, and surrendered to the Allies on the 25th. The liberation of Paris lifted spirits across the allied countries.

August 24, 1944

Dearest Doris:

I was thinking about you yesterday morning while going on the bus. I was trying to remember what your voice sounded like. What does it sound like? And I was thinking about you yesterday. On a bicycle trip with the Baptist minister and his wife we stopped at a large farm. We were showed around and finally visited the dairy. They get 36 cents a gallon for their milk. They sterilize their own milk cans, cool their milk by running it through a cooler, and sell the milk for half its market price. She actually gave us a glass of milk, the first raw milk I have drunk since being home in May. We have powdered milk for cereal and canned milk for coffee.

I had a great longing for you today. I just wished I had you by me, that's all.

Naturally the people of England are very enthusiastic over the liberation of Paris. I heard the Marsellaise played several times yesterday. I heard a very jubilant commentator declare the immensity of the victory in northern France. Seeing these headlines in the English papers telling of complete routs of the German 7th Army makes me wonder what the headlines in American papers might be. People of England have a special stake in this victory because it may mean the end of these pilotless bombs that have done so much destruction. Well, I hope the good news continues. General Patton is on the rampage again and that is always bad news for the Germans. With no more Rommell to chase Montgomery will have to find some other objective. It may be Goering this time.

August 25, 1944

I had lunch in a restaurant on the third floor of a department store. It was a large place into which people were admitted by

11:30 but not served until 12:15. I never saw anything like the patience of these English people. They'll stand in line for an hour at a time to get into a store or a tea room and when they get seated they'll wait more. They never ask a girl to hurry or worry a waiter or clerk by odiously comparing him to a snail or still life. Well I waited a half hour before being waited on. Finally I was presented with the bill of fare and ordered mock turtle soup, fried fish, mashed potatoes, Haricord beans (merely navy beans parboiled) and plum pudding. Everything was good. A middle age couple right next to me explained that my dessert was not really plum pudding but plum dumpling. I recognized it as dumpling, the pastry of which was similar to my mother's apple dumpling. The coffee was not good. The rest was OK and it only cost 2/3 [2 shillings and 3 pence] *which is about 45¢. I tipped the waitress with a package of Camels instead of the usual sixpence. She was very pleased.*

In the evening on Friday I attended the Jewish service. I'm not making very rapid strides with my Hebrew but I have hopes. We had a discussion about the Jewish home life and marriage which very soon resolved itself into a discussion of marriage and divorce. The argument for a time was heated and lengthy and came to no conclusion. You would have enjoyed it. Next Friday the discussion is going to be on the subject, "Do Jews want a Homeland?"

I made my trip today all right. I drove myself to the Camp and had a service there. Only six were present. I got back just in time for my 9:45 service here. Fourteen nurses, 2 officers and three men were out. Obviously our men are not church minded. I went to the Church of England service at eleven and felt it was time wasted. However, the service was well attended, very well. But all the churches have this abominable habit of presenting visitors with hymnbooks without the music. So, as far as the service was concerned I was a spectator, not a worshipper.

We've a new major now. That's bad news for me for it confirms the uneasy suspicion that Col. King is leaving. Boy! Am I sorry to see him go!

I'll answer your letter tomorrow.

Yours with great love,
Jerry

August 28, 1944

I am glad you've told me all about your lameness. I hope you're wrong about being lame all fall. It seems that this war is much harder on you than it is on me. I'm sorry for that, especially when I think of how much extra work I'm responsible for in persuading you to have another (girl?). I sometimes wish I could look into your mind and see how you feel toward me on that account. Will you tell me truly? I care most for your good opinion of me. I'm so sorry for you, my dear.

I'm glad to hear that the littlest fellow is getting along all right. Of course I have just the vaguest idea of what he looks like. And this gives me another idea. If you have in mind getting me a Christmas present here's what I wish you could do. Take your whole family to the photographers and have a picture taken of the whole family <u>*as well as one of yourself*</u>*. That means two pictures, doesn't it? Two Christmas presents. I have before me the picture of our family with Anthony completely invisible, you know why. I love that picture. But I'm awfully greedy and I want one of you looking your prettiest and one of you all with Anthony visible this time. I can think of only one present that would mean more to me and that, of course, would be to be with you. But we mustn't expect that for a long time to come.*

France & Belgium

On September 1-4, Gerald's unit convoyed to Dorchester, sailed from the port of Weymouth, landed at Omaha Beach and convoyed to Carentan, France, at the base of the peninsula that has Cherbourg at its tip.
Gerald mentions breaking his glasses. These would have been for reading, since he was far-sighted. He could get around and drive without them, but reading would have been hard.

V-mail, 3 Sept. 1944

Dearest Doris,

I'm still too busy to write a good letter, but I wish you to know I'm still thinking of you. This morning I attended a service in a tent of a hospital somewhere in France. We are stopping here on our way to elsewhere. Our convoy drove through enough of France to make me feel awful. It is the grimmest ride I ever took.

We spent yesterday in a field, just the convoy of us, and the men had a grand time exploring around while waiting for orders to move on. Mostly we heated water for coffee over a grand fire, something we never could do in England. We ate three times there. We passed through ruined towns and people in them certainly looked as if they were ruined, too. How glad I am you and the children don't live over here.

I broke my glasses yesterday and now I am going to have a chance to see if I can get along without them.

I hope you are getting better and better and better, loved one.

Your Jerry

September 5, 1944

Dearest Doris:

Now that we've settled long enough to get my field desk unpacked I'll write an air mail letter. I can't tell you all that has happened but I'll do what I can.

We left England in two groups. About a fifth of our unit went with the convoy of trucks and the rest went to the marshalling area by train. I was convoy leader again so I went with the trucks. We had a nice trip down and I saw the English Channel for the first time. But when we arrived at the little city where the camp was at which we were to stay, - oh my! What a dirty place. The mess hall was so dirty it was enough to turn one's stomach just to look at the tables. And we slept in cold rooms without blankets. Were we glad to get away from there! Our convoy got off that afternoon and we had a ride down to the place where we loaded all our trucks on the L.S.T. boats. These boats come right to shore, wait for the tide to go out, let down their ramp and in we drive. There the boat stays until high tide and out she goes. This boat takes all our trucks (26) and us, too. We officers had better quarters than when we crossed the ocean. Two of us to a stateroom. And we had complete freedom of the ship.

If you will get Kenneth to look in magazines until he finds a L.S.T. boat you'll see that it is a Diesel motor ship about 300 feet long and drawing about 12 feet of water. Being flat-bottomed it rolls violently, especially in this choppy Channel. I lost my breakfast. I never had anything come up so easily in all my life but I didn't feel sick. After that I spent some time in my bunk and then went on deck. We rode for about a day and saw many ships and some airplanes. When we arrived at our destination we had to wait for the tide to be right and when the time came we drove off under blackout conditions right onto the beach and to our parking area. We stayed there in the rain until daylight.

We spent most of the day in that area. It was cold and wet but after daylight the men built a fire and found their way into the rations. They found cases of K rations, two cans of turkey and two cans of Spam, sugar, coffee and condensed milk. So they decided to make a picnic of the affair. One can of turkey was left on the fire too long and the same thing happened to that that happened to my Barbasol in Westfield [i.e. it exploded]. *But the other can was rescued in time and we had coffee and turkey sandwiches. It wasn't long after that before they found a 10 gallon can and started heating water in that for coffee for dinner. That with K rations and Spam made up dinner. They didn't let the can get cold before they started heating water for supper. And in between times we explored around. We dug shrapnel out of trees, discovered air-raid shelters and plenty of foxholes. There was a donkey that attracted a lot of attention because he was so tame.*

When we received our orders to move and finally were on our way again. I didn't enjoy that ride at all. After four years of occupation the countryside was nearly all untilled and more than half the buildings in every town were destroyed. Most of the people exhibited no interest in us at all and gave the impression of being dirty, dejected and degenerate from infancy to old age. We all agree that we don't wish to stay here long.

I guess my V-mail has informed you of our present status. We are merely waiting. Rumors of all kinds are abundant and speculation as to our ultimate fate is rife. So far we have to live each day as a unit and leave tomorrow for itself.

How are you, my dear? Our mail hasn't come in for over a week now so I hope your next letter will tell me about great gains in your health. And are you getting enough money to get by? Let me know something about your finances. And if you haven't sent the box yet leave out the tea. Now that we are out of England I won't need it.

Yours with love,
Jerry

September 7, 1944

Dearest Doris:

...Now and then we try our French on the kids that come around here. One lad comes around soliciting washing for his mother. He knows enough English and the six of us in our tent know enough French to get by. But when my four handkerchiefs, suit of underwear and towel came back I decided I wanted to do my own after this. As we are really in a cow pasture and as cows are in the field below us their owners come through frequently we have a chance to throw an occasional bon jour or comment ca va at them. But we are a little suspicious of these French. After all, we are an army of occupation and I don't believe Vermonters would be very cordial to foreigners of a different religion who overran their country.

...In my last letter written to you from England I spoke of buying things for you all in England and leaving a deposit for them. Well, we pulled out without being able to redeem them so all I have actually is the beads of seashells I bought in the applied arts shop. We haven't been paid yet so I'm afraid when I do it will be too late to send the money to the Baptist Minister in our English village for him to try to get them. But I think I shall be able to buy something before I get home. If I can't I'll send Edna some money and have her shop for me in New York....

Priscilla remembers Mrs. Baylis, mentioned in this letter, as a know-it-all parishioner in East Arlington who criticized our parents a lot.

September 11, 1944

Dearest Doris:

After almost two weeks without mail our letters caught up with us on Sunday evening. How glad everyone was, including your devoted husband. In that mail were two letters from you, one from Mrs. Baylis (Ugh!) a V-mail from Gladys and a circular letter from the Acacia Insurance Co. Mrs. Baylis gave me a long harangue on the general subject of the worthlessness of men and the lovely qualities of women. She also suggested she was planning to make you a visit. Please, Doris, don't submit to any more torture than you already are subjected to. Be firm. And don't think because she can talk a lot Mrs. Baylis is either keen or deep or wise. I consider her a bigger fool than almost anyone I know. Otherwise she wouldn't exercise her talents of making enemies and imposing on friends....

I wonder what you do in your spare time. I assume that you do have some spare time because you can't possibly work all the time? Or does the work you can do take every minute? If you have long rest periods do you lie down and sleep or are you able to rest while reading? If you do read it occurred to me that now might be a splendid time to acquire a taste for good literature. I'm trying to do the same and I find that re-reading Great Expectations gives me moments of exaltation that I never get from anything written today. Can it be that these weeks and months are presenting an opportunity for laying the foundations of a new interest we can enjoy together? I loved those hours we used to spend reading aloud to each other. I hope there is something like that ahead of us. [I suppose he was reading the same tiny, leather-bound copy of Great Expectations that I read in Hinsdale, NH, around 1962, and which Priscilla now has at her house.]

We are still here in the old cow pasture. Yesterday we went from sun to sun without any rain, the first day in France without rain. Today is a lovely day, just like Indian summer. The officers spend most of their time making themselves comfortable. They forage around for boards and boxes to put things on, for stones to make soakage pits, for sticks to hang things on and for cans to put things in. Mr. Patterson, who has been in the army longer than anyone else in our tent, rigged up four sticks about 1½" thick and four feet long. He tied them together at the ends so as to form a square. Then he suspended them from the apex of the tent and, presto, we had a perfect frame for our coat hangers.... One of the captains had an anniversary celebration in our tent one night after dark. Bottles of whiskey were produced from bedding rolls and before long apparent adults were transformed into obvious children; children with very filthy minds and silly ideas. It lasted until about one o'clock and one of our tent mates talked in his sleep for about an hour afterwards. His conversation appeared to be entirely between him and a girl he was vainly trying to seduce....

[Gerald wasn't militant against drinking, but he was a teetotaler. I can imagine him watching men deteriorate into drunkenness and shaking his head.]

I went as officer with a truckload of men to the movies in town on Saturday night. What fun! The theatre was patronized both by American troops and French civilians. First there was a film showing General De Gaulle visiting Dekar. All the comment was in French. Whenever the French flag appeared the Frenchmen applauded. Whenever the Stars and Stripes appeared we applauded. Then came a new film called, "The Battle of France." It showed scenes taken in Paris. It showed poor old Marshall Pétain [Philippe Pétain, a hero of World War I after an astonishing victory at Verdun, was seen in 1944 as a German collaborator as Chief of State of the German-dominated Vichy government] *and there was a vague murmur of displeasure heard among the French. A little later it showed Laval* [the Premier under Pétain]. *Boy, what a mass of Boo's greeted his picture. There's no question of how the French feel about him. Next came a series of songs played by the U.S. Army Band in Washington. The picture was made before we adopted the present helmets. When General Marshall was shown everyone applauded.*

The feature picture was "The Gold Rush," with Charlie Chaplin. Chaplin's little antics, such as walking right to the edge of a cliff without realizing it is there and wrapping a shoe string around his fork and eating it like spaghetti tickled everyone. I could understand his popularity throughout the world for one didn't have to understand any particular language to enjoy the fun. I think he is the foremost movie comedian of all time.

...We had a nice service yesterday. I had the use of a big double tent and we set up the altar, had our field organ [a collapsible reed organ pumped by the player's feet] *and hymnbooks, and most of the people sat on cots. It worked out very well. We had about 50 out. I am planning an evening communion service for next Sunday if we are here. I'm purposely putting it in the evening so it can be by candlelight and only those will be there who really believe*

in communion and really wish to come. I certainly hope it will work out as I wish it to.

September 14, 1944

...My assistant is busy as usual doing nothing in particular but appearing to do it very impressively. He brings me complaints men have passed on to him, mostly about things I can't help any such as an order to pitch their pup tents in a different way or the hardness of the ground that makes digging latrines anything but a pleasure. He puts up notices and forges my signature to them and rearranges the stuff in my field desk so that it gives the appearance of never having been used. He likes to impress people with lots of pictures and a clean desk. Bandbox appearance seems to be his motto. I like to have something that is handy and gives the appearance of being used and useful. If I had an office he'd fix it so people wouldn't dare to come into it. I like to give the effect of "If you spit on the floor at home, do it here." Whenever there is really something that ought to be done someone else brings it to my attention. Ah me!

...One of the staff sergeants, whom I have worked with a lot during our bivouac days, showed me a note from his wife. It expressed suspicion that he was carrying on with some dame in the village we occupied in England. Someone probably had a spite against him so he wrote to the girl and told her stories about Leo playing fast and loose with this English girl. Well, there are girls in England that will go the limit with any man who has what they want but it so happened that the girl in question I knew. I met her the very first evening we pulled in and admired her looks and considered her O.K. She is a London girl that came to that area about four years ago for safety. Her husband is in the English army right here on the continent. Leo dated her for dances and went walking and cycling with her and, so far as I could see was doing what I would have done had that girl been one of our own nurses or Marian Nichols. So I wrote her a letter and showed it to him. He was very pleased about it. "That's a beautiful letter, Chaplain," he said. You never can tell how the Chaplain can help, can you.

I think Kenneth did real well with the letter he wrote. With the exception of the conclusion his English was good and his punctuation all right. I'm glad he wrote the letter and I hope he agrees to be your amanuensis as often as you are unable to write yourself.

Let's see, by now, I mean by the time you read this, you have been going to Dr. Samson for a month. What luck? Has he located the real trouble yet and put you on the road to recovery? Your condition makes me long to be there to help you. When Kenneth suggested that he and Priscilla would go one way and Bruce and Anthony another I wondered what they were going to do with you. Are you contemplating a stay at the hospital or a sanatorium? Just what did he mean by that?

I am still reading "Great Expectations." I have come to the place where Pip's benefactor has revealed himself and what a shameful revelation it was for Pip. This is the third time I've read this great book and I find myself enjoying it more than ever. I'm sorry it is the only book by Dickens with us for I should like to read Dombey and Son again. I wonder if Kenneth would care to have you read Oliver Twist with him. Dr. Martin of Bangor told me his boy read it when he was ten. Pretty young, but you know how exciting it is if one has the guts to stick to it. Is Kenneth still interested in good literature in the Bookhouse or have the comics taken over again? [*My Book House* was a 12-volume set of children's literature we had.]

When he wrote about your being so lame it was a triumph to be able to scratch your head I thought "How I would love to be there to take care of her." We started our married life together with you in trouble with arthritis. Perhaps we are going to have our second life together in the same condition. Well, I don't know of anyone that was happier with his new wife than I was with you and if it is to be that I should wait on you and carry you from place to place and help you all I can, I shall be happy to do it. Remember the shower where

Perley Crampton and I carried you across the living room so you could unwrap the gifts? Just so we do get together again, and soon. We'll take the last half of life in stride just so we are together. That's what counts with me.

September 18, 1944

Dearest Doris:

...I find myself wondering how you are and what you are doing. The mailman isn't as good to me even as he was at Camp Swift so any word I get from you I have to imagine. Our mail situation is bad anyway although some seem to get an abundance of mail and packages. It seems that I don't have letter-writing friends.

So I wonder how you are. I wonder if you are still in bed and unable to even comb your hair. I wonder if you are too lame to go down stairs and so you worry about how clean the kitchen is. In optimistic moments I dare to hope that each day shows progress, and that somewhere in the mail is a V-mail letter, written in your own handwriting stating that you are much better and are going to be well soon. And each morning and each evening I pray more earnestly for you that I ever prayed for anything before. I love you so much, sweet Doris. And I am thinking of you all the time. Please get well.

...I went for a ride on Saturday with two nurses. Lt. Engle has a brother whose grave she wanted to locate, so we visited four U.S. cemeteries in two days. We didn't find the grave but like the man who "went to the cemetery just for the ride" we had an interesting ride. We passed through several large villages and saw how people carried on their normal activities right in the midst of the ruins of whole city blocks. We would see a meat market with the meat hanging up, some women inside and what used to be a window now entirely open so customers could be served from the sidewalk. The small amount of stock suggested that there was no need to lock the place at night. Another building proved to be a banque and from my jeep I could have tossed an orange right through the opening that

was a window onto the lap of a girl working there—if I had had an orange. In one section of the road we got ahead of a thirty-ton tank. Boy, to ride in front of one of those things in a little car like a jeep and to hear and feel him coming on is a shivery thing. We went to a city and saw lots of indications of German occupation. And we went by many apple orchards, but the trees, though loaded, had such small fruit that no one cares to eat it. I went to all this trouble just to satisfy this nurse. I don't know whether she is satisfied or not.

I have finished "Great Expectations." The last chapters gave me a good chance to wash out my eyes and since getting the last letters from you I have been close to tears most of the time. My eyes ought to be good and clean. It is a wonderful book and I'd like to read another as good. Are you doing any reading?

You loving husband,
Jerry

September 19, 1944

Dear Mother Leach:

We are still in this cow pasture awaiting orders to move and alternately cursing the rain and enjoying the sunshine.... As we have nothing at all of a professional nature to do our men and officers are quite intent on manufacturing reasons for visiting various places. Not far away is a place that was completely bombed out and nothing stands. On Saturday afternoon a truckload of our officers visited this place to see the ruins. Personally I have already seen enough ruins to last me. But there are people who like that sort of thing just like others like to talk about their operations and still others used to take delight in witnessing hangings....

Since we don't have legitimate work to keep ourselves busy I have to try to keep up the morale through my office. I have a small library, mostly of paper bound books, and they circulate well. Whenever any of the nurses want anything they almost always come to me first and I try hard to help them. Being girls they are put under greater restrictions than the men and I do my best to lighten the boredom of our inactivity.... In passing through a place about the size of St. Albans I noticed a young woman, well dressed, with a clean face, her handbag on her arm and what do you think she was using to transport her purchases? A big, heavy, wooden wheelbarrow. How do you like that? What she could buy in that shopping district that would justify such elaborate transportation I couldn't conceive of for the only things we saw displayed in any of the places were meat and bread....

I'm afraid I'm in the dog house with the chief nurse. I'm sorry, too, because I like her. She came in this morning and asked for a map of this part of France. So I trotted out the maps and located the place she wanted. We estimated the distance and she went on her way. Before going I said, "If you need an officer to go along with you I'd be glad to accommodate you." The rule is that if the nurses go out an officer goes, too. We don't want our girls to take any risks. She came back later and said she wanted me to go this afternoon. I said I would be willing to go after the ball game but as they were depending upon me to catch I didn't want to let the team down. Still she wanted to go at one. We had quite a time and I even got a ribbing from the Colonel about it. She finally boiled it down to the fact that, since she is a captain, she doesn't need an officer anyway so she's going to pack the jeep with nurses and sail away. Now what do you think? Has she a right to be mad at me? I don't like her look when I offer to help her in the future. Ah me.

We are getting along quite well with the religious services. The Catholics only have to go about a hundred yards out of our area to find a mass every evening and each Sunday morning. Arrangements with another unit across the road have provided for the Jewish services and on Sunday night I attended a Rosh Hashanah service where there were at least 400 Jews present. And I have my services in a tent. On Sunday we had 54 out, the best yet for our unit.

6:30 P.M.

Well, we had our ball game and our side gave the M.C.s an 18-2 walloping. They're coming back for more tomorrow. I asked some of the nurses if their boss was mad at me and they said she wasn't. It seems she wanted to go to this place to see a boy friend of hers. They said she looked happy when she returned. "You'd have to do something pretty bad to get any of the nurses mad at you," they said. So I can breathe easier again.

Today's mail brought me two V-mail letters. One was from my father in which he said he had to move from that nice little place in Boyntonville to a flat on the third floor of a building in Troy. Ninth Street, he called it. I can imagine that my stepmother has a lot to say about walking up two flights of stairs every time she comes back from the grocery, and I imagine the problem of hanging out the washing is a tough one.... I am sorry he had to leave that nice little place in the country because he did a lot of work there. But now it will be much easier for him and Charles to get together. A four block walk will bring him to Fifth Avenue and the bus and a two block walk from the bus will bring him to my brother's place in Lansingburgh. It's an ill wind that blows nobody good.

The other letter was from Edna. She crammed a lot onto that single sheet. She told about Junior's [i.e. Carroll Leach, Jr., Doris and Edna's brother] visit down in New York, her visit to Maine, her attempts to put me up a box and the vain quest for lump sugar and she ended up by saying, "I hope the doctors get busy and discover the source of Doris' trouble." How is Doris getting along? She finds it so difficult to write and when she does write she tries to be so brave about her condition that I don't know what to think.... Can you take time to write me a V-mail note and tell me just how she is and if there is anything at all I can do for her? I'm willing to face the truth no matter how bad it is, but this fragmentary information keeps me guessing, and I don't like the thoughts that come into my mind when I do guess. If you can do this for me about every two weeks it will be a precious thing.

Yours sincerely and with best wishes to all,
Gerald

September 20, 1944

Dearest Doris:

The mail man was good to me both today and yesterday. Yesterday brought me a V-mail letter from my father and another from your sister. My father writes that he has had to move from the nice little place in Boyntonville to a third floor flat on Nineth Avenue in Troy. Edna writes that she has had company, her brother and sister-in-law, and has been to Maine to see her new in-laws there. Today brought a letter from your mother, written on August 31, and one from you written on September 6. So I shall settle down to a mailless state for another week.

In a way I like hearing from you only once a week. It would seem that a weekly letter might give time for you to improve enough to be noticeable and in that way each week the letter would have good news. For instance, if when this last letter was written you could stick out your tongue and touch your ear perhaps the next week you could comb your hair, and the next you could walk around the bed and the next you could go up and down stairs and so on, little as it might be, we could both be encouraged. It is fortunate that your mother and Aunt Helen could help out with the children, although I realize that both are sadly handicapped. 1944 will be looked back upon by you and me as our blackest year, I suppose. Perhaps we can make 1945 bright and glorious in comparison.

Yes, what you say about Bruce growing away from you does make your sickness harder to bear, but if he grows away from you, imagine what he'll be like to me. But he is a little boy and we shall both have a long time to get acquainted again. Becoming acquainted with Anthony and re-acquainted with the other three children, and even with you, my dear, will be a very fascinating game. I'll be changed because having people jump to do things for me and having both men and women deferentially call me sir will make me very hard to live with. So while we are playing that game with the children we can play it with each other. Old Dr. Denio, after living with his wife for about forty-five years was still surprised at the things she would do and say. I guess we are in for lots of surprises and I'll try to make most of mine pleasant to you.

I read your letter first, of course, and I expected the one from your mother would be filled with gloom and woe, but it wasn't. It was clear, from the brevity of the letter, that she is awfully busy and having the children there is a hardship. But she spoke with pride of your bravery and courage. I am glad they put you in a hospital and now I feel a little more confidence in the hope that you will be put to rights. Your letter shows me what a fine, courageous wife you are. I am mighty proud to have you and some day I shall be there to tell you about it.

September 22, 1944

Dearest Doris:

Yesterday was quite an interesting day. I provided the escort for seven nurses. We walked into town. They wanted to see something of the place and buy something of value to bring home. So away we went. The town is about as far from our cow pasture camp as is from your house in E.F. [Enosburg Falls] to the creamery where Jr. leaves the milk. We walked down and were soon in town. The streets are narrow and dirty. Although most of the houses have no drinking water piped to them the place must be as big at least as St. Albans. We saw children with wooden shoes like those Caroline brought home from Holland. But there was no indication that their code of cleanliness required them to leave their shoes outside. In fact every home that we passed had the same kind of smell that reeked from Ryea's in Westfield, and the appearance of most of them was like the home we took Lillian out of in 1933. [Lillian was a girl my parents fostered. By the time I remember, she was grown up and married.] And I noticed that the little girls were not embarrassed by pants either and when they sit down-----! But all the kids are friendly and not above asking for gum and candy. We saw two girls on a corner. One had a 10 Fr note [almost worthless in 1944 after years of inflation] in her hand and the other was playing with – want to guess? A rubber overcoat like we have in the chest of drawers! Imagine it.

The nurses were hard to keep together and, as their average age was not less than ten years below mine I made no attempt to keep them so. The place most interesting to them was the beauty parlor where real French perfumes were sold. They all bought liberally of those. They looked in at the hat shops but, what's the use of looking at hats when you can't wear them? They visited a tobacco shop where pipes and cigarette holders were sold but Woolworth's could beat that place at half the price. They also found a place where lace was sold, and after looking it over, most of the girls thought it was made in America. The girls spent some money but not much.

The town was so dirty and that dirt was characteristic of the church too, that we were glad we were camping in a cow pasture rather than being billeted in that stinking place. It was good to be back in the clean air again.

September 25, 1944

It is fun to listen to the men discuss the food situation while they are digging a latrine.... Because of the frequent moving of supply dumps and the uncertainty of refrigerator ships our supply of fresh meat is limited. So the mess officer tries to use what is available and that is one of three things. Baloney, spam and the C rations which are either hash or meat and beans. Well, we have had plain sliced baloney. Next day we have grilled baloney, the next day we have diced baloney and this morning we had chicken fried baloney. Now and then we get a surprise in the form of chicken, steak, pork chops and pork roast. But usually it is one species of baloney or another. So the men talk about it. One of them said, "The latest rumor is that they are going to feed us food at the mess." I said, "You're lucky you don't have a vegetarian as mess officer. Then you wouldn't get any meat at all." They all agreed that we had. Anyway, the dog that pals around with us has got so he turns his nose up at baloney.

While I was at Camp Swift Chaplain Morford said that my subscribing to Esquire was my one redeeming vice. Well, I thought my subscription had expired but, no, my September copy appeared in the mail yesterday. I'm pleased to get it because it was forwarded from Camp Swift which means it is a U.S. copy and not an overseas copy. The latter is much abbreviated. Esquire goes over big in the army because of its pretty girls and its advertisements, and its cartoons. I am glad I have that vice.

There are more and more signs of permanence about our camp. For one thing here in the Hqs tent there is more furniture. True it is slapped together out of two by fours and 5/8 inch boards, but it has a bench and a sign on it telling that the Detachment Commander is supposed to hang out there. Don't ever look there for him, though. And as you look over the area there are other signs. One is that they are putting up the second basket for basketball. Perhaps as the nippy weather comes on the softball league will give place to a basketball league. And around the mess tent there is evidence of staying. One is the sand on the floor of the tents and the other is the crushed stone in a large rectangle about the three G.I. cans that form the mess laundry. And some of the men have a very comfortable set-up. One of them was telling about his puptent which he and his tent mate have fixed up with an electric light. They have an automobile headlight bulb and several flashlight batteries they picked up at a signal dump. All they have to do is turn a switch on the pole and, presto, they have an electric light for reading, writing and rithmatic. But does this all mean we shall stay here for quite a while? It does not. The army rule is that as soon as you begin to get comfortable, then you get orders to move.

6:10 this evening

I went down town this afternoon and now I am ready to send the package home if I can find the wrapping paper. Here's what I have. For Kenneth a real French Beret with the brown sweatband. It is the kind that millions of Frenchmen wear and with that on anyone looks like a Frenchman. Since he has a birthday this December, too I am sending a French pencil box. It isn't much but he can be sure that everything in it is French except the English half penny. For Priscilla I have the pretty seashells picked up on the coast of Cornwall, England and hand painted. For Bruce I have another Beret, blue but with a white hatband. And for little Anthony I have another Beret, grey and small. I hope it will not be too big for him. And for you, well, you wait and see. I hope you will like it.

I went to sleep dreaming about you last night and, sure enough, you entered my dreams. I hope before another six months is up I shall be dreaming of you with you.

Yours with love,

Jerry

On September 30 the unit went to Euden, Belgium and stayed until October 7.

V-mail, September 30, 1944

Dearest Doris:

We're on the loose again. I'm with the convoy again and we've been over 350 miles in a circle which took us through the interesting part of France. We are here now in a French hospital of immense size just long enough to find out where we go next. We've had a sleep on a real mattress on a real bed and under real blankets and in a real building. We've shaved with running hot water, too.

We spent about 52 hours on the road, lost our way several times, ran almost out of gas, and spent about 4 hours resting in the trucks each night. And I've changed my opinion about France, too. The country we went through yesterday was like a scene out of Millet's pictures and the people were most friendly. I'll write at length about the trip when we get settled so I can. We still have over 200 miles to drive today and tomorrow. I think we are in for real business now. When we get to our destination we shall be setting up to receive patients right from the battle front. I may even yet be able to earn a day's pay.

I hope you will soon be well, dearest. I expect it will be at least 2 weeks before our mail catches up with us.

Yours with love,

Jerry

V-mail, October 2, 1944

Dearest Doris:

In another cow pasture! But in a different country. Now I know that before long the training of eleven months will begin to be of use. Our present location is temporary and the rest of the personnel hasn't caught up with us yet but soon we shall set up shop and begin work in earnest.

We passed through some lovely country during most of Saturday and how friendly the people were! Children were anxious to shake hands with us and give us things. One man accosted me with a bottle and a wine glass and offered me a drink. People tossed apples, tomatoes, pears & peaches into the jeep. Everyone waved and gave the V for Victory sign. But where we are now is another story. We have to prove ourselves friends before they more than tolerate us, and wherever we go, we never go singly. But it is beautiful country! We spent Saturday night in what used to be a tuberculosis hospital. A large building on a hill.

I hope you are getting better all the time.

I love you dearly.

Jerry

October 3, 1944

Dear Kids:

I'm going to tell you about our trip over here.

We started at seven o'clock on Wednesday evening. There were 25 trucks including the 3 jeeps. We drove until one and then rested for two hours. From 3 until seven I drove a ¾ ton truck and trailer. We stopped and had breakfast then. They took the field range off the back of one of the trucks and one of the majors bought some eggs at 90¢ per dozen from a French farm. We had French toast and coffee and eggs for breakfast. Then we started off and drove until we got out of gas. We went through very uninteresting country and by very uninteresting people. At our first stop we found an abandoned German tank and it had lots of bullets for machine guns in it. I've a strip of them. I hope to find a German rifle that will shoot them but I don't expect to.

We waited about four hours in the place where we waited for gas until a gas truck came and filled us up. We took 950 gallons. Think of that! We got on our way at about seven and drove until about four the next morning. I drove from 1-4. When we rested this time we were in a different part of the country altogether. The people were friendly. Not the English type of friendship described by "got any gum, chum," but the kind where children and adults walked up and down our line of trucks in the morning and handed out ripe tomatoes and apples and eggs. One of the kids made a special trip back to the hen house to get an egg the hen hadn't quite constructed on a previous visit. And if you didn't offer anything in return, that was O.K. If you handed out candy, gum or cigarettes you were rewarded by a smile. My jeep was at the very end of the column and I gave them an exhibition of a Barbasol shave which seemed to interest them very much.

From then on until we passed through the last big city before arriving here the people were very cordial and friendly. We drove through country that was level. We saw one big airfield where there were Boston Bombers and on the other side of the road were potato fields and people in them digging pommes de terre. Instead of putting the potatoes in barrels, bags or baskets as we do, they dumped them into large two wheeled carts and carried them home that way. Sometimes they would have four horses hitched to these carts, two horses together in front of the cart and the other two, one behind the other before the first two. And they were nice, big horses, bay in color and usually fat and sleek. Although this was wonderful country for tractors we only saw three on our whole trip of almost 800 miles.

We drove through one city right beside a R.R. yard where there were several French engines, but they were all out of order.

American engines do almost all the hauling in France where we were. When we finally arrived at our stop, it was again after midnight and we stopped in a big French hospital taken over by an American general hospital. It was from there that I wrote the V-mail letter. We stayed overnight there and the room we were in was dedicated to the Americans from New England. There was a large picture framed behind glass. It showed a tree with several branches and on each branch was a sign in French. One said (I translate) "Foundation made in memory of the men of New England killed in France in the country's service." There were as many as a dozen signs and they mentioned all the New England states and several cities such as Boston, Newton, New Bedford and others. I felt quite at home.

We were on the road again (Saturday) at noon. We gassed up again and drove through more of France. There we met the same friendliness and near the border we came to a series of long hills. Strategically situated where the trucks had to go slow were children with bottles of what they called beer. I guess it was a specie of home brew with a kick like an ostrich. So far as I knew none of our men bought any. Along this stretch of road for about 40 miles we saw tank after tank (German) abandoned by the roadside. In one city a big Mark IV was towed to a little park and left there as a monument. Quite expressive of German defeat. And there were so many cars turned up-side-down and all burnt off them that will burn that you think of the scrap drives back home.

When we crossed over into Belgium we found a beautiful country. We didn't stop at any place where we could verify the rumor about the 27 different kinds of ice cream, but we passed through one city where there was more on display in the store windows than I've seen since we left New York. As we penetrated deeper in this country we saw women out washing the sidewalks and the front of their houses! Some different from France. In one town there was a woman about Mother's age with a basket of fruit and she tossed some into every vehicle that had an opening. These people were offended if we didn't take something and shake hands with the kids.

Where we are now it is different. That's all I'm allowed to say.

We shall soon be set up to receive patients. When that time comes I'll write another letter.

Yours with love
Daddy

Holland

On October 7 the hospital moved again, to Maastricht, Holland.

October 10, 1944

Dearest Doris:

My last letter to you was finished on Saturday morning and here it is Tuesday already. Since I mailed your letter I have been the busiest I have been yet in this man's army. On Saturday I had to make arrangements for three sets of services and see the chaplains that would take care of the Catholic and Jewish services. That took a lot of running around. I also was given a room for an office, a huge affair, about as big as a kitchen in a five room apartment. When I put in my field desk, a table and three chairs there's not room for a cat to chase a mouse in the clear space. But it is cozy and warm (in the summer) and I like it. It took all of Saturday to get that done.

On Sunday I had to get ready for my three services. This is a Catholic high school and, hence, has a chapel. But the Germans in four years of occupation have so desecrated the chapel that except for a few of the windows that have recognizable religious symbols such as the lamb of God that looks as if it had been shorn, and a grape vine that refers to John 15, and a cross, and such, there is no resemblance to a place of worship. In the place where the altar was is a hole and on the wall behind is a large mural with three German soldiers, a woman with a baby and a man with a pick all in front of a background of factories. So I decided to arrange the seats so people wouldn't have to look at that picture. It took about an hour to clear a space for the service because the chapel is being used as an assembly point for surgical supplies and operating tables, boxes of dressings, anesthesia machines and cases of instruments take up at least half of the room. But the major in charge was careful that they left ample space for the service so we had ours there on Sunday.

On Monday I visited another evacuation hospital set up nearby. The Colonel wished me to talk with the chaplain there to see how he worked and especially to familiarize myself with the method of caring for the dead. So I went over, followed the chaplain through the wards, talked with him about the work and then I went with his assistant while he disposed of three bodies. Boy, that was something that a man needs good guts to do. It took the whole day to make this visit and when we came back it was supper time.

I had a nice, long discussion with one of the men last evening on the subject of morals. I think it is a healthy sign when they begin to come and talk things over with me. I was not greatly impressed by what a chaplain can do with the patients he has in a hospital like ours because he has them such a short time. But I feel that if I can reach my own men and nurses (the officers are mostly hopeless) that will be my great work. On Sunday evening I had a discussion on religion with another man and, although I don't claim to have helped him much, I do feel that this discussion is only the first of many.

Naturally I think a great deal about you and hope very much that you are winning your little war with arthritis. We haven't had any mail since we left Normandy and perhaps we shall even move from here before our mail catches up with us. So I am hopeful that the mail, when it does come, will have some good report on your physical condition. If it doesn't I know it will have a letter from you which will reveal again what a dear, sweet and courageous little wife I have back home. Yesterday, just before supper time at the other hospital I smelled some sort of a cheese concoction. It smelled good and it reminded me of the delightful smells that used to come out of your kitchen just about supper time when I would be reading to the children. It gave me mighty pleasant thoughts, that smell did, and the suggestion of homesickness it brought didn't spoil it either. When I get home again and get you back in it I am going to have a new sense of values. To be able to sit down with my own family at my own table every day and look across at my own wife all I want to is going to be a mighty precious thing.

Writing to Doris's parents, Gerald compares the school chapel to the church they attended in Enosburg Center. It seats about 150. This was the first parish he served as minister, and after marrying Doris he thought it best to seek a new parish and move away.

October 10, 1944

[to Carroll and Ruth Leach] Dear Folks:

...We are now in a large high school building. It was a Catholic High School of considerable size. I imagine it accommodated five hundred students in the pre-invasion days. It is a nice building with a chapel larger than the Enosburg Center church. It has two main floors with a gymnasium and a basement and an attic. We occupy the attic and the second floor as sleeping quarters and use the first floor for offices and places for our equipment. There is a fair sized playground paved with brick and fenced in on three sides by a fence and two gates and on the fourth by the school. These gates as well as the entrance to the school building is a guard post and guarding that post is no sinecure. My assistant is on guard today and it is fun to hear him tell about his futile attempts to keep the kids off the steps. In spite of what I wrote Doris this morning about there being no school it seems that in this city there is school so the work of keeping the children off the steps is not so bad until after five and then.... oh my! The children are curious and they want to see the lions and hear them roar. And they are friendly and they want to handle and be caressed by their deliverers. And they are starved for the little luxuries such as a bit of candy or a little gum or a trifle of some kind of ration. They say these people get so little of what we think essential to our wellbeing, butter, fats, meat, sugar, that a man with candy or rations that contain these things really has purchasing power. How I hope that some of the persons I asked to send me packages of candy, gum and the like have responded. Well, Figlioli would chase the kids down off the steps but he would hardly be back on the top landing before back they would be. He's too good natured to hurt the kids and he can't look ferocious to save his life. So his two hours on guard out of every six are really a hardship. I went out to see him this morning and found him talking with a couple of boys, one about Kenneth's age and the other a little older. He can't talk Dutch but by means of pantomime he made them understand that his boss would like a German rifle (I've picked up about fifty of their cartridges on the trip) and a souvenir for his kids. So, sure enough, this evening in came a delightful pair of wooden shoes, too small for Bruce so they must be earmarked for Anthony. By the time I get home he'll be old enough to wear them. The rifle will come later. I don't know what he used for money for these people so abhor anything German that they won't touch the invasion Marks we are now paid off in. So we began to accumulate stuff for barter. I went up and got a breakfast K ration. It consists of a can of eggs and meat, some Nescafe, sugar, a fruitbar and a package of four cigarettes. I gave him one unit of the D ration which is a highly concentrated bar of chocolate, fats and cereal, weighing about four ounces. They were delighted with that. I'm going to save all my cigarettes and candy that I can buy or are issued through the P. Ex. for such an exchange. To exchange is so much better than to give because it helps these people keep their self-respect, about the only possession they still have left.

Gradually, but surely I am beginning to get a hold on the affections and respect of my people. On Sunday we had three services. The chapel is used as a storeroom for medical supplies. It has operating tables, anesthesia machines, cases of bandages, of instruments, and it looks very much like a hospital. But the major in charge was careful that the material and equipment was not brought up beyond the half-way mark and the other half I used as a place for my Sunday service. We had about fifty out for the morning service, thirty for the communion and for the evening service we had about twenty-five. The evening service was a venture. I announced it as a song service and discussion meeting. It was a success and those there, mostly nurses, with six enlisted men, decided to make it a weekly affair. We are going to discuss topics with teeth in them and

I think they are going to fill a need. You see, in a foreign country and so very far from home many of the people, probably 85% of them, let down their bars and forsake their moral standards. They do things that they wouldn't do at home. And those with a little conscience left become quite belligerent about it. They try to rationalize enough to make it seem right. So they ask why this isn't all right and why that isn't permissible. So, why not discuss it? Next Sunday, if our program allows us to, we are going to have a discussion on "Should we forsake our pre-war moral standards here?" I think that has teeth in it and if they will discuss it I believe we can clear up a few things. At least they will know that they have a Chaplain who is alive to the existence of the problems and is willing to help.

Somewhere in Holland
October 10, 1944

Dear Gladys:

...I guess it won't be long before we shall be getting the patients from the battle field not very far away. If the Germans take a notion to fight for their country city by city and town by town and field by field I guess we shall have plenty of wounded and dead, too. Besides giving comfort to the wounded it is also my duty to clear out the dead. I saw how it was done yesterday and it is not pleasant. However, it is all in the line of duty. The average is that out of every one hundred patients we get three will die. So you can see, if we take in one hundred a day I shall be making trips every day. I wish every man and woman in America who has anything to do with a union who orders a strike in these times would have a detail like we had yesterday morning when we took our three dead away and left them at a place where there were a dozen more. If that wouldn't put them to shame I'd like to have the power to make them change places with those who died.

Strikes and other labor disputes resulted in the loss of 8,721,000 man-hours of work in 1944. This was about 0.09% of the available working time. The automobile, iron and steel industries were most affected, and since these manufacturing industries had been converted to producing airplanes and other war materiel, even a brief stop in production would affect the war effort. (U.S. Bureau of Labor Statistics, Bulletin no. 833, *Strikes and Lockouts in 1944*.)

October 16, 1944

Dearest Doris:

Mail call came on Saturday afternoon just before chow. Chow was good, but even if we had steak and French fries, peas and mashed potatoes, apple pie and ice cream, which we didn't, even that would not have been so acceptable as the mail for in it were the two letters from you, one a V-mail written October first and the air mail written on the third. Mighty fine it was to read that you were home and that you were so hopeful. Perhaps you will be able to do some Christmas shopping after all. And I hope the package I sent you will arrive by that time. It went out two weeks ago.

...I had to go down town on Saturday to see the Corps Catholic chaplain and on the way passed several stores. There were Ford, Chrysler, Chevrolet garages on the way, and many, many stores. In one store were many candy boxes. Gee they looked good, but they were empty. Purely window dressing. In another store there was an exhibit of pears and behind bunch after bunch of bananas, probably twenty in a bunch, all made of wood. In another store was a large square covered with eggs on end. Each egg was stamped and I guess they were real. Food is so closely rationed that a candy bar would probably sell for a dollar and probably cause a riot if offered for sale. Cigarettes sell for a dollar a pack. If they could buy these eggs they would be one dollar each. I guess perhaps those eggs weren't real or else the honesty of these people is much greater than ours. Milk here is distributed in five gallon cans and each person brings out a pitcher. I haven't seen milk bottles since England. The milk is just for the children. It seems that most of the food consists of potatoes so you can see that a K ration or a D ration or a C ration really means something to these people. The men who are associated with this school and help us so much bring the whole family to eat here and they don't waste a thing. How any of these children would delight in the kind of a breakfast that Bruce sits down to with real eggs, real sugar, real eggs, and whole milk. Sugar is rationed at the rate of one ounce per person a week.

Yesterday was a pretty good Sunday. I had 42 out at the morning service and there were twenty more for the evening service. We had a little difficulty because we had to have the meeting in the officers' mess room where there was considerable noise. But we had our discussion, nevertheless, and it gave us a chance to exchange opinions. Next Sunday, by their choice, we are going to talk on the topic, "Does our Christian morality condone a married man keeping company with a single or married woman other than his wife?" This subject is one of four dropped in our suggestion box for discussion. It has been given rise to by the fact that some of our officers are very sweet on some of our nurses. One in particular is seen with his nurse affinity just about every minute that the day will allow. They sit together at meals, they are seen talking together at very frequent intervals and whenever there is a walk to somewhere where they are permitted to, they are seen together. Well, what of it. He likes her, she likes him. But does Mrs ____ know of it? I guess that is the crux of the matter. Another officer, much younger, has a clandestine association with another nurse. They aren't often seen together but in Normandy he almost never got in before midnight. What they did in the dark out in the fields, but not with God, is left to the imagination. This fellow once asked me, "What is wrong about having sexual relations with a woman?" I expect it is these examples that gave rise to this question. I told them to come with an open mind for this question was debatable and there were angles that ought to be brought out. I don't want the only people who care enough about spiritual things to pass up a Sunday evening movie to be the ones who are like Mrs. Grundy or Mrs. Hard. [Mrs. Grundy, originally an offstage character in a 1798 play by Thomas Morton, was the archetype of a prudish and judgmental woman.] The men who were there told about the discussion we had and if they give us a good place to meet in our new quarters we ought to have a real good meeting.

There is a great poverty of men in this unit who are willing to talk about the moral aspects of our Christian way of life. Most of them do what they want to do and then challenge you to tell them why they haven't a right to do it. The nurses seem to be a fine group on the whole and their keenness of moral perception is sharp. The officers never have any moral qualms about anything. If they don't do anything it is just because they don't want to or lack the opportunity. That is what war does to them and that is why work with the enlisted men makes up practically all of the Chaplain's time. As far as officers as a whole are concerned there is no such thing as the Ten Commandments or the moral law. All they are concerned about is Army Regulations and military directives. With the Chemical Battalion I had quite a few who were interested in a group like this. I know that if it were not for the nurses I couldn't have any evening meeting at all. And it is needed because there are so many things that are tearing down every good ideal that they have started with.

...I am glad Bruce has a farm to run on and I'm sure he is less bored there than he would be at home with no one to play with. How is Mother Leach standing up with two little boys extra to think about? Or has she become reconciled to her fate as the people of Holland have to the big guns that fire at the Germans but break all their windows in doing so? It seems from your report that Anthony is doing mighty well to weigh so much so early.

Your letter had so much love in it that it did me a lot of good. All I need to know while I am over here is that you are getting better, the family is well and that you love me. I can fight my part of the war on that kind of news. Please keep it up.

Yours with love,
Jerry

October 19, 1944

Dearest Doris:

We've moved again! I'll have to see the Colonel about paying the rent more regularly so we can stay in one place for a longer period of time. But the place where we are now is a fine place, another Catholic school, of course, but the nicest building by far we have yet been in. Nothing has been set up as yet and I haven't any office. But I expect this is our last move until there is a very substantial advance in the front around here, which doesn't look at all likely this fall or winter. As it is we are the most advanced evacuation hospital in the whole U.S. Army, and us without a patient and past running out of patience.

"Ninth Army headquarters opened at Maastricht (Netherlands) on October 22, 1944… (General William) Simpson's headquarters now occupied a former Netherlands Army post and a Catholic school on the outskirts of the city." (N. Prefer, *The Conquering Ninth*, p. 43)

Here and Now [postmarked October 24, 1944]

...That morning a priest was brought to me and said that the resident priest asked him to say Mass for our troops on Sunday. So I met him and he asked if I could arrange transportation for him to his school from which he had been driven so he could have the books he needed for the service. So I took him to the adjutant and we made the arrangements. They wanted me to go along too because we were coming so very close to the German border that they didn't dare to let the men and vehicle go without an officer. So we went.

When we arrived at the school he took me around. It is an immense place with forty priests, twice as many nuns and four hundred students. But the proximity of guns and gunfire made the students go home and many to flee. Some, however, stayed it through and were there when we came. He took me into the church, the crypt was built in 1100 and the founder of the church is buried there. I was reminded of Mark Twain's, "Is he dead." The church was in good condition except for a hole in the roof and under that hole was a tub to catch the rain water. He took me to his room and showed me how all the doors were forced and the cupboards and desk drawers were all forced. He took me to the bishop's room where four other priests were enjoying a pitcher of hot chocolate. They gave me some. Boy, it was good. Almost as good as your mother's. They told of one priest who was driven out as he had been and lived in our city, six miles away. One day he thought he would like to go back to his room and see how his belongings were standing the occupation. He couldn't get a ride on any truck or car so he managed to borrow a bicycle. He rode the six miles all right and arrived to within fifty yards of his destination when, boom, a shell landed in a barn not far away. That was enough for this holy cyclist. He dove for a cellar, rested two hours and then rode back without even giving his belongings the once over.

On Friday night we had a party to celebrate our first anniversary as a unit. The officers had a dance with the nurses and each officer could buy a bottle of champagne. And what do you think? They asked me to look after icing the champagne. It was such a surprise to me I didn't know what to do. It was just announced at mess that the Chaplain will look after icing the champagne. Well, the chief nurse and I did it together and it was good and cold. I didn't take any and when I saw what it did to the officers I'm glad I didn't.... On Sunday when I called attention to my literature table I said, "Those who had a headache after the party on Friday night are invited to take the booklet on this end of the shelf." It was entitled, "How much do you know about Alcohol?" The enlisted men gave a show at six o'clock and it lasted about an hour and a half. It was a dandy, all thought up in about two days time and depicted the history of the organization. What it really was was a series of scenes ribbing some of the officers and some of the higher non-coms. It gave them a fine chance to get some of the things off their chest that have been bothering them for so long.

On Sunday night we had our discussion about married men in the army going steady with some woman. We talked about an hour on the subject. There were seven enlisted men, three nurses and I. They all decided it was all right for a married man to go out with another woman if he let his wife know about it, but they were unanimous in their opinion that it was a mistake to always go out with the same one. Interesting. So I guess I won't fall in love with just the chief nurse. If I fall in love I'll do it on a grand scale. Then there won't be any complications. Right?

I am, in a way, a privileged character. When everyone else is restricted to our area, wherever that is, I am usually permitted to roam at large because the assumption is that I have many kinds of business to perform. So I can go to Corps headquarters and get chores done. So far I have made four trips there for the purpose of getting marks changed into guilders for nine nurses. The people here have been ordered not to take any German money no matter who prints it so any trading that is to be done must be in guilders. A guilder is worth 37.8¢ of our money. Yesterday I went down on behest of the medical officer who is in charge of the post mortems. He wanted me to find out what we were supposed to do with the arms and legs of the dead when they were cut off. As far as the soldiers are concerned the army makes no provision. They are burned up. But as far as civilians are concerned, that is something else. The general hospital that was near us in Normandy got into a turmoil because a civilian was brought in, his leg cut off and his life saved. Some time later someone came around and asked for the leg so it could be buried in consecrated ground. When he was told the leg was burnt up with many other amputations he was scandalized. So our officer doesn't want any trouble here. Makes me think of Mark Twain again. Remember the subterranean monastery they visited where the bones of the monks were draped on the walls. Mark Twain said, "There will be a mighty rattling here when Gabriel blows his trumpet." We meet some pretty cockeyed situations, what?

Well, good-bye for now, dearest. My love is all for you.

Jerry

November 2, 1944

One thing has happened after another. On Saturday we went to a concert. I'll enclose the program. I would like to enclose the ticket but that would tell where we are so I couldn't do it. You can puzzle over the Dutch all you wish. I enjoyed the concert very much and was surprised to recognize the "Fantasie-Impromptu," by Chopin. We had a record of that, remember, and it has that theme made use of in the other war song "I am always chasing Rainbows." The pianist was good and we went to a large theatre to hear him. He is a Dutchman, well known in Holland but without an international reputation like Percy Granger. However, I think I can enjoy a recital by him as well as by the best because I don't know enough about technique to understand the difference. We paid 5 guilders and ten cents for the seats, that would be about two dollars. There were five of the officers, one nurse and one enlisted man of our unit that went. At the "pauze" we went out and smoked or talked and there was a bell, like a telephone bell that told us when to come back in. Just like the opera. Mighty fine.

I have been doing quite a lot of running around for the people here, especially the nurses. I've been to the finance office twenty times, I guess, to get money changed for the nurses. They are the ones who have the money. I get money changed from marks to guilders for one and she tells her room mates. Then they come down and I get it changed for them. I also have errands to run and I keep my eyes open. So when they want to have a watch fixed they ask the Chaplain where to go. If they want to buy a map or some ink or some Christmas cards or some perfume or get their hair done, or if they want some silver coins for a bracelet, I find out for them. It's like the want ad bureau.

Very soon, however, we shall be doing what the army pays me for. Yesterday four surgical teams arrived and I don't expect I shall have to do chores much more. Patients will begin to come in and they will be needing me. So will my own people when they see at first hand what war does to fine young men.

November 6, 1944

Dearest Doris:

On Saturday the mail that had been following us for a month caught up with us and just about everybody received something. Even I got one air mail letter from my sweet wife, a V-mail from Edna, another from Father, and a package from Gladys. It was my first package and I was quite pleased. Although I opened it and saw a collection of assorted candies I haven't sampled a single one yet. I hope to wait until there is a famine again, when there is no fruit to be bought and when the P.Ex. isn't functioning well. One man received 53 letters in that mail, many of them received more than twenty. Your letter, if it had only been able to get here on time would have helped me a lot because it told of your return from the hospital and your assurances of love that always mean so much for me.

Still we haven't yet any patients although every indication is that we shall soon. All our officers and nurses that were on detached service at other hospitals have returned, and we have been assigned ten officers, five nurses and six enlisted men. They have moved in and one of the officers is a Lt. Woodruth of Barre, Vermont. Luckily he has been billeted to sleep in our room so once more I have the privilege of talking with a Vermonter. He knows some people I know and the territory around Berlin Corner is more or less familiar to him. So there are Vermonters in the army.

I sent out Bruce's little book and the story with it on Saturday. After I had made the story all up the local priest came in and I asked him to translate the printing in it. I found I had made some pretty bad mistakes. However, I had some fun making up the story and I hope you will have some more fun reading it to him and he will have some more fun listening and looking at the pictures. It seems that there is a whole series of those little books. I think I shall get one each week for him. And I am keeping my eyes open for something distinctively Dutch for each of the children. Many of our men are having bracelets made out of Dutch coins. Do you think you would like that? So far almost everything seen in the windows is very little different from what could be picked up in the stores back home, and of much poorer quality. But I shall keep looking and looking and looking. Has the package I sent from Normandy arrived yet?

Every now and then Figlioli goes off on a hunt to see what he can finagle from the Red Cross or Special Service. So far he has done pretty well. He hasn't yet been able to pry loose from them what the men want most, cigarettes and tobacco, but he has brought home three cases of shaving cream, writing paper, envelopes, and his latest haul was to bring home blanks for sending flowers. That appealed to many men. The man fills out the blank, puts down his money, states how much he wants to pay for the flowers and then Figlioli each day takes the blanks to the office where the director has the message telegraphed and cabled to the place at home. They claim that it takes about two weeks for the flowers to get delivered.

We have also taken over the distribution of free rations. Theoretically each man is issued a package of cigarettes and a candy bar and a stick of gum each day. This comes with the mess rations. But the mess job here is a tremendous proposition because when we get in operation we have to feed people at any time of the day, especially patients. So the mess officer turned the business over to me. When the rations come in they are brought up to my office. Figlioli unpacks them and counts them. We figure out how much each man can have. Then we open each carton of cigarettes and empty it, open the candy boxes and empty them, and so with the gum. Then we have it announced over the P.A. system that the Enlisted Men will get their rations at the Chaplain's office at four and almost before the echo dies out men are at the door forming a line. We handed out the rations of five packages of cigarettes, one of lifesavers and one stick of gum per man to 200 men in less than an hour. It really was wonderful what genius Figlioli has in figuring out ways of doing things easy. And I let him alone. All I did was to sit by the table and check each man as he came. It's a swell way to get on to the names. I find that there are still about thirty names I don't yet know. But I'm picking them up day by day. With the officers' rations I go from room to room and distribute each man's ration on his bed. With the nurses I give the whole business to the chief nurse and she passes them out.

Figlioli is quite impressed with our duties with regard to the dead. I told you about our visit to another Evac several weeks ago. Well, we shall have to take over that work. But Captain Green, our officer in charge of the morgue, raised some question about when to do with..... I've been over all that, haven't I. They've given us a tent and I think we shall have a weapons carrier to take away the dead soldiers.

We had a good service yesterday. I put special care into the preparation of the sermon and I guess it showed it. We had about fifty out, which is good for this unit, and we had it in the officers' mess where there is a piano, so the singing went much better. I finished with a poem I found in Advance called "Look, God." One of the nurses came down after dinner and asked if I could get some copies made. Every Sunday in her letter home, she said, she would tell her mother about what the sermon was about. This time all the girls in her room were interested in getting a copy of that poem. So I asked Lieberman to cut the stencil and Figlioli is going to run off about fifty copies. I'll send you one. It does me good to have some recognition of my religious services. When we get to work I expect attendance at services will be pretty slim but I hope my work will be effective in a different way. It certainly pays to put plenty of preparation into the sermon.

I'm glad that every letter I get from you gives me a little good news about your improvement. The letter I received on Saturday was dated 27 and it told of how you were so very lame. A letter I received two weeks ago told how you could go up and down stairs without wincing with pain, and the letter of a week ago told how you were planning to start housekeeping again. If only each week can show progress like that I shall be so pleased. I hope that when I do finally get home we can do things together, go places together and enjoy our companionship once more as we used to. It was always such a pleasure to go anywhere with you. I loved it and I know I shall never tire of it.

I think I'll write Priscilla a letter when this is done. Think she can stand it?

Good-bye, sweetheart. My love goes to you.
Jerry

November 8, 1944

Dearest Doris:

This is a commercial card made by a local printer. The other one was designed and drawn by Davis and he and Fig turned them out. The poem is Fig's too.

I'm sending out 100 of this kind and if we have any left after the rest of the unit has its chance (we made 2000) I'll send some of them.

Merry Christmas,
Jerry

November 8, 1944

Dear Bruce:

I've been working on another story today which I hope to have done by the end of the week. I got stuck on my anniversaries and had to wait until I found what the tin anniversary was.

I hope you have a merry Christmas and I expect there will be many nice things for you.

Your Daddy

November 8, 1944

Dear Kenneth:

So many have been in for Christmas cards that I find myself believing Christmas is coming even though it is 57 days away.

I hope you have a good Christmas and that you get the things you want the most. Perhaps when the next Christmas comes we can celebrate it altogether. That will be grand, won't it.

Your Daddy

November 8, 1944

Dear Anthony:

You don't know me but I am your Daddy. Your Mother says you are a fine boy and by your picture I can see that you are as handsome as your Dad who almost won a baby contest when he was about your age. Some day I'm coming home and you can see what all your beauty amounts to after 42 years.

I hope you enjoy your first Christmas and make your mother very happy.

Your Daddy

November 8, 1944

To wonderful folks,

Your Hubby is a great guy. But see what you can do to sort of stop him from beating his poor assistant (P.S. joke).

You're a great family.

Your Husband's Assistant
"Fig"

On November 11, Gerald's unit moved to Heerlen, Holland, and began operating as an evacuation hospital, supporting the Ninth U.S. Army.
Doris sought and hired a young woman to help with the household and children. At this point Gerald only knew that she was trying to find a girl to help her.

November 14-15, 1944

Dearest Doris:

Your letter, written on October 29 and mailed on Halloween, arrived today. It is very precious. Precious it is because your letters are so few and far between. Precious, too, because of the news from home and you. I have become almost callous about the mail situation when day after day goes by and there's nothing in my box. So when I do get a letter, especially from you, it is really an event.

I am trying to send out ten Christmas cards a day with a personal message on each. So far I have sent out 35. You may be surprised at that because of my attitude towards that in the past. It seems that my army life is making a different kind of a man out of me.

We have started working at last. Some of our cases have been very bad ones but most have been the kind that go to the medical ward where there is a great deal of good cheer. I go around to the wards twice daily with Red Cross stuff and in the wards where they are well enough to enjoy company I visit the patients and do things for them. I also have considerable outside work to do.

One of the extra tasks was to solve the problem of what to do with amputated parts. There is an army directive instructing us to bury these parts under six feet of earth. This sounds very simple on paper but the question was where and how. So I went to Civil Affairs to see if I ought to hire a Dutch farmer's field for this purpose. There I was sent to the Corps Surgeon's office. I went there like the man looking for a pail of steam and found three colonels talking about something. A major talked to me for a while and said any place I could find would be all right. Then he suggested I go to a signal Construction Battalion and ask them to send a post hole digger down and dig my holes. That struck me funny for this machine has a huge 16" drill they use for digging holes for telegraph poles. But I went there and asked them. Sure enough, they'd do it. So the next day, which was today they sent their machine down and dug about 25 holes for me. They dug them at least seven feet deep. It would take two men at least a week to do that amount of work. So this afternoon I carried the leg over and buried it. You don't know how much good it did me to solve that problem.

Yesterday I took a little tour with a chaplain from Texas named Schrader. He is the Protestant Chaplain of an Artillery Group that has its big guns along the German border for several miles. I met him at the Chaplains' meeting last Thursday and we just fell in love with each other. We walked from the meeting to the Mess Hall together, bucked the chow line together and sat together at the same table. He is 31 and I am 42 but we are about the same in our points of view. He invited me to visit some of his big guns so I jumped at the chance. We set the next Monday for the day.

The first gun was what they call an 8" rifle. It was off in a field and under a net. It was hard to see from the road 100 yds away. It would be impossible to see 1000 feet up in the air. We went down and looked at it. It certainly was big. They showed me the powder used to propel the shell. That was in a cylinder about 4' long and it weighted about 100 pounds. In another hole in the ground was the projectile. That was 8" in diameter and about 3' long. It weighted about 250 pounds and that gun could shoot it as far as 16 miles. The other day they were shooting at a bridge 14 miles away and they hit it.

We visited a second gun which was about five miles away. It was called the 240 mm. That gun had a little shorter barrel but it would throw a 340 pound projectile 14 miles. They were cleaning it out when we got there. They had several cloths on the end of a ramrod about 20' long. A man sat on the gun near the muzzle and poured water down into it, then ten men pushed the ramrod up and back. This process goes on and on. They have to clean it every day it is fired and for the next three days after.

We came through a village that was partly in Holland and partly in Germany. The German part was blasted to destruction. People on the street were not at all cordial and we knew we were not wanted. In the Dutch part of the city everything was intact and some of the shops were open for business. The members of the Underground were patrolling the streets and everyone seemed glad to see us.

When we came back to his office he introduced me to the Catholic Chaplain's assistant and who do you think it was? Cecil Park of East Arlington! I don't know who was more surprised, and we had quite a long talk about Arlington people. He told me that Ellery Laurence and Oliver Warner are over here somewhere.

I had a service this morning and it was at a replacement battalion nearby. In fact it was in the same building we occupied for the first five days we were here. When I came back I was told I had more of the leg to bury. The man whose leg was cut off yesterday had to have more yet cut off. So what was left of that and some of the other stuff that is offal of the operation room was put in a 12 qt pail. So I poured that into one of the holes the Sig. Const. Bn. Dug for me yesterday. But the hole had water in it. Now, just like the fable of the crow and the pitcher of water, when I dropped in stones and dirt, the water level rose and brought what I was trying to bury up with it. So, if I kept on we would have the hole filled up and the offal right on top stinking to high heaven. What would you do?

Well, yesterday we received seven cases of cigarettes for our men. Each case has a covering of waterproof paper on the inside. So I threw two of these down the hole, covered it with a lair of dirt and, presto, the stuff was buried.

That is what makes my job here so fascinating. Whenever there is some problem to be solved that is not covered by an established army policy they put me to work on it. It takes quite a lot of thinking. If I had the brains your dad has I'd have been a major by now.

The weather is bad and bad weather means few patients. If we have a few days of clear weather there will be a lot of activity, and that means we shall get many, many patients and probably I shall have to bring some to the Army cemetery.

Now to answer your letter.

I'm glad you have hopes for a good girl. I am sure that if she is willing and able and agreeable she will earn a place in the home. I hope she earns her money and I hope you pay her what she earns. You know something about what it is for one to work for another person. If you think she earns ten dollars a week, give her ten. If she earns twelve, give her twelve. Remember, the standard of living has changed and $10 doesn't buy what it did in 1931. Besides, I *have been getting twice what I have earned ever since I got into the Army.*

Pretty soon I shall be so busy I won't be able to write you as much as I would like to. If quite a while elapses between letters don't feel bad. I'll be loving you whether I am busy or not.

November 20, 1944

Dearest Doris:

I don't believe this will be a very long letter but I feel I must steal a little time to write to you even though I am so very busy. I wouldn't want you to think I ever forget you.

We are taking in patients steadily. Some are minor cases and we send them right on back to a general hospital. Some are medical cases and we doctor them up so they can go right back to duty. Others have more severe wounds that require blood or plasma. And some are so severely wounded that anyone outside of the medical profession would swear they couldn't live. Some don't. But out of more than eight hundred patients we have received not more than twenty have died.

Would you like to follow me around for a day? Suppose you did yesterday [Sunday]. *I got up at seven, shaved and was right on hand for the 7:30 breakfast. After that I made ready for our morning service which was to be at nine o'clock. But only the organist and our chief clerk, T/Sgt Flickinger showed up so we didn't have any service at all. I left pretty downhearted but I tried not to show it. I went back to the office to arrange the work of the day and our adjutant brought in a Miss Duncan who is the director for Red Cross work in the hospitals of the first and the Nineth Army. She talked with me about Red Cross workers, supplies and the conditions we would have to meet before they would send us any workers. I finally got rid of her and went about my business.*

My first business was to get every body ready for the trip to the cemetery. That meant checking with the laboratory to see that they were all ready to go. Then I had to uncover their faces and see that the dog tags were around their necks. Then I had to go to registrar and find out the number of the bag their valuables were in, go to supply and see if they had any there that were not in bags. These had to be matched up with the bodies. Then I had to get a truck assigned and arrange so that the driver could get early chow so we could get an early start. Then chow. After chow we loaded the bodies and I had to be right there to see that the two that were to be left behind were not taken. Then I went with them to show them the way and offer my services for any burial service they might wish.

There we unloaded our cargo. It was five Americans and one German. While we were there a load from the battle field came. Ours were bad enough but those were even worse. They were unloaded by colored soldiers and their nonchalance in handling these poor, mangled bodies is a sight to see.

When I came back I tried again to have a service in the afternoon. Still no luck. In the evening we counted our free rations and got them ready to give out the next day. I visited some of the wards again and the place where they come in and go out. Then to bed.

We are shaping up very well and living up to our expectations. One lad who had his leg cut off has asked me to write home for him. Considering the fact that our patients are not allowed to say they have been wounded or are in a hospital they don't know just what to write. So I have to make up most of the letter myself. Yesterday (it is now Tuesday) I wrote again. He said, "I can't tell them I'm all right because I'm not." So I said, "We'll start in by talking about the weather." So I wrote about the rain, rain, rain and compared it with the perfect weather of New Mexico. Then we said, "This weather is good for ducks and Baptists." That made us think of turkeys and turkeys made us think of our Thanksgiving dinner. So, we filled the page with small talk which really said nothing except that he was alive. He'll be home and riding a horse on his brother in law's ranch before the rest of us will.

I guess I have rambled on long enough to let you know I'm alive and thinking of you. I would love to be with you for good but until then I'll be loving you.

Yours with love,
Jerry

P.S. Give my love to Kenneth and Priscilla and Bruce and Anthony. I'm always thinking of them, too.

November 28, 1944

Dearest Doris:

I've been planning for three days to write you a long letter but I'm so darned busy I can't. So I'm just sending my love and reminding you that I think of you always. I work from eight in the morning until eleven at night so I'm pretty tired when I go to bed.

I received a box from Edna Saturday and in it was a fountain pen, two typewriter ribbons, a fruit cake, lots of gum and a jar of candy. I'm writing a thank you letter now.

How are you all.

with love,
Yours
Jerry

December 2, 1944

Dearest Doris:

There's an hour before supper so I think I'll use it to bring you up to date on my carryings-on.

We are now starting our third week of operation and everything has gone pretty well. We are still well below our three per cent mortality rate and we have hopes of keeping there. Church attendance is very poor but everything else that I do meets with a fine response. Our ranks have been swelled by the presence of several surgical teams, an ambulance platoon and a collecting company so I am the chaplain of about as many as I would be if I were in a regiment. I am gradually getting into the routine of the work of hospital chaplain and I hope next week to follow a definite schedule of calling on the wards from ten till twelve and two to four, getting bodies ready for their ride to the cemetery from twelve till half past, of getting the daily paper called The Stars and Stripes at four and distributing it then, and having the evening for office work such as writing the letters that pile up, processing belongings of the dead, and studying. If I can work that out I'll be effective.

I wrote before some of the things I have to do for these patients that are little things but that loom so important to them. Did I tell you of the man I took to the town his outfit was in before the push so he could get the boots he had had made for his wife? Well I did. It took about the whole morning but his pleasure at getting the boots and some other things was worth all the time we spent. We found a money order on the body of another soldier. The name of the person it was to be sent to was on it but not her address. So I wrote to the A.P.O of his division and secured the address. Now the money order is in the mail and the girl whom he wished to favor will have twenty-five dollars just before Christmas. Another patient was concerned about his belongings so I called up his company and they said they would send them over in a jeep. Another was concerned about the Sixth Commandment. He said he did a lot of thinking while he was in a fox-hole about that. It worried him and he wanted to know if God held it against any soldier for shooting someone in this war. We talked about that for some time and I pointed out that we had come to such a bad state of affairs in our man-made mix-up that one had to choose between two evils and the greater one was to allow the enemy to kill not only him but many more of his comrades. Like Mrs. Fisher [the author Dorothy Canfield Fisher, whom they knew in East Arlington] says, the discussion didn't produce any definite answer but it did us both good to talk about it. And so it goes. Every day there is something different to do.

One of my most exacting jobs is the care of the dead. The first thing I have to do when a patient dies is to go to the registrar's office and get his name, serial number, and the number of the bag his valuables are in. Then I get the valuables. On the way back to the office I stop in at the morgue and check the names and serial numbers by looking at the dog tags on the bodies. That is the final authority. If there is any mistake in the name or number I report it back at the registrar's office and they make note of it for it might result in the wrong widow or mother or father being notified, and that is serious. Then I dump the valuables in a wash dish, go through them and again check the name, wrap them up and tag the package and put it on the body of the man it belongs to. Then we load them up in a truck right after lunch and off we go to the cemetery. Figlioli and I went with the truck driver and the motor pool sergeant on the first trip and we got stuck in the mud right in the cemetery so we passed the night in the village with the Graves Registration Company. They treated us well, provided our men with cigarettes, invited us to a movie and made a very favorable impression on my enlisted men. So when we went again I brought along a carton of cigarettes to pay them back. I have also brought some magazines and books for them so we have made a good impression on them. I went down today to straighten out a mistake and they asked about a Protestant service. So I offered to come down tomorrow and have one on Sunday afternoon. They took me up so I'm going. "If we have a body we'll send it on to the cemetery and I'll stop off here for the service. I like to combine business with pleasure." Sometimes we have a mix-up like one time we sent the wrong valuables with a man. The man's dog tags said he was A and the valuables said he was B. Which was he? So I look into that and found the dog tags were right and I brought back the valuables of B and took A's valuables the next day.

Being so far away from home it makes it hard to realize how my family is growing. Once in a while I stop to write something to the children and I find myself thinking of them in terms of the children I knew before I entered the Army, and that isn't right. So won't you help me out in the letters and tell me what they are interested in. If the package I referred to has arrived and in good condition and in good time I'll make up another. But unless I hear that it has, I won't. Does your hand hurt you when you write now as it did before. Your handwriting is about the best of any that comes to me and the easiest to read. I like to see a lot of it.

Well, good-bye for now.

Your with love,
Jerry

December 6, 1944

In the mail from time to time there come messages from our Denominational Headquarters. Usually they are so general that they mean almost exactly nothing but this time there was one that interested me more than the others. It told about the probability of many servicemen and women entering colleges and universities and the need of good men, especially Chaplains, as University pastors. So I applied for the job. So far as I know there is no such thing as a University pastor but there are churches in college towns that call their ministers mostly on the basis of his ability as a counselor of young people. I've had good luck here in the army and I get along very well with all the army personnel of both sexes and of all ages. I think, with the army experience behind me, I could swing a church in a college town. How would you like that?

I received the letter from Priscilla in which she stated that she was using both hands at once [when playing the piano]. *Is Kenneth still sticking to his music, too? I would like to see them practicing.*

How are getting along in your war with Old Man Rheumatism? Are you able to make gains from week to week our Nineth Army is over here in Germany? Or have you both settled down to a winter stalemate? And how is your heart nowadays? Do I still have a portion of it or has that handsome Anthony moved in? I want to have a home there so that no matter where you are, I will be there, too.

We are not quite so busy right now. For a while we were working night and day. But now we are relaxing a little. Now we are listening to a Bob Hope program. Everyone uses my office for a place to read or write or listen to the radio.

Have you been getting along all right with your girl? Is she satisfied with her boss? And, since I'm asking questions, what about the picture of you I've been asking for for about a year now? Is it a hopeless thing to hope for?

I remembered Kenneth's birthday on December 5. Now I have an eleven year old boy. Right? Gee! Let's hope this part of the war will be over before the next birthday in the family.

Good-night my Queen,

Jerry

December 8, 1944

Now that I know you are getting the coins all right I will send some with each letter. I'll start modestly and send a ten cent piece. It is very much like the "fish scales" Canada used to have for their 5¢ pieces. Remember them? I will be on the look-out for coins. I can give the kids a collection they will be proud of. Just as soon as I hear that the package with the things I bought in Carenton has arrived I'll make up another of things procured right here.

A man has a right to tell his wife anything, hasn't he? I think so. I received two fine compliments in the last seven days. I thought I wouldn't tell anybody, but I want to tell you. One was this. Another chaplain of an engineer group who was at Chapel 12 in Camp Swift when we were there came in to see me last week. He mentioned that he had access to a secret document at Army Headquarters Chaplain's Office. The document contained a list of the chaplains in this Army and he said he noticed my name that I had a rating of excellent. Gee, that pleased me wonderfully. And last night when I went to my room one of the medical officers said, "We were talking about you with another man. I won't tell you who he was but he said he thought you were the best chaplain in the E.T.O. [European Theater of Operations]" And the other officers in the room said they all agreed. In a way this doesn't mean anything because no one has a large enough acquaintance of chaplains to make a statement like that. But it filled me with pleasure to have them say it. It showed that I am well-liked here. And I have always been susceptible to compliments.

I just got safely in bed last night when my assistant came over and said there was a patient about to be operated on who wanted me. So I went over and he was on the operating table. He was a medic who saw two soldiers injured by snipers and started out to get them. He stepped on a mine that blew off his left foot. He applied the bandage on himself and was sent to us with a bandage on the leg. But when it was time for our surgeons to operate he began to feel worried. So I held his hand and talked gently to him and almost like magic he quieted down. The nurse that gave the anesthetic said he took it surprisingly well. I stayed right by him for an hour and a half while they took off the rest of his leg just above the knee. It was my first night on the operating room and I did not enjoy it.

We had to terminate the discussions when we started working. They weren't very successful because, try as we will, when we get together our decency will not allow us to speak our minds. The things earnest people want to talk about they cannot discuss in a group. Only those who are very much in earnest can understand the moral turmoil that some go through. So now we have discontinued that and if we have a rest period my evening service will be a little different.

Yesterday I was just settling down for a quiet afternoon in the office when our warrant officer came in with a soldier who heard that his brother was dead and wanted his belongings. I had just sent them along with the body about a half hour before. So I got a vehicle and we chased the truck to the cemetery and got there about fifteen minutes after our load had been delivered. I looked up the lieutenant in charge and got his permission to turn the valuables over to the brother, which he did. When the man saw the picture in his brother's wallet of him, his wife and baby it was too much for him. He began to cry then and we couldn't get him away from that cemetery quick enough. Fig had gone with the load and he took two of the loudest talking boys with him. They, he said, had a lot to say about war not being anything. But when they took one look at the dead brought in from the field they had no more to say. Fig has a pretty clever way about him. That was smart, don't you think? Two went with me on the Wednesday trip and after looking things over they decided they had seen enough. We think we see some pretty bad sights here at the hospital but at least, the patients are alive when they get here...usually... But those who one second weighed 180 and the next were blown apart so that all that could be collected would weigh less than Priscilla, they do not look pretty.

Tomorrow I have another chore to do for a patient. He was brought in from a basement which was the company C.P. (Command Post). He had carbon monoxide poisoning. He left a letter in that basement that had a money order for $50 in it. So I'm to prepare a note to the officer in charge, ask him to check and see if that letter got mailed. That's all, but what a lot of comfort that will give a soldier who has nothing all day to do but worry over that. That's one letter I have to write. Another letter is for one of our barbers who is also a Tec. 5 in the motor pool. He has a brother wounded in a hospital in France, but what hospital? He wants to know and it is my job to find out. That's another letter to write. And a nurse, trying hard to hold back tears, told me that her boy friend was reported missing. Would I please do what I could to find out about him? Another letter to write. I can see now why standard equipment for Chaplains is a typewriter.

Gerald often addressed his wife as "Mrs. Girl." I heard this endearment many times growing up. I remember once telling Mother, to be fair, she should call him "Mr. Boy," but she never did. "The Wild Man of Borneo" was a comic song that built up over multiple stanzas in the manner of "The House that Jack Built."

December 11, 1944

Dearest Doris:

Sometimes known as Mrs. Girl. Here I am again with my typewriter on my lap snapping out a letter for you. I'm trying to take advantage of this slight lull in our activity to write plenty of letters. When they are a week or so apart you'll know we are so busy that my mind won't turn out a good tome.

This morning I came back from an errand and got to the Hospital area in time to see a funeral procession. Here they have the right idea about a funeral procession. Instead of having a procession of cars going along at about twenty miles per hour they have only one vehicle and that is a hearse drawn by horses. The horses are draped and the cross on the hearse is draped and the pall bearers are in black and walk on each side of the hearse and all the mourners walk behind the hearse in a procession two by two. This morning some of the women were saying some sort of litany with all the expression of a gate swinging in the wind. And you'd never guess what that made me think of. I hadn't thought of it for two years, I know. It was "The Wild Man of Borneo has Just Come to Town." So I sang that a little tonight. How well your dad used to do with that song.

Yesterday Captain Wright, our chief nurse said to me, "I'd like to go to the cemetery with you sometime. I'd like to see how they do it." So I invited her to go with me this afternoon, which we did. We had only two to take and ordinarily I wouldn't have made the trip, but Monday is a slack day with me so we went along. Along the way it was just another ride for her because she's been just about everywhere on one sort of business or another. The first thing about the cemetery I called her attention to was the flag. I happened to mention that when the princess of Holland was traveling in Canada her baby was born. The Canadian Government waived all claim to the hospital as a Canadian building while she was there so that she could technically consider that her child was born on Dutch soil. She thought that was silly. I suppose it's the same here. The land that the cemetery is on has been given to the U.S. so technically it is American soil. When we drove into the place everyone who noticed her stared and stared. When we stopped at the place where we unloaded there were only three on the boards. Two were already wrapped in their mattress covering sheets and ready for burial. But one man was as he was picked up from the battle field. His injury had blown off most of his head and the colored soldiers were trying to cut off his clothes without cutting him up, too. The job of separating blood-soaked clothes from human flesh was almost too much for them. I think just a glance at him made Captain Wright lose all her enthusiasm for sight seeing. She was ready to go right back.

Occasionally I find myself trying to make up my mind about how I feel toward these nurses and what would be my attitude if I were interested in girls as such. A few are very attractive but my favorites are not the pretty ones at all. I can't decide whether I like Captain Wright or not. Sometimes I think I do, other times I'm not so sure. I used to be the same way about Edna. They are alike in some ways. Both of them are 100% good listeners. Both of them are quick and hard workers. You know how capable Edna is. Captain Wright impresses me as being that way, too. Both are good dancers although Captain Wright's posture and gate are not good or graceful even if her name is Grace. I have an impression she is brittle and would blow up in a fit of temper if she were thwarted in her will.

I hope everything is going well at home and that you have a good Christmas. Be sure and tell me about it in detail.

Yours with love,

Jerry

December 16 was the date of the famous, or infamous, Battle of the Bulge.

No Congregationalist would dream of calling a minister "Father," as Catholics and Episcopalians call their priests. Hence the amusement over the local Catholic residents calling a Protestant chaplain "Father Miller."

December 24, 1944

Dear Mother Leach:

These Dutch presents I mentioned were given by the working girls of the city. Mostly sales girls, I guess. Two young women came to see me about it last Saturday and asked me if it would be all right to bring presents to our patients. Said it was all right and so yesterday they came with the presents. There were over 100 parcels wrapped in red or white paper and tied with red ribbon. One package was oblong and quite large. "If you have a patient who is very sick give him this present....... it's a bottle of wine." I told some of the men about it and several of them resolved to be patients immediately. Another present was labeled "Father Miller." The men, especially my assistant, had a lot of fun over that. Quite often now I am greeted in the hospital as "Father Miller." I expect we shall have considerable fun tomorrow distributing these gifts. I asked the committee if there was anyone I could write a letter to to convey the thanks of our organization. They said, "Oh no. Just tell the boys they are for our American liberators and we hope they get well soon and that soon there will be no more war."

It looks as if my prediction that this war would be over by Christmas was not well advised. Well, I didn't bet any money on it. There is considerable excitement about here, of course. It's an adventure taking a trip now, even in the line of duty. On a trip last week I was stopped five times each way and only twice was asked to show my card. Usually I was asked questions that required a knowledge of the comics, geography of our country, nicknames of cities, habits of radio stars, and other things that any American would know. You see these Germans are dirty fighters. They infiltrate somehow, either by parachute or at night, somehow get U.S. uniforms, and with forged identification cards steal a vehicle and away they go. Many have been caught in this clever way. For instance one soldier that stopped me said, "What state are you from?" "Vermont." "What's the capital?" "Montpelier." "How well I know it!" He was familiar with Vermont. You know, I'd like to question some doubtful person who says he's from Vermont. It would be exciting, and I don't mean maybe. I'd ask him about deer hunting, fishing season, 4-H clubs, January thaws, Lake Dunmore,

Camel's Hump, the Roller Coaster road. I'd have a good time and, if he were from Vermont, he'd have a good time, too. But if he were a German with a school book knowledge of Vermont, he'd begin to sweat.

I've heard the President. Back in the U.S.A. it was no treat to hear him begin with "My Friends." But over here....... it's different. To hear his strong, steady voice and to feel in it the strength and security of America, even though the Germans were doing their best to create electrical interference, it thrilled me as nothing has since we left home.

Doris says she has had her picture taken at last. I am eagerly looking for it to come. That will be my no. 1 present for this year. I hope you all are well and enjoy this holiday.

Yours sincerely
Gerald.

December 28, 1944

I have one patient here who does me more good than I do him. I got him to talk of home and the family. He has four sisters and a brother. He thinks a lot of his mother and in my prayer I mentioned her and the early teaching she gave him. He was very pleased about it and said "It sounded as if you really knew her because what you said was very true." Now every time I go in he is very pleased to see me. It does something to a person to have someone pleased to see him.

January 1, 1945

The Germans paid us a visit at exactly midnight last night. The timing was perfect. Take that and the response our A.A.A. batteries gave him and our drunken officers coming back from their session with Rheims Champagne it was a memorable New Year's eve for me. Well, we have the pilot of that airplane down stairs as a patient. At least, so they say.

Saturday night the Colonel came in, stayed a while, looked over the literature, read for a while and when he went out he asked me to come and see him sometime the next morning. I said I would. My feelings were those of a high school boy who is told the principal wants to see him. I began to wonder what I had done and if he were going to bawl me out for letting the nurses come to my office or if I have been negligent in my care of the personal belongings of the dead, or if I had an office too untidy or if I were going to be transferred out. You know all the hopes and fears that come up. So I went and knocked on his door at ten, at half past ten, at eleven and at eleven thirty. At the latter time he was in. When he had said only ten words I knew all my hopes and fears were groundless. He wanted to talk about what the men were saying about how a few of the officers and nurses were carrying on. He asked me not to pull any punches but to tell just what I heard. So I told him the remarks the men made about how the nurses and officers, most of them from outside, were so thick on the stairway with their affectionate embraces that litter bearers almost threw out their patients trying to avoid them. One of the enlisted men was thrown out of a ward because he happened to have his hand on the shoulder of the Dutch girl that works in that ward. He was put on K.P for a week. The injustice of that punishment not only rankled him but was the subject of so much discussion among the men that it got to the Colonel. So that's how he happened to ask me about it. He said there isn't much he can do about an officer and a nurse who make fools of themselves. If they are the kind who will do that there is nothing that can be said to them that will bring a favorable response. We have three officers who are particularly sweet on certain nurses and they follow them around like love-sick swains. We talked about it for about an hour. Finally we decided to let matters rest as they were. "If things get too bad we can transfer the worst offenders out." So we left it there. He told me to be sure and let him know if the men talk about anything that bothers them a great deal and he said I was doing a fine job in keeping them contented with things as they are.

Well, in the interest of brevity I'll close now. I hope you get better. I'm very glad you love me because I love you, too. Remember how we used to sing, "Let me call you Sweetheart?" Every time I sing it now I think of you.

Yours with love,
Jerry

January 3, 1945

Dearest Doris:

Take a good look at this paper. Know what it means? Right! Your package has arrived. I hit the jack-pot yesterday. Your package, your parents' package, one from Charles and Florence and the fourth from the Red Mt. Lodge at Arlington. Not bad! Your brownies were mighty good and kept well. The maple sugar is moist and good.... Was it Kenneth who wrote "Look in every part if you want to [know] *who it is from." I found the tag in the little compartment in the top.*

The mail also brought an answer to my inquiry concerning the album lost here. Did I write you about that? I think I did. Remember I said we found an album with about 100 pictures, snapshots of a soldier's wife, his children, his sisters, brothers, their children, other soldiers, etc. If I lost a collection like that I would hate to lose it. The only clue was on one baby picture. On the back of that picture was stamped the name of the studio where it was taken, and a number on the back. So I wrote to that studio and yesterday the answer came back. A Mrs. A. B. Correll of Bristol, Tennessee had the picture taken. So I looked up the name and, sure enough, a S/ Sgt A. B. Correll was a patient here on Nov. 16 and was sent out on Nov. 17. I found out which hospital it was he was sent to and it was the one that was across the hedge from us in Carenton. I had met the Chaplain, Powell by name. So I wrote to him to look up the man so I can send it on. Wonderful, wasn't it. That did me a lot of good.

January 11, 1945

Guess what I did this afternoon. I went to see Sergeant York again. The last time I saw it was in East Arlington and you were beside me. I thought of that during the picture and after I thought of it I had tears in my eyes. It was at the Royal Theatre where I went to hear the piano concert in November. It was the first time I had been to a show there and to be mingled with a Dutch audience was an interesting [experience]. The music and dialogue were in English, but there was the Dutch translation flashed on the screen with each sentence. It was good to see it again and there was the added interest of seeing it with Soldiers and Dutch civilians. They screamed with pleasure when York captured the Germans at first, and they didn't have to have any words on the screen when the German major spoke to his men. When York ordered the major to tell the second batch of men to surrender, that pleased them immensely. They made so much noise in their excitement over the action that they didn't hear York give his turkey gobble and attract the interest of the two Germans who were perpetually keeping their heads too low. But try to imagine what superb propaganda it was. Here was a Tennessee hillbilly with eight men taking 132 prisoners of the Master race, and these prisoners were taken out of trenches where they had perfect protection. And just about ten miles away as the crow flies are similar men from the similar territory holding back the Germans who have overrun all Europe.

How are the little Millers about now? I hope they are all well and happy. I was just thinking, suppose I'm in the army for two more years and then come home. Then suppose Kenneth and Priscilla and Bruce should say, "Daddy, fool with us." Poor daddy! Are the kids growing tall at all? And are they showing any special interests? I think I would like to develop my archery hobby after I get home. Perhaps I will feel like spending the money it takes for a good outfit. We can't tell.

January 14, 1945

There is a radio in my office and, being so close to Germany, most of the broadcasts we hear come [from] *there. Naturally their stations come in much better than broadcasts from the B.B.C. Their music is excellent and if I could understand German I would be content to keep it there. When we get the various Allied Forces programs they come in well but are often bothered by electrical interference. When we do get one of our own programs well it is almost sure to be good, whether it is English or Yankee. The English have a splendid program at 9 o'clock. There is 15 minutes of news and then there are recordings produced at different sectors of the battle front. It might be in an American truck where you hear them printing maps for immediate use, or it might be at an observation post where you can hear conversation between observers, punctuated by artillery shells landing near enough to give the listener the shivers. Or it might be in a tank on its way to take a pillbox. American programs are usually musical with plenty of swing. But we heard Jack Benny last night. We hear Charlie McCarthey, Bob Hope and even Amos n Andy. All this without advertisement. It's going to be almost pleasant to hear the ballyhoo about this or that product again.*

The Armed Forces Radio Service (AFRS) produced entertainment programs for service men and women, often using performances by leading movie and radio stars who donated their time. These and the shows aimed at the civilian audience were transcribed onto 16-inch, 33 1/3 rpm phonograph records, flown to Europe, and broadcast. These transcription discs were expensive to produce, but offered greater dependability and better sound than the short-wave broadcasts used early in the war. Hearing the entertainers they knew from home boosted troop morale.

January 23, 1945

Dear Priscilla:

Right now, somewhere in the United States Mail is a package. In that package are presents bought here in this city. Some of those presents are for you and some for your brother Anthony. Now when that package comes I want you to deliver it to your sweet Mother and ask her to take care of it for you. It is my suggestion that she open it up at some time when you and Kenneth are at school, wrap the presents up separately and put them away for your birthday. I packed them altogether. Your Mother is not only sweet but she is very smart and she will be able to tell you which is yours and which is Anthony's. I'm afraid Anthony is getting the short end of this deal but he is magnanimous, I know, and will forgive me. When he is old enough to ride one I will get him a bicycle. Tell him that if he says, "Priscilla, I think our Daddy is just a lady killer to give you all those trinkets and me this junk." Just think, when you and Bruce and Kenneth are out earning their own livings we'll have Anthony to give all the presents to. Tell him that. If he's still mad tell him I will send him a wooden shoe full of bullets to play with. That'll fix him.

Now, little girl, don't expect too much from this package. Nice things are hard to find here because the Germans took all the nice things away. But I want you children all to know that I think of you very often and I would like to send you something good every week, but I can't....

It was nice of you to write the V-mail letter telling me that you liked the necklace. I thought it was pretty, too. Those shells were picked up on the coast of Cornwall and colored by hand by some English person. You ask Kenneth to show you on the map where Cornwall is. Perhaps someday you will go there and see the place. And you may pick up some shells just like those....

Oyesiforgotit. There is a little sign among the presents I sent. I saw it in a hardware store I went into to buy a dustpan. It was with several other little signs and I thought it would be fun for you to have in your room. People will see it and look at it and ask, "What does that mean?" And you will tell them, won't you. When you put that sign up you try to figure out what it means yourself. If you don't, you ask [Doris's cousin] Don Eldred if he can translate it for you. It is in Dutch but Dutch is enough like German so that I think he can tell you what it means. But if you can't tell him what it means and he can't tell you what it means you just write me a note and I'll tell you. Will that be all right?

I'm enclosing a letter for Mother. It is for her and for her alone so don't ask her what is in it. I'll write her again soon and tell her whatever news I think she might be interested in.

Yours with love,
DADDY

Here Gerald discusses the German V-2 rockets, or "buzz bombs." "As soon as the Ninth Army established itself [in Maastricht], Colonel John G. Murphy, the Army Antiaircraft officer, made plans to defend the area against a rocket attack…. [S]ometimes a hundred rockets a day passed over Ninth Army headquarters. Many of them passed over the city and exploded nearby, but none ever landed in the city directly. Despite German claims that Maastricht was being destroyed by the rockets because Ninth Army had its headquarters there, no bombs exploded within city limits." (N. Prefer, *The Conquering Ninth*, p.81.)

January 25, 1945

...Yesterday Chaplain Simmons, 102nd Division Chaplain, who is a Lt. Colonel, came in to see me and asked me how I would like to be a combat chaplain.... Chaplain Simmons told me he had lost three chaplains and wasn't having any luck in getting replacements. Would I like to join them? I said I would be glad to. But when he asked my age, that was against me.... Colonel O'Brian will fight for keeping me because he likes my disposition, my method and the results. However, if I'm needed on the line more than I'm needed here, that's where I want to go. Boy, those are the fellows who see what this war is really like, and, what with buzz bombs as they are, a chaplain up there is just about as safe as in a city fifty or a hundred miles back.

Of all the methods of fighting a war the buzz-bomb is the most cowardly and fiendish. We haven't had many here, but on two occasions we heard one go over, cut off and in a matter of a few seconds we heard the blast. It is a cowardly way to fight because there is no telling where it is going to land. Bombing by plane is done with a certain mission in mind and the intended victims can use their ingenuity in hiding it by camouflage or they can defend it by anti-aircraft. In artillery fire there [is] an objective but with a buzz-bomb it is just launched against a city which it sometimes misses three or four miles. We had a V-2 bomb land about three miles out and the vibration from that thing shook our building.

...The shortage of mail is beginning to get the men down. I censor some letters and practically everyone tells about how long it has been since they have heard from home. The average is a month. That means it has been a month since the last letter they have received has been written. That is about true with me, too, for your last letter was written just after Christmas. When the mail does come in I opine that we shall need hours off duty to catch up. I shall expect at least three letters from you and I hope each one tells me that you are getting better and better and better and that the present I had sent you has arrived and that you liked it and that you love me and that you are anxious to have me come home and that you are looking forward with pleasure to being a minister's wife, this minister's wife once more. That's a lot to hope for, but I do.

February 1, 1945

...Don't tell him, but I am going to buy, through our P. Ex. a baby panda for Anthony. Not a live one, of course, but the teddy-bear kind. It will take two months to get there but I hope it will arrive by his birthday. I'm sure Bruce will like it, but tell him not to get jealous. I'm sure Anthony will let him play with it. [This must be the teddy bear, not in panda black-and-white but gray with brown snout and paws, which I eventually named Theodore. I still have him.]

Yesterday I took a trip about fifteen miles due east into Germany. I went through one good sized German city, passed through part of the Siegfried Line where the Dragons' Teeth were seen and noticed one pillbox that had been blown apart. This city was a very sorry sight. Bigger than any city in the vicinity we found very few people there. Hardly a building was intact although block after block was standing. It is hard to imagine how people could possibly live there and it gives me an idea of what every German city of size and importance must look like. We went through smaller towns that weren't badly hit because the Germans didn't defend them. I imagine the places on the Eastern Front that try to withstand the Russians are much the same way. It is the worst I've seen yet. I don't care to see anything worse than that.

February 4, 1945

I'm glad your picture is on the way and I hope it gets here soon. If you like them I am sure to. I made out the order for the baby Panda for Anthony. The order goes to Paris, they send it to New York, they send it to the manufacturer and they send it to Anthony. All that takes two months. But that ought to get to him in time for April 10.

...It is now Sunday evening. I've had my daily service. Only 25 came out and we had the service in the mess hall. I could see loaves and cakes and we all could smell chicken cooking. I decided we'd have our other services elsewhere. Incense is part of temple worship but the odor of cooking fowl is not part of my service if I can help it. It is very discouraging the way people don't come out. I'm getting pretty sick of it. They all like me and I do things for everyone indiscriminately. The Colonel is satisfied with my work as Chaplain but the monthly report looks mighty bad with four Sunday services and a total attendance of 122.... Combat Chaplains list four or five Sunday services and five or six week-day services a week and that looks darn good on paper. By reports like that the chaplains are judged. Somehow I never look very good on paper. And I can't get any cooperation from the men here. But I guess I shall just have to consider that my problem and work on it.

...Yesterday Grace Wright, our chief nurse told me she planned to get married and asked me to perform the ceremony. I told her I was honored. She holds the rank of captain in the A.N.C. [Army Nurse Corps] *and her husband to be is a captain in the signal corps. She wants a church wedding. Now getting married over here is no cinch. Each member of the armed service has to get consent of the C.O., the general of that corps or army and the O.K. of the head of that branch of the service. Captain Wright is all set. But it will take her man two more months. Now here in Holland the bride and groom must get a civil marriage first. This is done by going to the mayor of the city and getting him to marry them. That makes them legally married. Then the religious ceremony is performed. Now I have to see the minister of the Dutch Reformed Church, ask for the use of his church, make arrangements for Lieberman, my organist, to practice on the organ, and then sit tight. The chances are that we shall be deep in Germany in two months' time but we are going to make our plans as if we expected to spend our lives here. So that is something to look forward to. I've been hoping I could get through this overseas duty without any wedding, but I guess I can't.*

I would love to be on hand to carry coal & wood and oil for you and to shovel snow and make breakfast and admire your cooking. I'd like to look into your eyes again especially after something had pleased you. There are lots of things I'd like to do and you [are] *concerned with them all.*

Pretty soon it will be time to look for Bruce's present to arrive. I hope it gets there for his birthday. Say "Happy Birthday" for me if the present is late.

Yours with love,
Jerry

February 8, 1945

Dearest Doris:

Laugh and grow fat. Is that why I've gained thirty pounds in this army? I do a lot of laughing and a lot of gaining. Fig is a good provoker of the former, anyway, and his comments on the men and to the men who come in here are a cure for the blues. So, if I keep on laughing I guess it will be very hard to recognize me when I return.

I have just returned from a long trip. Do you recall my writing to you about Lt. Helen Hight Van Sickle, the nurse that reminds me so much of you? I wrote about her to your mother and I think I told you about how she came to me just before Christmas concerning the quickest way of getting a message through to her husband who was in the Seventh Army way down east of Metz. Anyway I got a letter through by courier for her. I was glad to do that little thing and I wondered if I wouldn't be called upon to do more. I was. Well, if I had to choose which nurse I would rather do something real big for, it would be she because doing something for her would seem the nearest like doing something for you of anything I could do. Does that make sense at all?

On Monday afternoon after coming in from an outside errand concerning the impending wedding of Captain Wright, I heard over the P.A. system this announcement, "Chaplain Miller, please report to Hospital Headquarters." So I reported to the same and was told the Colonel wanted to see me. So I went to the Colonel's Office and he told me to sit down. "Relax, you must have hurried to get here. You're out of breath." So I relaxed. He explained that he wished me to take Lt. Van Sickle down to see her husband. He had talked it over with Captain Wright and they both felt they didn't want her to take the trip unless an officer were along and I was the choice of both of them. So he showed me on the map where I would have to go to get there. The route took in places made famous by the last great counter-offensive of the Germans that made our positions so uncertain all through the last half of December and the first half of January. I suppose it would not be right to trace the route for you but I will mention that we were to pass through Bastogne, famous for the determined stand of the 101st Airborne Division. We should also go though Metz for his position was east of there. On the map it looked simple enough but we weren't sure whether that road would be safe. I did what investigating I could and we decided it was all right. I was then to tell Lt. Helen that she could go on Tuesday morning or Wednesday morning. She was to have one day to get there, spend the night of that day with her husband, have the next day with him, spend that night and come back the third day. It was a mighty large order for yours truly to fill.

Well, I told her and she chose to go the next morning. "There's no time like the present," she said. It is well she made that choice.

So we started out on Tuesday morning. We planned to get away by nine but when we got around to sign out we didn't know how to do it. The ordinary V.O.C.O. is good for only 24 hours and that obviously wouldn't do for three days. So we fixed it up by making applications for leave which would not be granted unless something happened that would require a leave to cover. If, for instance we should be injured by a motor accident or be hit by shell-fire so that an official leave would be necessary to make this line of duty, then they would grant the applications for leave so that we would be officially covered. For me it wasn't leave because I was on very heavy duty. It took a half hour to get that all straightened out so we didn't get away until 9:35. But we did get started.

We headed for Liege first of all and I was quite interested in that city because it had been hit by so many buzz bombs. Some said there wasn't much of the city left. But there was. A very small section was hit. Going through the main part of the city we saw regular trolley-car service, trackless trolleys [electric buses powered from two overhead wires—these were still operating in the Boston area in the 1960's] like those we saw in Cambridge when I was going to Chaplain's School, the railroads were busy and there were tug boats on the Meuse River towing the barges around. We passed well-dressed people and street after street of department stores. Just like Boston or New York, only smaller than New York, and smaller than Boston, too, I guess. But Liege is so big it takes about a half-hour to drive through it. We headed south from there to our destination and passed through the Belgium that was occupied by the Germans for a month. What a sight! We went through one district where it was quite heavily wooded and not a single tree could we see that not pitted with shrapnel from exploded shells or bombs. We saw tanks of every kind, half-tracks, trucks, jeeps and even airplanes and gliders smashed up. We had to admit that a great majority of the tanks we saw knocked out, some of them up-side-down, were American. In one field we saw three tanks dug in, all facing the direction the enemy came from, and we could see that they had faced the enemy and fired at them until they were rendered useless. Occasionally, however, we saw one of the famous Tiger Tanks knocked out with its big .88mm gun forever silenced and its arrogant cross a symbol of death to itself. We passed many a building smashed to pieces and (this would make you dad and brother sick) we passed field after field and barnyard after barnyard where cows and horses were lying dead, some with their legs sticking up in the air, others on their sides and their bodies ripped open. Surely the crows of Belgium won't be hungry for many a day. We went by one little plot of ground where there were eight or ten rude crosses and on some of them were German helmets, mute token of the price the attackers had to pay. When we passed through Bastogne we saw what we expected, a city knocked to smithereens. It was a terrible sight, Doris, and I am so glad you don't have to see it and similar places. But the people of Bastogne were still there. How they survived and where they live now is a mystery to me. Mercy me, what a war! We saw one place where there was a pipe running out of a heap of rubble that once was a public building. By some miracle the plumbing of that pipe was still intact and people came there to get their water. Only the strictest medical discipline can keep these people from a scourge of typhoid more deadly than war. We passed through the town and it took us an hour to get out of that area where it was still unsafe to go two feet out of the road. We still saw tanks that were out of action but we saw some more that were raring to go. And we came to many craters in the road that had been filled in. We went over at least six of them and right beside each crater was the wreck of some kind of a vehicle. I don't know whether these vehicles hit mines or whether the bombs of the American planes were so accurate that they hit the vehicles and made the hole in the road at the same time. I have a feeling the latter is true for these Yankee pilots are real marksmen.

When we got into France things took on the appearance of more peaceful times. We passed through several towns and some cities and we saw the French in their natural setting. We were stopped by French soldiers and asked the password but being from the Ninth Army we knew only that password. But Redman, the driver, showed the trip-ticket, which is our authorization for the vehicle, and he studied it intently for about thirty seconds and handed it back with an "O.K." "What does he know about a trip-ticket?" We had a Sgt. Along who went with us on the chance we might be able to put him close enough to his brother to enable him to find him. I secured him a three-day pass after I guaranteed the Detachment Commander that I would not leave him unless we found his brother's unit. So we had that chore to do, too. When we came to the town where his brother's unit's A.P.O. was we planned to find out if his unit's truck had come for the mail. If it had not and would we were going to let our Sgt. stay there and wait for it. So we inquired at the M.P.s depot. When we came in there was an argument going on between a couple of M.P.s and two Frenchmen, one of the latter a French major. It was about black market gas. It seems that the M.P. had caught the man with the gas and wanted to run him in, but he wasn't allowed to. How mad he was! "At home my mother has two cars in the garage and can't get gas to run one of them. Here this Frenchie takes gas and goes out with a woman whenever he wants to." Later on he said, "These guys take everything. I'm just waiting for the time when I get orders to shoot someone when he tries to steal gas. I'll knock him out with a crowbar." The M.P. in charge was trying hard to get some order out of the confusion, without much success, and at the same time keep the Frenchman from going away mad and the soldier from being too mad. When we could get a hearing we asked about the unit our Sgt. was interested in and he looked through and through his list of local units but it wasn't there. He also told us the A.P.O. had moved to a town north of there, a town we had already been through. If we had stopped there we might have connected. But, as it was too late to go back we had to take him with us, quite disconsolate.

We wended our way onward through French towns, stopped occasionally by French guards and finally darkness overtook us. We were then in Seventh Army territory. When we came to a village we were halted and told to put out our lights. When we hit the highroad we put them on again. We had passed through Metz, famous as the most fortified city in the world and were now heading due east. French villages were made up of houses made of stone with the house and barn all in one building and the manure pile with hens scratching it is right at the end of the barn and beside the road. This goes on and on. Finally, when we were about a dozen miles from the place where Lt. Helen said her husband was supposed to be and where we were occasionally alarmed by the sound of a big gun going off right beside us, or so it seemed, we were stopped by a guard. He asked for the password. I couldn't give it so he told me to dismount. I couldn't give him the satisfaction he desired so he called the corporal of the guard. They decided to take us down to the Hqs. for examination so the corporal sat on the side and we went, in total darkness. I was taken into the Hqs. and there, to my surprise I saw lots of rank, a Lt. Colonel, majors and such. I explained to the Lt. Colonel that I was looking for the husband of a nurse we had with us. He wanted to know what unit. I couldn't tell but asked if it were possible to bring her in and she would tell. "Is she a U.S. Army nurse? Is she an American?" When I assured him that she was he said, "Bring her in." So I went out and brought them all in. So she told him her husband was in the --- Regt. The – Bn. And the – company. "Why that is this Regiment," he said. "What's his name?" "Lt. Van Sickle." "Why, I know him. Come into my office and I'll call him up." So we went into the Colonel's office and met Colonel Morgan. They put a call through to the Lt. and he was on his way. Boy! Talk about answers to prayer. If we had gotten to the village we were heading for we wouldn't have found him that night, if at all. The Colonel Morgan and the Lt. Col. Russell entertained us for the three-quarters of an hour we waited. Lt. Helen sat right on the edge of her seat all that time and when he did come in they hurried into a clinch. Then I had completed half of my mission for I had delivered her into her husband's arms. They had a room together by turning out a captain and everything was perfect for them. And, believe me, the officers in that regiment were mightily impressed. "How would you like to have your wife walk in on you like that?" was the standard question. "Boy, that would be great," was the standard answer. Say what you want in fun about the nuisance a man's wife might be, these army men are unanimous in their opinion that they would like nothing better than to have her come in and see them.

After that I was ready to go to bed and they put me up in that very building along with two majors and two other captains. I had my bedding roll with me and just laid it out on a couch and slept very well considering guns, big and little were pounding away all around me. The next morning I just killed time. I slept most of the afternoon and let the young people have the day to themselves. Lt. Col. Russell arranged for Lt. Van Sickle to go back with us if I could arrange transportation back and I mulled it over in my mind pretty thoroughly and came to this conclusion. If he were to come back with us he could spend one more night with her if Captain Wright would let them be together. I had my doubts about that. Then on Friday he could ride to Liege on an ambulance and from there to Paris by connection with the Blood Bank truck or some other vehicle that makes the run right through in a day. I explained that to Col. Russell and it was contingent on when the convoy coming back from Paris would arrive. For Lt. Van was slated to go to Paris on Wednesday morning and if we had come on Wednesday instead of Tuesday we would have missed him. Wouldn't that have been tough?

That night there was a counter-attack on that front by the Germans. I was in the Regimental Hqs. when it happened. Messages kept coming in about this platoon and that platoon, this company and that company, this battalion and that battalion. Boy, they were excited, and by the way the officers sent out messages I could see how they disposed their men to meet the attack. They would tell this company to fall back to a certain point and that company to stand in reserve, they would call up the artillery to lay down a barrage at a certain point and they would ask some other officer to send some bazooka teams to meet the tanks. It was quite a show. I saw how important the work of the signal corps is for the telephone was might important about then. After a while I received a call from Lt. Van saying they would be down at eight the next morning and that they were all right and safe. With that off my mind I went to bed and stayed and let them work out their counter-attack without my interference.

We got started back the next morning two hours late because he didn't have a way to ride down to us and didn't let me know about it until after nine. I sent my driver after him and they came down. We talked the practicability of his coming back with us and discovered that the convoy that takes the members of his unit back from making whoopee in Paris started on Saturday morning at eight o'clock instead of Sunday, so he decided not to come. We came back another way that took us through the City of Luxemburg and part of the Grand Duchy of that name. One interesting thing we saw was a little, narrow-gauge train that had a little engine on either end. It ran right on the road, practically, only to the right and a foot above it. Luxemburg is a pretty city, what we saw of it, without much war damage. In fact, we didn't see so much damage in Metz in spite of that being a fortress city. Along the way we saw forts with barbed wire around them but by some military strategy they were made useless without being taken. So they were harmless to us. When we returned through Bastogne we found that progress had been made in cleaning up the town and many of the tanks and other vehicles had been towed away and some of the cattle buried. Frost had also heaved the roads so the driving in places required all the traction these four-wheel-drive, low range geared army vehicles are capable of. But we got back in two hours less than it took us to get there. On the way back we went through parts of France, Luxemburg,

Belgium, Germany and finally arrived home in Holland. It was a long, hard trip to take in a jeep and I think that for the first time in my army experience I earned my daily salary. It was no small thing to take a girl down to an uncertain destination, deliver her into the arms of her husband, take her out again after they had been thirty-five hours together, and get her back intact and reasonably happy. But I did it. Mission accomplished.

And the latest development from this is that the Sgt's brother we were trying to find came in to see him this morning. His unit has moved into an area not far away and he looked up his brother. Now what do you think of that? But our Sgt. said he was glad he went on the trip just the same. He took several snap-shots on the way of war's damage along the way and came the nearest to the front any of us have ever been.

February 13, 1945

Dearest Doris:

...Tomorrow will be Valentine's Day. I wonder if you all received the valentine I sent you, the one Fig made up for me. I expect the children had a fine time on this day. And by the time this gets to you Priscilla will be nine. Did her presents from her Daddy arrive on time? I have several postal cards Fig bought in town for me and I'm going to pick out the very best and send it along with this letter. Wait a minute, it's Bruce's birthday, not Priscilla's. Whatsamatterwith me? Bruce will be my seven year old boy, and it's his card I shall have to pick out. So I hope you all have a good Valentine's Day and Bruce has a good birthday.

We are going to have a Jewish discussion group in here to-night. These guys are the champion discussers of the world. They can discuss on any subject. They could discuss on the subject, "Ash trays make good coffee cups," and find plenty of pros and cons. Gosh, they started a discussion on Zionism way back in October and the next to the last discussion was still on Zionism. Tonight Father

Van Wersch, my assistant Chaplain, is to speak on the "Position of the Jew in Europe before, during and after Nazi occupation."

Our office is a little different now. The Colonel ordered me to take out the tables so the men wouldn't use the office as a lounging place and letter-writing room and some of the nurses wouldn't be associating with the men here. Now the men come to read and get supplies but there aren't nearly as many and at times it seems very quiet. Fig doesn't like it one bit. When he comes in here and sees me alone in the room he says, "It's so quiet here it's just like our other office." He refers to the morgue. I censor his mail for him and the letter he wrote to his father and mother just after we cleared out the tables and benches was the most pitiful letter he ever wrote, or that I have ever read. But we've got used to it. I don't like it so well as it was but professionally it is much better.

I saw a boy from Vermont on Sunday. He had stepped on a shoe mine and blown off his foot. He was from down Bethel way and I asked him if he knew Mr. Berry, the minister at Sharon. You remember Mrs. Berry, I'm sure. She was the one who was so jolly at the Middlebury convocations. He said he did. I asked him if he knew Earle Phelps who went to high school in his town in 1928. He said he was only three then. That would make him only nineteen now. I talked with him quite a while and promised to look him up later. I looked him up and so far he has been irrational. But I expect we shall become better acquainted.

Captain Wright's boy friend was in to see her Sunday. We went to church together, Captain Wright and I, at the Dutch Reformed Church in town here so's she could see what it looked like inside. She liked it. Then her man came in the afternoon and they had some time together. I saw her the next day and asked her if she had told her husband about the conditions that had to be met before he could become legally married by the mayor. She said she did and he didn't want to go through all that. He said they would be married in Germany where things would be simpler. But she wants to get married in the church right here. And she wants me to marry them. Apparently she's a little more anxious to marry him than he is to marry her. Gee! She is close enough to being an old maid to do a little worrying. Remember how anxious I was to marry you? I would have met almost any conditions. And if by getting married again I could have you now and always I would do it quick. I enjoyed our wedding and I enjoyed being married to the girl I married. Best wife I ever had.

Feb.15, 1945

Dearest Doris:

Back from a Chaplains' Conference this afternoon. I went down to see if I had any mail. I did. A letter from you. I liked the way the letter started, "Jerry, you Darling!" I certainly go for indications of affection and joy from you in a big way. I would certainly like to play the part of an ardent lover with you while you were wearing that gift. And playing the part would not be hypocrisy, either. Perhaps you had better eek out enough from your allowance to supply me with some silk pajamas so I can be dressed for the part, too. Or do you think that will be necessary? I certainly hope it won't be long before we can be together for keeps. We belong together, don't you think?

Feb. 18, 1945

...I received my very best Christmas present. The pictures arrived. [See next page.] *They're wonderful! Thank you so much, my dear. How proudly I show them off. Everyone admires my pretty wife. "How did you ever get a nice looking girl like that?" I wonder myself. They are surprised when I tell them that the little fellow is only 9 months old when this was taken. One major said, "It looks as if he were driving, doesn't it?" And they remark how pretty Priscilla is and how manly the other two boys are. My, what a change time has made in my little family! I love the pictures and I love you, too.*

Studio portraits of Doris (left) and the children: Kenneth standing behind Priscilla, Anthony, and Bruce.

The boy from Vermont who came in last Sunday died this morning. I had no idea he would but the blast did more than take his foot off. It hurt him more severely than we thought. He was worried about losing his foot. I'm going to write to his mother. Since we are both from Vermont I think I can make the letter a little less formal than the usual letter of condolence.

28 February, 1945

Well, did Brucie have a good birthday celebration? Being seven years old does deserve a little extra, it seems to me. Have the knick-nacks I sent arrived yet? I hope they have and that the lot for Priscilla and Anthony are well on the way. It is tiresome to send something and feel that it will be months before it arrives. Won't it be great when I can be home and help celebrate these birthdays when they come around? Back last fall I was quite confident that I would be home to celebrate our wedding anniversary, at least. But I don't think so any more. Probably this war in Europe will be over by my birthday but I have a feeling that every chaplain who is good for anything will be kept in. I think that the men who get dismissed when Germany folds up will be those whom the army is quite anxious [to get rid of] or those whose denominational big wigs will be clamoring for. No one in our denomination gives a darn about me and so far, except for one brush with the Colonel, I have made a good record in the army. So, if I keep well, I expect to be in for the whole of this year, at least. But we can't tell. Anyway, I hope that I get a chance for some time with you all before 1946. Wouldn't it be nice if we could celebrate Kenneth's birthday and Christmas together? I would certainly love to be with my family again, to say nothing of holding you close in and out of your new nightie.

March 12, 1945

The Jewish Chaplain from the nearby Corps Hqs comes in frequently for services. I have worked hard for him to see that he got something like a square deal here in his services. He appreciated it, apparently, for he had two bracelets made out of local coins. One was for me and one for Fig. I am sending you this one. Probably you will wish to give it to Priscilla. If you wish it please keep it. If you would rather Priscilla would have it tell her it is from her Daddy. I think it is kind of pretty, don't you?

We have been assigned a Red Cross worker from Chicago. Her name is Mary Vernia. My work is going to be different from now on. She will take care of much of the distribution of supplies to patients and letter writing....

March 20, 1945

Dearest Doris:

Your V-mail of March 6 arrived today. I am glad you have found my idea about paying the bills was good. Remember how I used to brag that I had a good idea twice a year. Perhaps that was the good one for 1945. When you have cashed in all you need to tell me how it feels to be free of debt. I'd like to be there to help celebrate.

Now let's see. What's been going on here? On Friday night we had three Britishers come in as patients. One was a man 57 years old. He died here. The second was a captain. The third was a woman they called Lady Margaret Stewart. She was a red-headed dame who didn't look nearly as much like a lady as you do. She was put in a ward with a Red Cross Girl who was a patient here. When I went in to call she didn't pay any attention to me because I was a Yank. But the Captain was very glad I called on him because I was able to get a message through to the Press Camp for him. I made a special trip to the city to get it through for him. And I spent a lot of time on Mr. Rippon, the correspondent who died. I went through his belongings and inventoried them. Then I rescued a pair of pants that belonged to the Captain and had them repaired. They cut one leg right up to the crotch but the other leg was intact. When this was finished the next job was to put the clothes on him, which was not easy. I put the pants on him on Saturday morning up as far as I could alone without dumping him off the stretcher and left him until I could get a shirt. On Monday I got two men to help me and we put the shirt on. He had a Thomas splint on his right arm because that arm was broken between the shoulder and elbow. We took that off and put the sleeve on that arm. It seemed queer how limp an arm broken where that was could be. Then we cut the shirt up the back and put the other sleeve in. That went on harder because the arm was stiff. When we got that on we slipped the collar over his head but in order to pull his pants up in back and to get the shirt together in back so it could be sewed we had to roll him over. When we did that some evil smelling stuff gushed from his nose. Usually they plug up the nose and mouth, the rectum and tie up the penis. They didn't on this fellow. About that time the men who were helping me said,

"Boy! I wouldn't want your job. You have to do all kinds of disagreeable things, don't you?" Then we loaded him on the truck for the graveyard.

This city is becoming more and more like communication zone where Army Service Forces take over. We see American soldiers wearing cloth caps and that doesn't seem right. We are all anxious to move up to the Rhine and across where an Evacuation Hospital belongs. But we are well known for our sitting ability. We sat a month in England, a month in Normandy and we sat here for a month before we received our first patient. But since November 11th we have been in operation. I saw two street cars yesterday, the first I've seen here. The tracks, until lately, were used for piling ammunition.

We started a German class last Sunday. I am taking the course. Father Van Wersch, whose profession is teaching, is giving the course.

Yesterday morning a soldier came in to ask advice about some trouble he was in. He had made a girl pregnant and she is about two months along. He is willing to marry her but she is not willing to make her home in America with him. Coming from here she is a Catholic so it will mean meeting the church requirements as well as the civil ones. Well, I said I could advise him on the question of getting married but they would have to talk with Father Van Wersch about the church end of it. He brought his girl in in the afternoon and they had a long talk. It was old stuff for Father V.W. He told me that in nine days ten cases of that have come to him. The girl that works for his mother has been made pregnant by a major. He says he has had between thirty and forty come to him since he started with us. Not our men but just soldiers. He thinks that not less than 15% of the Dutch girls in liberated Holland are carrying within them embryos that are half American. There is a saying here that in the next war the Americans won't have to send over any invasion army. It will be here already. He told of a factory district where the girls are paid such low wages that prostitution is especially tempting as a means of getting money for nice things.

With the coming of colored troops these girls made themselves easily available so that there is a ribald rhyme to the effect that "I am waiting in great expectation to see whether my offspring will be white or black." The implication is that they don't care which.

All this has its tragic side. These girls will begin to expect their offspring in about May or June and later, figuring from the first liberation in September. Most of the maternity homes for expectant mothers out of wedlock are in occupied Holland. Perhaps the war will be over by then and they can be taken care of. But the facilities of liberated Holland are taxed to the limit now and if the hospitals already crowded have to take care of 40 or 50 thousand girls for two weeks it will be terrific. Besides that all the soldiers who are responsible for these unfortunate situations will have to get their friends at home to send a few Liberty Ships loaded with baby clothes or else the little fellows will have to go naked all summer. Clothes are a critical item, here.

March 25, 1945

Dearest Doris:

We are going to move soon so I'll just write you and go to bed. We are going to move into Germany where we shall be in a rest camp in tents until we are needed elsewhere. My next letter will be somewhere in Germany, probably not far from the Rhine. This week of clear weather has helped us wonderfully.

We've been here for almost seven months and that is too long. I haven't tried to make any connections in town but some have and find it hard to leave. I like the place here but the Chaplains that used to come in and talk with me and take away books and magazines for their men have moved up so far they can't come in any more. I don't feel right in the midst of these Communication Zone Troops with their slick uniforms. I'm too used to steel helmets, O.D. [olive drab], *field jackets and coats and muddy boots. So I'm glad we're moving.*

I saw the Queen on Tuesday or Wednesday. They had a big gathering here in the square before the City Hall. She, just like some other women, was two hours late. But the crowd waited quite patiently for two hours until she arrived escorted by Dutch police and English and American M.P.s. I thought the thing kind of risky myself. Just one German bomber over head could probably have landed a lucky bomb in that square and perhaps killed a thousand or two. But none did. She is very short and dumpy looking and wore a hat without a brim and a fur coat. She didn't look nearly as much a queen as your mother does when she's dressed to go places. I'll bet her daughter isn't nearly as nice looking as you, my queen.

Chaplain Gerald Miller, somewhere in Europe, 1945

Germany

The fighting front moved into Germany itself, and the 111th Evacuation Hospital followed it. Lieberman's map shows that on March 27, 1945, the unit moved to Dülken, Germany, and on March 28 to the Sports Platz, Dinslaken. They supported XVI Corps elements, 17th Airborne Division, and the 75th Infantry Division.

April 1, 1945

Dearest Doris:

This is Easter Sunday in the evening. We are set up in a tent right by the exit from this area so I hear all the traffic that goes by on this busy German road and what goes by from our hospital itself. Considering we have ambulances coming in with patients continually and other ambulances going out with patients, too, and that we have twenty-six of our own vehicles to come and go you can see that our own traffic is not light. At the present time there are six men here just enjoying the radio and just sitting.

Believe me I had a tough time in the service today. We were in a double ward tent right behind the sterilizer, a big machine for sterilizing instruments. That thing goes intermittently while operations are in progress. It sounds like an outboard motor when it is running. That thing just kept starting, running, stopping, starting, running and stopping through the service. Then there was a bulldozer, a great big one to the right of the tent. That darn thing would start up, amble by, turn around, amble back, stop, mutter and then go through the routine again. Added to this was the water truck, a seven hundred gallon truck, stopped across the way at the mess tent. There is a little gas engine used for pumping the water out that sounds like another outboard motor. That thing came at about that time. Added to all this trouble my regular pianist was sent away on a run to the quartermaster for supplies. So, the only thing about the whole service that was any good was the attendance. We must have had over sixty out. Afterwards we had a communion service and we had to have that in the midst of all that noise, too. When we sang all I could hear was the three men on the cot right close to me, and one of them was very, very flat. When I led in prayer it seemed as if God must have been a long way off I had to yell at him so. And when I preached I am certain that it made no difference at all what I said because no one could have heard it. It was Major Elias' idea to put the meeting place behind that darn sterilizer. He isn't called the Black Turk for nothing. Sometimes I find the commandment "Thou shalt love thy neighbor as thyself," very hard to keep when a fellow like that is my neighbor. I asked Fig if they had the same competition in Mass right after my service. He said they did. I spoke to our new Colonel about it afterwards and he said, "I'm sorry. They didn't need to run that thing during the service."

We are deep in Germany now. I had to go back to Heerlen to marry Captain Wright on Wednesday so I stayed over night with them the next day. Now we are set up in tents operating within artillery range of the front. Things are moving so fast, however, I think we shall be moving about every two weeks. I like it here. We are in a German city and yet we don't see very many Germans. Of course there are some but I expect all who could retreated behind their own army. There is a refugee camp near here where over a thousand persons of all nationalities are living together in what used to be a stockyard. Father Van Wersch was over and said… these people are living under conditions so bad that the cattle that preceded them there lived like kings in comparison. Both men and women are there living in unbelievable unsanitation. He said he thinks every third one is either a victim of syphilis or tuberculosis. Now that we have taken over as many are being evacuated as possible daily. Some come from the western countries and can be returned with comparative ease. But the Russians and Poles present another problem. I'm glad it isn't my job to take care of them.

The trip from Heerlen to here was more interesting to me than the trip to the first area where we expected to have a rest. We went from Heerlen to Sittard, from there to Roermond, still in Holland. We crossed and went from there to Muchen-Gladbach and headed east and north. I can't name any more places. Most of Germany where we went was badly shot up, but like Bastogne and many French towns, persons still live there. We stopped at one place and parked in a city. Two of the men in the truck happened to throw away the butts of the cigarettes they were smoking. Two German men scrambled for those butts like two hungry dogs would go after a bone. We are strictly ordered not to give anything to any Germans regardless of age or sex. It comes hard for up to now one of our chief pleasures has been to give candy and gum to children and tobacco to young people and men. We can't any more. It is part of the army policy to show the Germans that, since they chose total war they shall have to endure it. It must be torture for them to go by our army installations and, at chow time, smell the delicious aromas of cooking food and not be able to get a bit. There are some exceptions. We have some German men working for us about the mess and we feed them. But we are not allowed to be friendly. I don't know what would happen if one of our cooks slipped a German a candy bar for his kids. He might lose his stripes. War is no fun! When the instincts of generosity have to be stifled it is really a bad thing. But I suppose this policy has come out of a great deal of thought.

Just think, by the time you get this Anthony will be a year old and Priscilla nine. [My birthday is April 10, and Priscilla's, April 15.] How our family is aging. Is Priscilla still well preserved? I'm afraid I shall stand very much in awe of her when I get home. I hope she will still be nine at that time. And will I stand in awe of you, too, my lady? How about it?

Well, I bid you a fond good-bye for now. I'll be anxious to hear from you soon.

Yours with love,
Jerry

April 4, 1945

Dear Carroll and Mother Leach:

Here we are in Germany, about seventy miles in, I guess, although a hungry crow would fly from here to Holland a much shorter way than we came by truck. You see, this is our second trip into Germany. Last Tuesday we started out for a place south of here and about a dozen miles from Muchen-Gladback and when we arrived we found that the tents were set up in a sports park with an amphitheatre made of terraced earth held in place by large slabs of stone. We expected to rest there for a week or a month until we were needed at the front. There was one little bomb shelter dug in the side of the hill that I picked out for my office. We were all set for a long time. We had stoves for our tents and looked forward to softball, volleyball, long nights of sleep and long days in which to do out our washing, read and enjoy life as much as any person in a concentration camp ever could. That was Tuesday. On Wednesday I had to go back to Heerlen, Holland (now it can be told) where we were set up from October until March. Captain Grace Wright, our chief nurse was going to be married on that day and she needed me. So I went back with her man and his two soldiers to tie the knot....

I got Captain Wright safely married off in Heerlen. First she and her man had to go to the city hall and be married by the Bougermaster. He had them sit down before him, read the ritual to them which consisted of the statement that Grace O. Wright was the daughter of Mr. and Mrs. Wright of Winston-Salem, North Carolina, that she agrees to be married to the man of her own free will. That Alfred Kraas is the son of Mr. and Mrs. Kraas of Indianapolis, Indiana, and agrees to marry the woman of his own free will without the insistence of a shotgun or bazooka. He reads this in Dutch and then, as well as he can, in English, and they are married. Ten guilden please. Two Dutch girls witnessed the wedding. Then we went over to the Dutch Reformed Church and I married them a la American style by using the ritual out of my little black book. The two soldiers that came with them were witnesses. I made them promise a great deal more than the Bougermaster did. But I think they intended to keep every promise they made. The two Captains had until Saturday together. They had a small apartment in the home of one of the members of that church, a very wealthy man who had a mansion. Pretty nice.

I stayed the night back at the place where our hospital was because we still had an officer and twenty-five men there to clean up the place. The next afternoon, Thursday, right after chow, we started back. This time we went to Sittard, still in Holland, followed the road to Roermond, still in Holland. There we crossed over into Germany and headed for Muchen-Gladback. All along the way we saw signs of war and a very depressing sight it is, even in enemy country, even an enemy such as Germany. Farmers were getting in their spring's work. Occasionally a farmer was fortunate enough to have two strong horses for his ploughing. But usually a horse will be yoked with an ox. Sometimes the ox is harnessed with the ropes or straps hitched to the horns. At other times there is a similar harness to that used on the horses. The fields looked very good and the soil rich and black. Often we came across groups of people with wagons of varying sizes all the way from a two wheeled affair pulled by one man and pushed by two or three women to single wagons pulled by one horse. Apparently these people were going back to what was their homes. I suppose someone had gone ahead and discovered that there was some possibility of retrieving something out of the almost hopeless waste that is the result of the kind of war they elected to fight. In some towns everything was pretty well intact and the reason was evident. In every house window there was some kind of a white flag, a towel, handkerchief, table cloth, part of a sheet, anything white, to show that they gave up. In the Stars and Stripes there was mention made of one little city that wanted to surrender by telephone. Some one called up the colonel of the regiment about to make the attack and asked what they must do to give up the town. He asked for the mayor and when the mayor was on the line he said have every home show a white flag within twenty minutes. Well, talk about your evening primrose blossoming out all at once, that's just what the town did. In an unbelievably short time there were white flags all over the place. Some women even used their slips because they didn't want to take time to unset the table. But for the most part just about every house had to receive some token of force before the people in it gave up.

We crossed the Rhine on a pontoon bridge. That river is about like the Hudson at Albany but not nearly the mighty stream that the Hudson is down by the Catskills and West Point. Of course, once across that river there was no doubt that Germany was invaded. I think the Americans outnumber the Germans here. There are many civilians that are of other countries, forced to work here to help fight Germany's war. Lots of them are now being sent back. Near here is a place where such persons were kept all together like a bushel of beans. I haven't seen the place yet but those who have say it defies description. Suppose you have a building about like the Opera House at Enosburg Falls [which seats 120 in its main hall] and make some two thousand people live there with no attempt to segregate them because of sex, age, diseases, nationality or religious heritage. That's the way the Germans do things. If that sort of thing had to be done in America or by Americans they would put up tents and dig latrines and have a dispensary and make some effort to allow the people to keep some of their self-respect. If you live here long you see what our authorities mean when they say no fraternization. The people here may be basically the same as any other people, but their methods might well come from the Dark Ages.

Our Hospital is set up in tents. When I came here on Thursday they had the hospital set up and the tents for officers and the tents for the Enlisted men but none for me. We got ours up the next day and now are very comfortably settled. The responsibility for moving and setting up in a new area and being ready to receive patients by five o'clock was too much for our Colonel. He became sick and had to be evacuated to Aaken. Now we have a new Colonel, Anderson by name, and like every new Colonel, he has to change everything to show who's boss. He has had the poor men taking down tents and putting them up until the men were about worn out. It worked well before because we have men here that know how to lay out a hospital in the field as well as he does because we received all our training with the idea of operating in tents. But, you know how it is. Probably [Carroll] Junior [Doris's brother] has made changes in your set up, too.

There were two men in the tent just now and we discussed the mental demise of our late Colonel O'Brian. One was his orderly and the other was one of our X-ray technicians. The orderly told about the last day Colonel O'Brian was here. He suffered from what the doctors call schizophrenia or dementia praecox. Also from exhibitionism. It was worth a dime to hear the two men tell about him. For about eight months now he has treated the enlisted men as if they were made of dust and the officers as if they were made of gold dust. Every effort I have made to help the men has met with either cynicism or objection from him. And the men knew it. Braude, the X-Ray man said he could see signs of the breakdown three weeks ago. Trisorio, his orderly told how on the last day he and Redman were trying to rig up a stove for him in his little tent. It was hard because in the small tents the opening for the stovepipe is out the back and we didn't have any elbows for our pipes. Naturally the stove smoked badly and the Colonel said, "I know I'm a ham but I don't want to be a smoked ham." Coming from a colonel who has never said anything to men except to give orders, that was amazing. Next THING HE KNEW when he came to the tent again was to see Colonel sitting on his cot wrapped only in a raincoat. His clothes were outside on the grass in front of the tent. Said he to Trisorio, "I want you to burn my clothes for me." Trisorio looked at him in amazement but he saw the bottle there and thought that perhaps he had drunk a little too much. He said, "Yes Colonel." Then the Colonel said to him "Have a drink," and handed him the bottle. Trisorio waited for the Colonel to offer him a glass to drink out of but after waiting over a minute the Colonel said, "Go ahead. Tip it up." Trisorio thought, "Well he's never offered me anything before in all the time I've been waiting on him so I may as well make the most of this." He tipped it up and had a drink. Then the Colonel said, "When are you going to start burning my clothes? Here, start in with these boots." He handed him his best shoes. Trisorio decided either the Colonel was crazy or he was but he ought to humor him so he said, "I think I had better get a good bed of coals so it would burn better." Then came in Major Boudreaux, the handsome and worthless dental officer, special pal of the Colonel's and when he could he whispered to Trisorio, "Pack the Colonel's clothes." Trisorio was even more confused. Either two high ranking officers were crazy or he surely was. So he didn't do anything. Boudreaux took the Colonel to his tent to talk with him awhile and Trisorio just killed time trying to collect his senses. Then Major Hutcheson, the executive officer came in and said, "When are you going to pack the Colonel's clothes?" Trisorio realized that it was true so he said, "I'm beginning right now, sir." Later on they took the Colonel away.

The new Colonel is a regular Army man and that means that he is a law unto himself. No matter how well things functioned before, and they functioned so well that we received special commendation from Nineth Army Headquarters, it has to be changed. The men are almost frantic. They aren't used to working hard. They aren't used to being pulled out of latrines or stopped from going where they are going to pitch tents. One fellow said no one will venture out of a tent now without looking both ways to see whether the Colonel is within sight. One fellow said he had to get up something awful but he stayed right there in bed. Figlioli, my assistant, was supposed to show a movie at four in the afternoon. I went out to the Military Government on some business and when I got back Fig told me he decided not to have a movie because at least twenty of the men begged him not to. They reasoned that if the Colonel heard the movie going on he would come in and say, "I want twenty men to pitch two tents. I'll take the first twenty beginning with this man here." So Fig didn't show any movie. For myself I think the change will be all for the good. There will be a weeding out of the old Colonel's favorites and I expect we shall function better for it. I have been hearing rumors that he has volunteered for the whole unit for service in the C.B.I. [China, Burma, India theater of operations] Our men don't like the sound of that at all. Says Fig, "He doesn't have to volunteer for me. I can speak for myself." I don't put much stock in that. The morning radio report carried a statement by General Montgomery to the effect that we should not look for any clean-cut surrender of the Germans on the Western Front. Probably we shall be another six months cleaning them out. Front line men say they aren't afraid of the Germans in front of them but the ones that hide and then come out about a thousand yards back and shoot when one isn't looking. So probably by the time we get through here they will be about through over in the C.B.I. (China, Burma, India) theatre.

The Colonel asked me yesterday if I had any ideas about getting the laundry done. I said I hadn't, but I would work on it. Fig said there was a colored Quartermaster Laundry set up nearby. They would take our stuff but they would make no attempt at keeping the garments of any individual together. We have about fifty officers, forty-five nurses, three hundred enlisted men. Can you imagine the fun we would have when the laundry came back? The old fashioned shoe race where everyone's shoes were mixed in a pile would be like A.B.C. compared with that mess. What it would amount to would be that the first to the pile would get the most desirable garments. Besides, a laundry like that would reduce the size of our O.D. pants and shirts by two sizes each time they did them. The Colonel didn't like that idea. So I visited the Military Government yesterday. I asked what could be done. The result of our conversation was that the Bougermaster could get us ten women who would be willing to come here and work daily at washing clothes. We are going to set up a laundry for them. Most of it will be improvised but with plenty of hot water and soap we can do much better for them here than they can in their homes that are, for the most part, without electricity or water. I told the Colonel about that and he was pleased. It will mean that the women will get their noonday meal here which is a mighty big thing. We are to pay them in our invasion marks at the rate of from seven to ten marks per day. We are to pay them in our paper money and in nothing else. If they are found with anything American on them be it candy, gum, tobacco, cigarette, soap, or clothing they are in for trouble. The lieutenant in charge there said he hasn't given a child or an adult a bit of candy or a single cigarette since he came to Germany. It's mighty hard to act that way.

Our Hospital has been receiving patients steadily for a week now. I don't know just how many have come in but if we are keeping below our three percent, like we always have, we must have had about four hundred because we have had ten visitors in the morgue. I have already made two trips to the Collecting Point and today I have to make another. This is where we leave bodies to be buried here, if German, or taken back to the Nineth Army Cemetery in Holland, if American or Allied dead.... We are getting many German P.W. patients, nearly as many as American. They have a thirteen year old boy there now. Soldier of the proud Reich. Two days ago there was a man 67 years old. Also a soldier of the proud Reich. One came in yesterday who was 55 and had been in the army only two weeks. Of those who have died here there have been two Germans, two Russian civilians, forced laborers and six Americans.

Good-bye now. Thanks for being so good to Doris.

Gerald

April 8, 1945

Dearest Doris,

Here we are at the beginning of another week. I had a better day today than last Sunday.

We are working hard enough so that only two officers, six nurses and three E.M. of our personnel came out to church this afternoon. However there was a major up the line who brought his men, about thirty, down so my attendance was about 40.

I'm kept busy with many things. Tomorrow I am to help set up a laundry and get 5 German Fraus to do the washing. I also had to arrange for the burial of a Polish woman whom a G.I. raped and

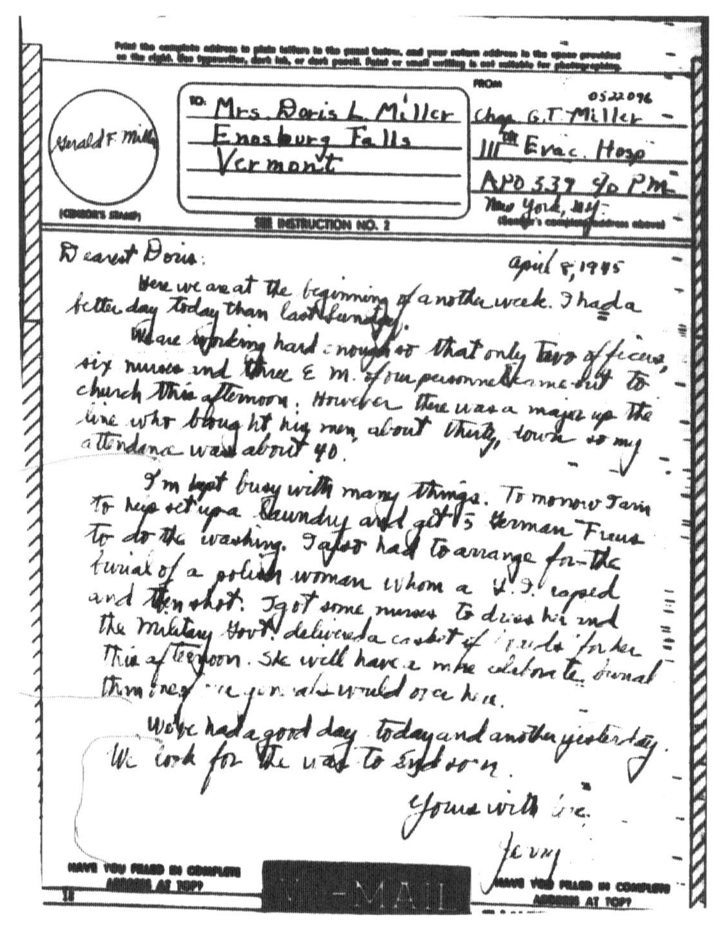

Print the complete address in plain letters in the panel below, and your return address in the space provided on the right. Use typewriter, dark ink, or dark pencil. Faint or small writing is not suitable for photographing.

TO: Mrs. Doris L. Miller
Enosburg Falls
Vermont

FROM: 0522096
Chap. G.T. Miller
111th Evac. Hosp.
APO 339 % P.M.
New York, N.Y.
(Sender's complete address above)

Gerald F. Miller
(CENSOR'S STAMP)

SEE INSTRUCTION NO. 2

Dearest Doris: April 8, 1945

Here we are at the beginning of another week. I had a better day today than last Sunday.

We are working hard enough so that only two officers, six nurses and three E.M. of our personnel came out to church this afternoon. However there was a major up the line who brought his men about thirty, so my attendance was about 40.

I'm kept busy with many things. Tomorrow I am to help set up a laundry and get 15 German Fraus to do the washing. I also had to arrange for the burial of a polish woman whom a G.I. raped and then shot. I got some nurses to dress her and the Military Govt. delivered a casket of boards for her this afternoon. She will have a more elaborate burial than one of our generals would over here.

We've had a good day today and another yesterday. We look for the war to end soon.

Yours with love,
Jerry

HAVE YOU FILLED IN COMPLETE ADDRESS AT TOP?

V-MAIL

HAVE YOU FILLED IN COMPLETE ADDRESS AT TOP?

Gerald's April 8 V-mail, actual size

then shot. I got some nurses to dress her and the Military Govt. delivered a casket of boards for her this afternoon. She will have a more elaborate burial than one of our generals would over here.

We've had a good day today and another yesterday. We look for the war to end soon.

Yours with love,
Jerry

On April 12, 1945, President Franklin Roosevelt died at the Little

White House in Warm Springs, Georgia. The *New York Times* reported that our English allies mourned him as one of their own, and in Russia the Soviet flag was flown with a black border, a sign of mourning seldom used for a foreigner. The German authorities hoped that FDR's death would cause a breakup, or at least lessen the Allies' determination, but newly sworn President Truman reiterated America's determination to fight to the end.

German soldiers had begun surrendering to American forces in large numbers. Nathan Prefer wrote: "In the first two weeks of April, 10,464 prisoners were taken in by Ninth Army. These had to be removed from the combat zone as soon as possible. As a result, every truck convoy bringing up supplies was to take back as many prisoners as it could carry. In many cases, there were 'potential' prisoners of war wandering behind the lines who had yet to be officially 'captured.' Many American units had no time to process prisoners, so many groups of Germans simply wandered along the roads until some officer directed a truck convoy to load them up and take them to a collecting point in the rear. Oftentimes, a single military policeman in a jeep would guard hundreds of German POWs as they marched west.

"One driver…came up with a method to get more POWs to the rear quickly. He loaded his truck to capacity and then moved forward, stopping suddenly. The inertia of the stop pushed the prisoners forward just a little bit more, allowing for additional prisoners to be hurriedly loaded into the truck…. None of this seemed to disturb the prisoners, most of whom were only too happy to get out of the combat zone as quickly as possible." (N. Prefer, *The Conquering Ninth*, p.216.)

On April 16, the Soviet assault on Berlin began.

April 16, 1945

…I am becoming the key trouble shooter of this outfit. Whenever anyone comes in with a problem that Headquarters can't solve they send him to me. I had the arrangements made for the burial of the Polish woman I mentioned last week. On last Thursday a woman came in and through an interpreter she told me that there

was a girl, her daughter, I think, who had tuberculosis and needed to have injections weekly. Only on Saturdays was the team in this town and she wanted transportation for her daughter. I had to handle it because no one else here could. Ours is a military hospital and we handle soldiers of any army under the sun. But we can't handle civilians. It was very simple. All I had to do was to get into my jeep and go up and get her and take her to the hospital and bring her back. But nothing in the army is as simple as that. The way I figured it all out was like this. I would have to go to the Military Government and tell the tale. Then I would have to get them to ask me to do it for them. That would cover me in case an M.P. stopped me and said, "How come you [have] *two Germans with you?" Or if the Colonel heard of it I could explain and say, "The Military Government asked me to do it." That would give it official sanction. So I did and they did and I did and the girl, a beautiful child about 16 years old, received her injection.*

They call on me when an ambulance comes in with the body of a civilian and our Collecting Point won't take it. They call on me when they are short on rations and I fix them up. And so it goes.

Tomorrow we are going to move again, this time our trip will be towards Berlin and we shall travel from seven a.m. till about 9 p.m. We'll be closer to Berlin when we get to where we're going than you are to Burlington [about 50 miles by road]. *Whew!*

Lieberman's map shows the 111th's route heading toward Münster, turning east and passing south of Bielefeld. They bivouacked (camped) the night of April 17 at Bad Selzuplen, then on the 18th drove south of Brunswick and bivouacked until April 27 at the Volkswagen factory in Hesslingen.

April 20, 1945

Dearest Doris:

Here it is Friday and here we are in a swell place, swanky as Weston, Mass. [a Boston suburb known for wealthy residents, large estates, and low population density compared to other suburbs] and only five miles from the front. We had a wonderful trip over here even if it was hard. We went from Dinslaken, where I wrote you my last letter and came almost due east to the present location. The place where we expected to come hasn't been taken yet so we settled for this place which was a sanatorium, I guess, for there are many one story buildings with the Red Cross over them. [A sanatorium, a hospital for treating tuberculosis, used fresh air and isolation from others to help patients recover, hence the many small buildings.] In fact we evacuated the remaining civilian patients this morning to a hospital eight miles away. We are put up in a fine two-and a half story hotel with about fifty rooms. We have a wonderful dining room and civilian help to wait on us. We are living the life of Riley for a time, I don't know how long.

Our trip yesterday was full of interest. Of course much of the way the usual signs of war were in evidence. We passed one factory that was so thoroughly blasted by bombing that it was just good for nothing. I think it was an arsenal but I'm not sure. I saw what I thought was a big siege gun barrel split half-way down. It may not have been but it looked like it. We headed towards Hanover but we didn't get there the first day. We met thousands of liberated prisoners, both men and women trudging back from their areas of concentration. We thought our trip was long in trucks but those poor souls, some walking and pushing or pulling carts with their personal effects, or riding on commandeered bicycles, or in wagons drawn by a horse or two, both commandeered, or in wagons drawn by tractors or even in G.I. trucks. These people often wear or fly the flag of their nation, France or Russia predominate because they are the largest nations to have forced laborers in Germany. But we also see Dutch and Belgian flags, and we passed one group which claimed to be Roumanian. It is a pathetic sight, Doris, to see these poor people, so far from home, constantly on the move. What they do for food I can't imagine unless they filch as they go along. To farmers who live along the way they must be a constant menace. I just wonder what a German farmer could do if four or five of these displaced persons should happen in just about meal time and help themselves to everything edible in sight and endeavor to catch a hen or rooster on the way out. There is no government here to stop such a thing. Yet these people seem to keep to the road and press steadily to the rear. They go just about so far and are stopped by our own Military Government that rounds them up and puts them in large buildings, where there are any intact, and they stay there until they can be taken to their homes. Load after load leaves these places daily, but the Poles and Russians just have to wait until the road is clear to their homes in the east. In just another month, I imagine, we shall be able to send them East, right through Berlin to Poland or Russia and south to Czecho-Slovakia, Jugo-Slavia, Greece, and not long hence, to Norway and Denmark. Near where we are now is another camp where these people, workers in a nearby factory, are housed and the French and Russian flags float proudly where once the Swastika was monarch of all that could survey it.

This is wonderful spring weather and almost everybody who belongs here is out farming. The earth here is rich and black and looks almost as if the seed planted today would be up tomorrow. The work is done mostly by hand and it is a family job. We saw children, women and old men working these fields and the neatness with which everything was finished off was something to remember. I guess it was potatoes they were planting in many places. They hilled them up in such a way that they had the rows boxed up with the dirt so that they look like long low buildings of dirt. To associate such care with farming gives me an inkling why they are so easily ruled. They certainly haven't any time to do any thinking if they are going to make a Babylonian architectural landscape just to plant a field of potatoes. And we see the same thing in the small vegetable gardens. They cultivate a strip about four feet wide, and then they have a path sunk down about eight inches, usually about ten inches wide, but sometimes wide enough for a cart. Then another strip then another path. It looks good but it gives the impression that these people take more joy in planting the garden than they do in eating the produce it provides. And when there is not a plow they spade it up. They don't use a fork like I do, but a slim spade. They just turn over the soil. It looks fast the way they do it. I'm going to try it that way when I get home. And they try another trick. With the shortage of animals for harrowing I saw several cases of a small spike harrow being pulled by two people. Can you imagine Kenneth and I pulling a harrow over spaded ground as a quicker way of getting the ground ready than raking it?

One of the interesting experiences was the ride over the super-highway that Hitler built for military purposes. The Germans call it the Reich Autobaun. It is not any more impressive than the highway approaches of New York City but it is good for heavy traffic. It consists of two, two-lane strips separated by a stretch of grass-sown land about twelve feet wide. Where there are cross roads they either go under or over this highway and if one wishes to get off it to the left he has to travel on a side road to the right and circle around under the main highway and under or over it to get to where he wants to go. I had read of these roads as too good for ordinary traffic because they were so expensive to build but we were glad they built them for a slow convoy ten or twelve miles long can stay on the right lane and the faster vehicles like ours can use the left one. We rode on that road the last part of the first day's trip and part of the second.

At first the Colonel planned that we should make the whole trip in one day, well over two hundred miles, but he thought better of it so we went about 150 miles to a summer resort called Bad Salzuflen, a very famous summer resort for those afflicted with asthma. Boy! what a swell place that was. No sign of war damage anywhere. The streets of the town were teeming with well-dressed Germans going about their business, the stores had their wares displayed in show windows behind plate glass, the only unbroken glass I have seen in any quantity over here in the Third Reich....

The next morning my truck was about an hour and a half late pulling out because they had trouble starting it. So I had to lead the convoy that remained, about four trucks. It is not easy because if you ask a German for directions he might tell you wrong. But I had certain objectives in mind. Hanover was one and every sign that pointed to Hanover was in point. Hanover is a big city, about

450,000, and so almost all roads would branch into one leading there. Before we got to Hanover, however, we caught up with the convoy and we were all right. My goodness, what a plastering that place has received. Some of it is still intact but other parts are just piles of ruins. We saw women going from place [to place] gathering scraps of firewood from the shattered buildings. Here in Hanover were many liberated persons of various nationalities wandering through the place. Now and then a German vehicle, a three wheeled affair, with one wheel in front and with a small wagon box on back would flit through the place. And we saw the smallest automobile I ever saw, just big enough for two, go popping by. Germany is paying a fearful price for carrying on the way [it did]. Multiply Hanover by the number of all her big cities and the destruction is too enormous to conceive of.

...We feel that we are really in the army now with a Regular Army man for our Colonel. He has already straightened things out with regard to my jeep and Figlioli is so happy about it for he is the official driver. We are given the right of way in religious services, too. But he can lay down the law and I know I don't want to do anything to get him after me....

I have some nice things here that Fig liberated in one of his trips to Munchen Gladback, something in the linen line. I think I'll send it along to you and you can enjoy it. There is also a long pair of shears that Fig says is for cutting blue prints. I may include that, too. And there is the thing we found inside the cabinet for reminding you what to get at the store. I think I'll include that. We are not allowed to send any packages right now but when we can I'll remember you. I also have succeeded at last in getting a German rifle. I've been wanting one ever since we passed that stalled flame thrower in France in October. At last I have the rifle, a splendid piece, which I hope I can carry home with me. I may not make it but I shall try. It will look quite impressive in my study when I get back in the parish. [I remember Dad's German rifle. He had a few bullets for it, but I never knew him to fire it.]

...I love you just as much in Germany as I did in Vermont.

With love,
Jerry

On April 21, the German army in the west surrendered to Allied forces. The Reich sought to withdraw its remaining forces into two redoubts in the north and south of Germany.

April 24, 1945

Dearest Doris:

I'm afraid I am using you as a guinea pig, and that is no way for a man to treat his wife, especially when the wife is lovely you. But sometimes we treat those we love the mostest the worstest. Ain't it the truth? You see, we picked up an Italian typewriter and it found its way into our office. I've learned by now never to ask Fig about the hows or wheres or whys of anything that makes its appearance nowadays. My policy, finally established after much protest is to accept the inevitable for if we don't get the benefit of these things in the service of the men someone else will in the service of himself. So I accept. This is a swell typewriter but a few of the letters are different and lots are in a different place.... the carriage turns by half spaces instead of single spaces. But the big thing is the y and z. They are in the opposite places from what I am used to in our American standard keyboards. I hope, however, I can get used to this for it is a swell typewriter and perhaps it can be taught to spell better than the American one made by Remmington.

...I suppose by now that Priscilla has opened her package and seen the contents. Did she discover what the little sign said? It says, "Have you forgotten anything." [The little sign in Dutch hung in the workshop or back room of several successive parsonages during my childhood.]

We are still resting in this quiet place. Fig and Captain Zarecki went off on a little trip to the refugee camps yesterday in search of binoculars for the Colonel. Fig is Italian and he was a real help for it was the Italians that had them. They went after five and came back with six, one for me. They picked out the very best pair for me and they are perfectly swell. If I can get them home we shall enjoy them hugely when we take that Long Trail trip together. [The Long Trail is a spur off the Appalachian Trail, from western Massachusetts through the Green Mountains to northern Vermont. On average it is steeper than the A.T. and has rustic shelters along it, grandly termed Lodges.] They will be good to see distant places with and will also be lots of fun when we wish to watch birds without getting close enough to scare them. This was really a wonderful find.

I hope you will explain to Kenneth that he mustn't expect his Luger. Besides being very scarce they are much more dangerous than a rifle. When the war is over there will be plenty of them on sale and I'll buy him one for his sixteenth birthday or something else just as good. Rifles are different and are a dime a dozen over here. Already I have two. I don't know whether I can get them home or not. I have a lot of bullets for them, too, and probably I'll have some target practice on the Leach Farm if they can stand it. Crows, look out!

The war's end drew closer. On April 25, American forces, coming from the west, and Soviet forces from the east, met at the Elbe River.

On April 28, partisan forces caught Italian dictator Benvenuto Mussolini and his mistress, along with other top Italian fascists, trying to escape to Switzerland. The partisans tried them on the spot, executed them and hung their bodies upside-down from the roof of a gas station.
Also on April 28, the 111th Evacuation Hospital moved north from Hesslingen to Altenmedingen, to support the XVIII Airborne Corps, 8th Infantry, 7th Armored and 82nd Airborne Divisions.

[V-mail]

April 29

Dearest Doris:

Moved again! This day we are set up in a wheat or oats field. We are in the "Mid west" type of country with rolling topography and large grain fields and towns and villages far apart. We are now in a sector where there are many British soldiers and they have to stop war operations twice a day to have tea. If anyone is unlucky enough to be behind a British convoy at 10:59 he has only one more minute to drive for precisely at eleven they stop for the above named custom.

The weather here is cold at night and in the morning with warm afternoons on days that the sun shines. Potatoes are in here and the boxed rows I spoke of in a previous letter were probably for celery.

I don't think I shall be having a service today as everyone is busy setting up and getting ready to operate. We open officially at noon. Where we rested for a week was just out of Wolfburg, about 15 miles from Brunswick. I guess you can trace our progress pretty well.

I hope you are all well and in love with me as much as I am in love with you.

Yours lovingly,
Jerry

The evacuation hospital set up in tents, probably in the field near Altenmedingen.

On April 30, Hitler and his mistress Eva Braun committed suicide in their bunker. A week later, on May 7, Germany surrendered unconditionally to General Eisenhower in Reims. A second surrender document was signed May 8 in Berlin, at Stalin's behest.

10 May 1945

Dearest Doris:

I have lent out my typewriter so I'm going to thump out another letter to you on this Italian machine. If you count two mistakes to the line instead of one, that's the reason.

With the war over over here we are still working about as hard as ever and still getting in patients. Some of them are from carelessness, such as killed our own Sgt. Fields, and some are from truck accidents and others are from celebrations. One lad died last night from the effects of drinking poisoned liquor that a German gave to him. We have a colored boy who declares he was an innocent bystander. Three were in the house occupied by a Polish woman. For three nights they were drunk and tore the place up generally until she finally complained to the M.P.s. They came along to straighten out things and when they did come the coons ran in three directions. The M.P.s shot one fatally and the others got away. The one we have claims he was merely walking by at the time and the M.P.s shot him by mistake. We accept that story with some doubt, however. This morning Fig and Captain Green took away four bodies. Besides the one who died of alcohol poisoning there was a captain shot by his own men and two other soldiers who were dead in the same room, we don't yet know the cause. Right now we don't have nearly the census of patients we had on Sunday evening, but I imagine we have well over 100.

Everybody is as curious as they can be about what's going to happen to us next. There is supposed to be a broadcast at six from Washington explaining a point system whereby men are eligible to be dismissed from the army. Naturally we shall all be around the radio to listen to that. We had a notice on Monday for every officer and nurse with dependent children under 18 to report to personnel section. I think that counts and we with our four children are right in there. But with Chaplains I have a feeling it will be different. As I stated a while back I think a Chaplain who is mustered out before the war with Japan is over is a Chaplain who just isn't wanted. So, I'm not hopeful of seeing the Statue of Liberty or you for a while yet.

Yesterday while I was giving out rations two soldiers came by and one had a P38 to sell. That is the Germans' best automatic pistol. He wanted fifty dollars for it. I counted the money and it came to only forty-one dollars. So I didn't buy it. I wouldn't have bought it anyway because I can think of what fifty dollars can mean to you right now with the operation [my hernia repair] to take care of. Next month, if we don't move to some place where living expenses are high I will send you some more money. I'd like to hold on to what I have now because it feels bad to be always so short of money that I have to borrow some all the time.

[He must have received word that I had had my hernia operated on.] I am glad you have little Anthony straightened out at last. Now I suppose you will be able to let him have his cry out as a normal youngster should. That will be good. I hope that makes your last dealing with a hospital for a long, long time. Me, too.

While we were at the rest place two weeks ago I noticed something that Dr. Denio told me about the Germans long ago.... Dr. Denio said that he passed German schools several times where there were children out playing during recess and they didn't make any noise.... I noticed the same thing in that model village where we were occupying that nice little hotel. I would see groups of children with eight or ten of them, boys and girls, playing together and there was practically no noise. A group that large in our back yard at East Arlington would have made lots of noise. Strange, isn't it?

...We have plenty of liberated prisoners here, most of whom are merely malnutrition cases. Those who have been prisoners for over a year and have been liberated by the Russians have strange stories to tell, not so much about the rigor of their suffering but of the wildness of the Russians. I was talking with a technical sergeant who had been captured after bailing out of a plane a year ago. He says the Russians go in for loot in a big way. Instead of doing as we do with liberated prisoners which is to send them back to America the quickest way possible they put them right up in front so they can shoot as many Germans as possible.

...I suppose by now life at home has slipped back into its usual routine and Anthony is getting along well. I am looking forward to getting acquainted with that lad and I certainly hope the Government decides I'm of more use on the home front than in the army, at least for a while. But one cannot tell. Perhaps he will, meaning Uncle Sam, let me go home just for a while. I would like to see how Kenneth and Priscilla are getting along with their music lessons and I would like to be around when Bruce starts school for the first time and see if he takes to it like the other kids did.

...Personally I'd like a church where the people think enough of their minister to pay him something like what the army pays a chaplain for it is going to be mighty hard to have you suddenly have to make one hundred dollars a month do for six what you have had two hundred dollars do for five. And I wonder how you feel about it. You say your mother says for you to tell me that I'm needed at home. I appreciate that and I hope it is so. Now suppose the army should give me a choice between discharge and continued service. Which would you like me to take? I have gotten along well in the army so far and I understand it. On the other hand you know the kind of churches that come my way when it is time to change. Seriously, how do you feel about it? Would you like to be dumped with me into a parish where they are enthusiastic about me for a year and then let go so I have to mow cemeteries, deliver ice, plough roads or work in a store to make both ends meet? I know it is great to be together and I want it to happen for I love you dearly, and I love my family. But if I had the choice, and I don't expect it, of staying in the army another two years with a possible furlough at home for three weeks, or of immediate discharge, which would you like? ...If I should be mustered out in the fall I would have to take just any church that was offered and the chances are it would be another East Arlington.

...I think anyone who gets out of the army before Japan surrenders is a quitter if he has any say about it. But I do respect your wishes and I don't want you to be called upon to endure more than you can.

Well, I hope you are getting along all right at home and saving plenty of room in that bed for me. Sooner or later I'll be asking for it.

Yours with all my love,
Jerry

Somewhere in Germany
May 11, 1945

...When I send you money my purpose in mind is to bring you happiness, not myself. If it brings you happiness to buy something for yourself, that's what I want you to do. If it brings happiness to you for you to buy covers for our much used overstuffed set [of couch and chairs], by all means, my sweetheart, do it. I don't wish to be a tyrant about how you spend your money. If you will get the equivalent in happiness to use 100 bucks on a bicycle for Kenneth, a new doll carriage or another bicycle for Priscilla (if you can get them), a little bike for Bruce and a kiddie car for Anthony that you would get in putting that much in a personal gift like a watch or a bracelet or clothes, please do it. Do I make myself clear?

So, sweet Doris, please yourself and you will please me. I know $100 won't get all the things I mentioned. I was only citing examples. I'm not sure I shall have that much for you, either, but I don't need much over here and to have it is a temptation to spend it. I remember how little I have managed to save over the years. My love for you will never take the form of a dictatorship for my love is tempered with a very high regard for your good sense and your love of our home. After all, it is only our money I give you, isn't it?

...I've changed my mind about the loot I mentioned in a previous letter. I wrapped it up in two bundles this afternoon and mailed it. I am anxious to know whether it gets to you or not so please acknowledge it if either or both bundles arrive. I got tired of the idea of carting it around in the bottom of the duffle bag and there is some talk of the possibility of our stuff being gone over by the U.S. Customs when we get home. So I took the chance. There are about 100 coins in the two packages and lots of paper money the kids can enjoy. There are a few good coins there and I wish you would save whatever looks like silver. The children may do just what they wish with the rest. [Germany had experienced very bad inflation, so the Mark was worth practically nothing.]

The point system has been announced and we have about twenty enlisted men who are eligible for discharge. I haven't seen it in black and white but I understand it is something like this. Each year in the army counts one point. Each month overseas counts a point in addition. Each child under eighteen counts twelve and a man needs eighty-five to get out. Figuring that way I have fifty-seven points because they only allow for three children. But officers have a different scale, not yet announced, and I think, as I wrote yesterday, all will be kept except those who will be allowed to go "for the convenience of the service." I can see that I shall have a lot of morale boosting here among all personnel for there is hardly a one who wouldn't be delighted to get on a plane right now and head for the U.S.A.

Yes, being away from home a whole year is a hardship for me, too. It was exactly a year ago that I was home, wasn't it. I hope there won't be much time go by before I am home again.

Altenmedingen, Germany
May 17, 1945

Dearest Doris:

...Did you notice how I headed the letter? Two days ago a notice came out that we are allowed to tell where we are now and so that's where we are, in a rye field (not wheat, as I said before) just outside the village of Altenmedingen. I don't believe you will be able to find the place but I can tell you where the big places are. We are fifteen miles north-east of Uelzen, a place about as big as Burlington, I suspect. [Burlington is the largest city in Vermont.] It is half destroyed. We are about sixty miles from Brunswick to the south of us. We are about twenty miles from the Elbe River, which I crossed on a trip two days ago to Hagenow. We are south of the Elbe. Luneburg, another goodsized place is about fifteen miles west of us, Hamburg is about seventy-five miles northwest. Do you suppose you could spot us?

...This P-38 I mentioned is an automatic pistol like the Luger, but not so well made. They sell for about fifty dollars, like I told you last Friday. This one, however, was left in receiving for Captain Sparks, the forty-eight year old M.C. who used to get drunk so much. He and Tommy Williams got drunk again after the new Colonel warned them not to so they were thrown out of the unit. Captain Spaulding, one of our youngest medical officers was going to his tent with this P-38 and I asked him about it. He told me it was for Sparky but he didn't expect Sparky would ever come after it and I could have it. I have talked with several other officers about it and they all agree we shall never see Sparky again. So, possession being nine-tenths of the law, I have a P-38. I asked some men from an Ordnance Company, whom I fixed up with rations yesterday, if they could get me some ammunition for it and I think today they will bring some in. I have about 500 rounds for the rifle and if I could get a thousand rounds for the pistol, that would be perfect. Then I am sure your mother will never invite me to your home in the summer anymore.

I am enclosing a couple of fancy handkerchiefs that Fig picked up somewhere. Fig is expected to have a week's vacation at the Riviera beginning on the twenty-fourth. Lucky boy.

22 May 1945

...Yesterday I took a trip with a couple of live bodies and a couple of dead ones. The live bodies were those of Sergeant Montross and Lt. Wilkens, a nurse. Montross drove and the nurse, whom he is sweet on, without a chance, I think, sat beside him in front. I sat in back and endured all the bumps, of which there are plenty. We went first to Peine, to get rid of the bodies, and then to Brunswick, where the Ninth Army Headquarters are. Gee, what a building that is. A four story affair with six hundred office rooms. It was occupied by the Seventh German Airforce and had some luxurious rooms that were occupied by Goering and his major generals. They have little elevators that run all the time and hold only two. You just step in as it comes up and you step out when you get to your floor. When the car gets to the top instead of turning over as you would expect so it can come down, it just slides over in an upright position, and down it comes. A novel way to save on elevator boys. These cars are made for two but when Goering went up or down I suppose he went alone. Brunswick is a city about sixty miles due south of us and is about the size of Worcester, Mass. A little larger, perhaps. It hasn't suffered as much war damage as most German cities and is quite a fine city, even during the war.

We keep seeing unit after unit pull out. The Seventh Armored Division pulled by us yesterday. They were one of the divisions we supported both here and in Holland.... In another week or two I expect we shall shut up shop and be on the road ourselves. It used to be said, "Join the Navy and see the World." We don't do so badly in the Army. If we don't go right home I expect we shall go to another part of Germany.

My official number of points is 78. I signed for them yesterday. With me I don't believe points make much difference. Being over forty I don't expect to see the Pacific. So one of three things can happen to me. I can be kept over here to serve the men in the Army of Occupation. I don't expect that because I think that job will be amply handled by the Fifteenth Army which hasn't done much of any fighting. Or I can be sent to an army post in the U.S.A. That will be good for I shall be able to get home for a furlough right off and if I am located in New England, I can have you come down to see me. And the third possibility is a discharge. Then you will have to put up with me for a long time.

I don't think much about how much I would like to be with you because it isn't good for me. That is why I don't let it get into my letters. So many people yearn to get home and can't that I have to be able to at least appear cheerful. If I thought how good it would be to be able to have you within call almost all the time, to be able to hold you close every night and kiss you hard the last thing I do each night and the first thing I do each morning; if I thought how grand it will be to see my fine children again and be with them and watch them grow and really be their daddy again; if I think about this I just won't be any good as a Chaplain. I'll be like Priscilla used to be when she would say, "I can't wait." I mustn't be that way because I have to wait. So, my dear Doris, if my letters seem a bit perfunctory it is because I really don't dare to tell you how much I miss you and love and wish to be with you. But you understand that I do, don't you.

May 28, 1945

...I think I mentioned that the climate here is just about the same as it is in Vermont, but with this difference, there are no frosts here. We have been here for exactly a month and, although the nights are so cool that I am not quite warm enough under four blankets, there is no frost. We have lots or rain, too. But the grain is now about three feet high and well formed. I know that oats and wheat in Vermont aren't more than a few inches high this early in the season. What seems strange here is the lack of corn. I never yet have seen a field of corn anywhere in Europe.... The trees we see around here are mostly pine with some hemlock. In small groves there are hardwood trees like beech, oak and locust. Some of the roads are lined with oaks and elms so that they seem like long, beautiful parkways.

Lots of our people are away on short vacations now. At Lake Schwerin, about 70 miles from here, the 8th Division has the complete control of a beautiful summer resort. Four of our officers, four nurses and 20 enlisted men go up there for two days' rest. They have boating, fishing, hunting and horseback riding as pastimes. That takes away 28 people every two days. We have two nurses, an officer and three enlisted men on their way to the Riviera. That is a long, hard trip.... There are two reasons why I haven't applied for a week's leave at the Riviera. The principal one is the lack of money. Good times there come high. My little forty or fifty dollars would be just chicken feed. The other reason is the tedious nature of the trip. There are only two places in the E.T.O. I care to see particularly. One is Paris and the other London. I think I shall get to one or the other in the line of duty. If they decide to keep me over here very long they will probably expect me to take some kind of refresher course. And the place where the school will be is almost certain to be Paris. So I'll just sit tight. If they decide to send me home soon I won't have any regrets about what I haven't seen.

The body we are taking away today is that of a lieutenant who was shot on Saturday by someone in his own outfit. After they had left with the body and been gone about twenty minutes a messenger from his division arrived asking us to hold the body for further investigation. This is the second one that has come to us for a post mortem since May 10th with the suggestion of foul play. Since that time we have taken nine bodies away. It seems such a pity, now that the war is over that we have to keep losing men.

Yesterday, with so many people away, I had only 10 out to church service. Next Sunday I am going to give everyone who should come a personal invitation. That is, if we are here. Medics are the world's most irreligious people. I'm getting sick of it.

Are you planning a garden for this summer? I suppose what little you did plan went unplanted with your hard luck of last summer. With your folks so near I expect you can let them raise the stuff and you can help them can it and have plenty for yourself. But a home without a garden hardly seems right.

May 30, 1945

Dearest Doris:

Here it is Memorial Day and we have a little Memorial service scheduled for all soldiers in general and for Fields in particular. It is a typical Memorial day, like the kind we are used to. Last night we had a thunder shower with all the fireworks, noise and heavy rain accompanying it. Today is the kind of day that we are so used to. Damp and cool with the sun breaking through the clouds occasionally but with the threat of rain constantly present. Gladys used to say that Old Mother Nature was very sympathetic on this day. She would think of all the soldiers that were killed and weep. Then she would think of the present and smile. Then she would think of all those who were wounded and weep, then she would think of all those who got better and smile. Then she would think of all who will have to go to another war and weep. Then she would think of all who would come home and smile. And so on and on all day. Weather would be smiley or weepy. And that is usually how it is.

...I tried out the German rifle two nights ago and it is a honey. I think I shall concentrate on that and forget the other things. I went out with Captain Axinn and he brought along his Luger. We shot with his Luger and then with my rifle. With the Luger the difficulty was to get near enough the target to hit it, with the rifle the problem was to get far enough away to be able to use the sights. The sights are set for a minimum range of 100 meters and they go up to 1800 meters. That is quite a distance. I don't think I can get particularly interested in pistol shooting so I wish you would ask Jim [Carroll Leach Jr., Doris's brother, was nicknamed Jim] if he would care for my P-38. If he would I will wrap it up and the ammunition and bring it along with me.... And as far as Kenneth's Luger goes, when he is sixteen and if he still wishes one I'll buy him one then. There will be plenty on the market. Fig says in the pawn shops in New York you can get just about everything that is going. Will you do that for me?

Gerald's unit moved again, heading south from Altenmedingen, according to the map passing through Brunswick, Kessel and Marburg, to Griedel.

[Griedel, Germany]
June 10, 1945

Dearest Doris:

Your package arrived on Thursday of last week. But as we were getting ready to move I didn't open it until we arrived here. We loaded up on Thursday [June 7] and had about forty trucks to take us and our stuff. All the tents were taken down except five double ward tents. We officers slept in one, the nurses in a second, our enlisted men in two more and the visiting truck drivers in the fifth. At three o'clock on Friday morning we were up, had a breakfast of toast and coffee and were on our way shortly after five. I was to drive my jeep and trailer so they put a nurse in with me, a girl about my age called Lt. Shearer. I was sent with an advanced convoy of four vehicles, the lead jeep with the lieutenant in charge of route, his driver and three nurses. Ahead of me was a truck loaded with sixteen nurses. At the first stop one of the nurses got off the truck and came in with me so I had myself, two nurses and two enlisted men in my jeep. Following me was an ambulance with eight nurses. We started a little early so we could deliver the nurses early.

Our route took us due south to Brunswick, then south to Sessen, south along the Autobahn to Gottingen, and then south and west to Kassel. Then we connected with the Autobahn and went about 100 miles on it until we turned off opposite Butzback to the place where we are now on a hill just outside the little town of Griedel. The whole trip was 265 miles and we made it in a day. My jeep quit work about sixty-five miles from our destination and we had to be towed in. But we finally made it.

June 13, 1945

The longer we stay up here on this hill the more I am impressed by our surroundings. It is certainly a beauty spot.

Griedel is a little village where probably a thousand people live in an area no bigger than East Arlington from Will Saffodd's to R.H. Walker's. Every house has its barnyard with its cows, horses, pigs, chicken, sheep and geese. These people are mostly farmers and they work the country around here. From our hill we can see scores of patches of grain, potatoes, strawberries and meadows. The land here is hilly with a mountain in the distance. My tent is on the loveliest spot here. If I can find time to go out and look at the view here is what I see. To the east is a castle with two tall towers rising from the midst of it. On the taller tower is a flagpole, visible to me through my field glasses. A few months ago I imagine the Nazi crooked cross was flying there, but not any more. This castle is surrounded by woods. As I swing my field glasses from East to South I see a great sweep of meadow land until at a point E.S.E. there is another village. I guess a thousand or two thousand people live here, too but the outstanding feature is a prison. I can see the grey walls from here surrounding a set of stone buildings. With the glasses I can see the tops of what look like cone-shaped sentry boxes inside the walls. Apparently they found their prisoners hard to manage. There is a church in this village with a steeple but no clock. Probably it is a Lutheran church.

As I turn further towards the south I see more fields, a railroad, a concrete highway, and then, at the foot of our hill, Griedel. Swinging towards the West I see a little of Butzback, the largest town in view, a little city about the size of Rutland. This is two miles from here and across the Autobahn. We can see from here a long section of this famous highway and, sitting up here on the hill, with our glasses can pick out a truck or jeep as it appears about three miles to the north and follow it right across our front about two miles away until it disappears from us in the south. Probably we can follow it for six or seven miles. Last night I was talking with Major Adams about this wonderful road, remarking that we had nothing comparable to it in our country. He is from Oregon and said out there they have even better roads all the way from British Columbia to Mexico. He remarked that here there were peas ready to pick, haying was started, strawberries were getting ripe and before long the grain would be in condition for reaping.

One of the most interesting sights here is to see the sheep dogs work. There will be a flock of about 200 sheep with one man in charge. He will have four dogs to help him and those black canines will keep those sheep in a compact group. As soon as one sheep breaks away the dog on that side will go dashing after him. He'll head him off, nip him and back the sheep will go. Those four dogs are worth as much to that man as the four wheels are to a car.

This hill we occupy was orchard and sheep pasture for 22 families here in the village. Perhaps there are sixty acres. Imagine 60 acres in Vermont being owned by 22 people. We are getting well settled now and as a token of his high regard for me the Colonel has given me a tent all my own right near my office. I sleep there and can have my morning devotional period in private. It is a splendid privilege. Apparently the Colonel thoroughly approves of me.

I have a radio in my office and it gets only one station, Luxemburg. Probably all the German stations around here are Kaput. Luxemburg is about 135 miles by air from here and it is a United Nations Station instead of the A.E.F. Station we listened to in Heerlen. The result is that at least 2/3 of the time the announcements are in a foreign language. A linguist would have a grand time. At about nine this morning the news was given in French. Then followed a "Voice of America" program with comments on the Pacific war. After that there was a transcription broadcast of the presentation of the Keys of the City of London to General Eisenhower. Now I am listening to a half-hour program of music for Displaced Persons. I have heard Spanish, German and Polish over the radio yesterday. Fortunately music is international.

Fig is back from the Riviera and our office has sunshine and cheer again. I hardly realized how precious he was until I had to put up with a poor substitute for two weeks. If we are going to stay here long I certainly hope my request for a pass to Paris or the Riviera is granted. I have been strictly on duty ever since we landed on the Continent and, unless there is a chance to go home soon I would like to get away for a week or two.

And now, dear wife of mine, how are you getting along with your problem? I surely hope you are finding a solution to your help problem. I don't like the sinister thought suggested by the big interval between your letters and the brevity of the letters themselves. They suggest that you are so dead tired that it is an effort rather than a joy to write to me. Now I don't want it to happen this year like it did last. I may call up one day and say, "Can you come to New York to see me?" If you say "I'm sorry, but I'm sick in bed," if washing curtains and beating rugs and washing woodwork puts you in bed I shall feel very hurt. I'm pretty sure I shall be home before the summer is over. But I may not be released for a trip home for quite some time after arrival. If you get a telegram saying "Be at P.G. Hotel by six on the tenth" I shall want you there.

I know you have a high code about your housekeeping and what remarks your mother or Edna may say will goad you on to even harder efforts. But if you could see the millions of homes over here in Europe that are just piles of ruins and millions more that are half ruins you might realize that the gift of health is more precious than a clean mop board and the privilege of receiving your husband back is something. So use your brains to cut corners and use your three older children all you can. If you don't get help use all the ingenuity you can to coordinate the efforts that Kenneth, Priscilla and Bruce can exert to do all that is necessary. And when I can come home I'll use all the energy I have stored up in two years in the army to put you on your feet. I want you to keep well, my dear.

Yours with love,
Jerry

June 28, 1945

Dearest Doris:

On Monday and Tuesday I took another trip. We have a nurse who decided she wanted to visit the grave of one of her old lovers. She had me find out where he was buried and when I got the information she got the Colonel's reluctant permission to go to the grave. It was in the cemetery made especially for those killed in the Bulge Battle last winter. The Chaplain of the regiment her friend was in wrote the details of his death and told exactly where he was buried.

Armed with this information we started out at eight o'clock on Monday morning and headed for Heerlen. We planned to spend the first night there. Our route took us through Cologne and Aaken. We saw how badly Cologne was destroyed. Cologne was about as big as Boston and it was the first city to have a 1000 plane raid. Now it is hard to tell which did the damage, bombs or artillery shells. It all looks bad. We saw the famous Cathedral from about two blocks away. It is still standing but it has some holes in the roof and steeples. I don't know what it looks like inside. We could see three bridges down across the Rhine as we crossed on an American made bridge. Aaken was inhabited more now than it was last winter but it still looks about as bad as last year's straw hat when the puppy has finished with it. We arrived in Heerlen at about 3 pm and found the city very much alive and all evidences of war damage taken away. I stayed at the home of a person who used to work for us at the hospital. I gave them my K rations and ate with them. What they had was not good. Coarse dark bread with greasy butter, an egg, coffee that tasted like the third time through the dripolater, some kind of jam on the bread. That was an ordinary supper for them. The girl told me that if they buy a bunch of carrots they have to buy two bunches of lettuce with it. So they get tired of lettuce. The Dutch look pale and thin compared with the Germans. And I can see why after eating with them.

On Tuesday we started for Foy, Belgium, where the cemetery is. We went through Aaken again and by Vivieres, Spa, Malmedy, all famous places in the Bulge Battle. We got to the cemetery at the noon hour. She went to the grave, took several pictures of it, picked some wildflowers, did quite a lot of brooding, took pictures of the whole cemetery from different angles and used up about an hour there. This cemetery isn't nearly so well made as our Nineth Army Cemetery at Margraten where all our patients that died are buried. This Foy Cemetery had on Monday 2700 Americans, 3708 Germans and 24 Allied dead buried there. Most of them were Bulge casualties.

We started back at 2 and headed directly for Koblenz. We went to Bastogne and from there took the road through the Grand Duchy of Luxembourg passing through Clervaux, Gerolstein, Mayen, and a lot of little villages along the way. The road through Luxembourg and the border area of Germany took us through mountainous terrain where the roads were narrow and crooked like going through Hazen's Notch. We saw hundreds of American tanks knocked out along the road in Luxembourg. But in Germany not only were the knocked out tanks mostly German but the villages were pretty badly used up, too. From Bastogne we climbed from about 1600 feet to around 2300 at Prüm. The mountain scenery was wonderful and if the villages were of wood instead of stone it would have reminded me of the Green Mountains.

Koblenz is located at the junction of the Mosel and Rhein Rivers. We made a mistake when we crossed the Mosel of thinking it was the Rhein. So we took our route along the east bank for about ten miles south before we realized our mistake. But it was worth it. Both sides of this river have steep hills coming right down to the river. These hills are terraced and planted to grape vines. These vines are supported by stakes instead of trellises and it is quite a sight. I imagine these grapes form the material for enough wine to float the Queen Mary. When we crossed the Rhein we were in Koblenz. That is another big city that has had a great amount of destruction. From there on the driver knew the way and it was plain sailing. We are about 100 miles from Koblenz. Altogether on Tuesday we went about 350 miles.

We are still waiting but now we are having a training program. We are supposed to have some form of exercise during the morning from 8:30 – 10:30. Then we have Military Courtesy and Discipline. In the afternoon we have our choice of French, German, Spanish, typing, sign painting, art, dramatics or public speaking. I chose French. That lasts till 3 when we can have swimming lessons. So, some attempt is made to help fill the day. I'm afraid we are going to have a great many days to fill. It burns me up to think we have to spend the best part of another year doing nothing.

I received your birthday card and one from the kids and one from your mother. I also received your note. I can imagine how busy you are without extra help so all is forgiven.

July 3, 1945

Dearest Doris:

Your letter of June 16th arrived yesterday. It was the best letter I have received from you in a long time. It was so full of pep and of ideas....

First, however, I want to wish you a happy birthday. I am enclosing a money order for $50 for your birthday. Please spend it for anything under the sun that pleases you. If you wish to get $50 worth of pennies and throw them over the dam, do it. If you wish to spend it for chewing gum, do it. If you want to buy rugs, pinking shears, button hole scissors or brown derbies, do it. I hope you enjoy it and use it for anything you wish.

July 9, 1945

Dearest Doris:

Well, we've lost our 85 pointers, our class D men and our married nurses and those nurses who will admit they are over forty. That includes some of the people I think a mighty lot of. Lt. Hight, whom I took to see her husband in Feb. was one. Major James, whom I used to ask for advice and the one officer who came to church more than any other, was another. Sgt. Montrose, one of the two Congregationalists I had and the enlisted man that helped me more than any other, went out, too. All in all we lost about 60. But since V-E Day we have lost 13 officers, 16 nurses and 55 enlisted men. Take that many out of a unit about 300 strong and you can see what a hole it does make. We are supposed to have replacements for all these people by July 15. I can see that I shall have a great many new names and faces to get acquainted with.

I received a two page V-mail letter from Edna yesterday with her new address in it. And in it was an invitation to visit her. So that makes two invitations. She also said she had invited Priscilla and Kenneth to visit her this summer. Lucky kids!

...Edna said she was in Enosburg for Uncle Roy's funeral and saw you. She said you looked well then. I hope it's true. She spoke of Anthony as a dark-eyed doll. He must be doing a little pioneering now in walking or is he still satisfied to be a quadruped? And has any of the stuff I have sent in the last three months arrived? There were four packages, two of linen pieces, one of a bolt of linen and the fourth of surplus clothes. I have in my foot-locker some white silk for you. I hope some of the stuff I sent has got to you by now.

...I wondered if you would have a garden this year. Apparently you have. I'm glad, even though it might mean more work it's nice to have your fresh vegetables. I could stand a mess of green peas cooked the way you cook them and enjoy it muchly.

...I'm enclosing a picture of one of our outdoor services.

July 12, 1945

Dearest Doris:

"Another day, another dollar," as they say in the army. We find it hard to fill "each unforgiving minute with 60 seconds' worth of distance run." I am following out my old habit of reading a chapter of a book and then writing a letter. Right now I am wading through Sumner Welles' book "The Time for Decision," and Leslie D. Weatherhead's "In Quest of a Kingdom." Yesterday I got through a chapter of each and hence, three letters. One to the kids, one to your mother and one to Skippy Grout Saunders.

This morning I'm supposed to give a sex morality talk. It's the old disgusting story. The medical officer tells them how to avoid V.D. if they have sexual intercourse, the Detachment Commander tells what will happen if they get V.D. and then the Chaplain tells them they'd better not do it anyway. If there is any better indication of the moral bankruptcy of the Army I don't want to see it. There is a V.D. poster showing a girl in a blue dress under which her ample breasts make a very plain impression. In the upper left hand corner is this little limerick:

"There was a young girl from Paree
As sweet and demure as could be.
She'd turn down a Fee,
For "I love you cherie,"
And give away syphilis Free."

Below in heavy capitals is "Of course she isn't safe. Use a Pro-kit." I've asked for the poster and I'm going to send it to the Seventh Army Chaplain with my comments. It doesn't seem as if our moral standards are so low [as] that. Not a sign of keep away in the whole business.

Our chief nurse, Captain Wright, left yesterday. I expect we shall have a new one soon. The Colonel is finagling to get one from the 27th Evac., one he knows. I expect that by Sunday we shall have our new men and women. Then I shall have to get acquainted with about eighty new people. Captain Wright took a picture of me before she went. Probably so she could remember the guy that tied her to her new husband. I liked her but most of the nurses didn't. Handling thirty-nine women is not an easy job.

July 13, 1945

...We had another party last night and I danced with four different nurses. It was a command performance because Colonel Anderson had a little more showing off to do. He presented another bronze star and brought a lot of his chums from other units over. There were more non-111th people there than there were 111th.

At supper last night the nurses were complaining about the Wacs. One of the nurses went to the Army Sales Store and asked for a pink skirt. They refused her on the ground that they were saving them for the Wacs. That made our nurses so mad that you can get them as excited by just saying Wac as you can get your grandfather excited by saying "New Deal." So they asked me to write to the Stars and Stripes about it. So I did. I wrote a short letter which I hope they'll publish. I showed it to one of the nurses and she approved of it. So we shall be watching the paper for a week or so to see if it gets published. That was the third letter I wrote yesterday for others.

14 July 1945

Dearest Doris:

It's so darned hot in my tent I have taken the typewriter out into the open and am sitting by a bush with the typewriter on my lap. Airplanes are flying about. Here comes a B-26, off in the hazy distance is a B-17. About a half hour ago a B-25 flew right over us. Sometimes the Mustangs and P-47s come so close we can almost recognize the pilots. They are frequently lower than we because they fly right by our hill instead of over it. The recon planes, Piper Cubs they call them, just show off to our nurses. They'll swoop down hoping to surprise a nurse out sunbathing with her suit on backwards and in the evening they will hover over their area like a dragon fly over a lilypad. And occasionally the big, lumbering C-47s will fly over. Sometimes I get out my glasses to give them a look-see and with the fortresses I can see the open bomb-bays. Quite interesting. These pilots have to have something like four hours a week to get their pay. They like, as much as possible, to combine business with pleasure.

Our Colonel gave us a little bad news yesterday. We are to move to Mannheim, about seventy miles south of here. We are to set up as a Station Hospital, which means we shall have about 250 patients, mostly medical, and will be kept over here two or three months longer than we expected. Tell your mother not to plan any picnic. We'll do well to be home by Christmas. Two Christmasses away from home is enough.

I'm sending home a photograph of the map that depicts our travels. [See p. v in front of book.] I'm afraid he had it done too soon. It's just like our Colonel to go off half-cocked like that. But it gives you an idea of where we are, anyway. Each break in the line represents a stop we made. This map was made by Lieberman, the man who plays the organ for me on Sundays. Swell job, I think. I wish I had the original. It represents quite a bit of traveling, doesn't it.

July 18, 1945

Dearest Doris:

We are in the process of moving. This time, instead of having a couple of truck companies move us we are moving ourselves. We load up about twelve of our trucks and they go out with about forty men. The first load consisted [of] several tents, some mess equipment and the carpenters. They pulled out on Tuesday. Now we load up trucks each evening and they pull out right after chow each morning. In this way we shall be all moved in a week and probably have our first patients by Saturday. It will be a 250 bed affair and most of our patients will be the kind that don't need operations. We are going 103 miles south and we shall be only 18 miles from Heidelburg. We shall be in a field right on the autobahn where we can watch the Fords go by. I'm trying to get used to the idea of working again. I tell myself that if we are busy the month or two we are working will go more quickly. I'm still a little mad we can't have that picnic in September.

...I expect that by the time you get this your birthday will be long past and you will have made up your mind about how you are going to spend your money. And soon you will have our anniversary to celebrate. Last year on July 31 we were at Liverpool anchored in the river and waiting for them to get ready for us. We spent the whole day there just waiting for the day to go by. I expect we shall be busy taking care of measles, mumps, bellyaches, sore throats, road accidents and such on the thirty-first this year.

The grain is getting ripe here, potatoes are nearly ready to dig, mostly all the farmers have done their haying and it's a good thing, too because Germany is facing a serious food shortage. The Germans we see don't show any signs of it yet, however. I saw a little fellow not more than two years old yesterday and the fat stood out on his little legs as much as any of our kids ever did.

Well, au revoir for now.

Yours with love,
Jerry

July 22, 1945

Dearest Doris:

Here we are in our new area. If you are interested in locations we are in a field just out of Karlsdorf. This is a village too small for any map you may have of Germany. But you probably have one that shows Mannheim. We are directly south of Mannheim about 20 miles. Heidelburg is about 15 miles to the north-northeast. Below us is the big city of Stuttgart, about 40 miles S.W. [This must have been Karlsdorf-Neuthart, not the larger city of Karlsdorf farther north and east. Stuttgart is actually southeast of Karlsdorf-Neuthart.] *Stuttgart in 1936 had 459,538 people. About five miles away on the other side of the autobaun is a place called Bruchsal, a railroad center. The R.A.F. made a raid on that place once and in 18 minutes tore the whole place apart.*

We are set up as a station hospital and we are now ready to receive patients. In fact, I think we have two already. Yesterday I asked the Colonel for some hard work to do. He took me at my word and told me to dig a soakage pit beside each of the officers' and nurses' tents. Well there are eleven tents occupied by officers and seven by nurses. Each hole was about two feet deep and 18" in diameter. I dug steady from 9:15 till 2 with an hour out for dinner. After that I gathered stones and put them in the hole. This army experience is going to teach me a lot about field sanitation. I guess I would be competent to direct a summer camp after all this experience.

Our field here is a very big one. It is owned by dozens of farmers. The length of the field is about 1000 yds and the width about 600 yards. It is almost perfectly level but from side to side through its width it has ditches and someone said these ditches represent the boundaries of each person's land. In a field like this it must be hard to find one's holdings, but I expect the owner has a landmark that guides him. This whole business is surrounded by a moat about 20' wide but sloping so that the bottom, where a little stagnant water is, is only about 6 feet across. On one side of the area is the road, blacktop, a main highway. On the west side is a forest with a nice, running brook beyond the moat. This brook has a very good dam a little upstream and we can go swimming there because the water in brook is about 6' deep in the middle. It isn't clean and the bottom is muddy. So far none of the nurses have been in but some of the medical officers have. I've been in twice and after a hot day's work under this July sun I certainly appreciate it. I went in first on Thursday evening and our millionaire medical officer liked my suit so well he asked to borrow it so he could make a pattern. Remember it? I got it of Sears, Roebuck back in 1938. I find it quite hard to get on now.

Having the moat around us as we do there are millions of flies and millions of mosquitoes. We find that there is grave doubt about which is to be preferred, to leave one's shirt on and be hot or to take it off and be bit. The flies get us in the daytime and the mosquitoes at night. We have a lot of men here from New Jersey and they ought to know something about mosquitoes but they declare the ones here are the old folks at home compared with the Jersey type.

The people around here have been working on the place to get their hay cut. They use mowing machines like ours only the cutter bar is less than four feet long. They use cows mostly to do the pulling. Cows, not being very intelligent, have to be led. They can be driven on the road all right but in the field where more precision is demanded, someone leads and another someone sits on the mower. This hay here isn't much good, too much wild caraway in it. But they load it in their carts & wagons and away they go with their 2 cow power engine. In this area they grow corn, too. On Friday we took a short trip and I saw field after field of corn. Usually the corn would be with something else like six or eight rows of corn with oats or wheat or rye. The corn was tasseled out and some had ears beginning to form. This is the first corn I've seen since we left America.

July 24, 1945

...We are now using mosquito bars over our cots to keep out these P-51's of the insect kingdom. [The P-51 Mustang was a one-seat fighter airplane used in both WW2 and the Korean War.] *I'll tell you about them when we get home. If we ever decide to really take that Long Trail trip together there will be places where we shall need them.*

...I had it explained to me Sunday evening by one of our medical officers why we had to set up again. It doesn't necessarily mean we shall be set up long. He explained that Congressmen have

raised such a stink about keeping medical officers in the army over here when they are needed at home that it threatens the plan of redeployment so carefully worked out by the Army. If they hear that 100 general hospitals with 40 medical officers and 50 nurses are idle over here and 50 evacs. with 30 medical officers and 40 nurses are also idle they'll have too much ammunition to be ignored. Hence they put us to "work." Then the Army can say to the Congressmen, "We'll discharge them as soon as they can be spared." That's why we're working. And remember, we haven't been in one place more than six weeks since we left Heerlen.

We all had to get up at five o'clock yesterday morning and have a "shake-down" inspection of the men's belongings. We were looking for guns, ammunition and loot. We picked up 42 guns. Those who owned them will all have to do extra work. In the afternoon we officers had to turn in our guns. We tagged them and got receipts for them. We'll get them back when we leave the unit. The purpose of this is to prevent any accidental shooting. [Based on my experience in Vietnam, I wonder if some of the shootings were not so accidental. Many enlisted men resented the treatment they got from their officers and sergeants, so much that there was a real possibility that during an attack, one might be shot by his own men.]

July 27, 1945

...Today I went to Heidelburg. That's a very famous old German university city. Remember the plaque we got for a wedding present from somebody? The plaque said, "Back yard in Heidelburg." I didn't see the back yard but I did see the church, the tower of which is shown in that plaque.

You see our Seventh Army Headquarters is located there and our Colonel sent me in to see the Seventh Army Chaplain about Army policy with regard to going to a civilian church on Sunday. I was glad of the chance to go because everyone interested in either education or music has heard of Heidelburg. It isn't a very large city and its main streets are narrow and quite dirty. But it's located on the Neckar River and is right at the foot of a mountain range. Houses are perched on the mountain-side much like they are in Montpelier. The river is quite good size there at Heidelburg, probably 100 yards wide but ten miles upstream it narrows to a width similar to the Missisquoi at Perley Crampton's. This river is not wasted at all. Besides giving wonderful scenic value to its surroundings it also is useful. Big barges are seen for miles up above the city and every ten miles or so there is a dam used for water power. Of course, the barges can go only up to the first dam but I guess they can go downstream to the Rhine and from there to the North Sea, if they wish. They won't go now because every bridge is down, stopping both land and water traffic. The University of Heidelburg I didn't see. It was founded in 1356. Boy, it lacks only eleven years of being 600 years old. I can't remember its football team ever playing Middlebury. It's older than Kendall's Spavin Cure.

We are operating now with regularity of old times but not so extensively. We have sixty odd patients, mostly medical. It gives me work to do so that I feel that I am earning my money again. I have to stop and think to realize how much money our government is paying me. Each month I get 42 + 90 + 200 + 20 dollars. You get 200, my G.I. insurance costs, 8.70, my Acacia insurance costs 7.28, my war bond costs 75 and my mess 23 dollars. The result is that I get 35 or 33 dollars a month for myself. I use about $10 monthly for P.Ex rations, and perhaps $2 monthly for postage. The rest goes for books or gifts. I'm flat broke now so that if I do get a leave I shall have to borrow about $100 from Fig. But my name's at the bottom of the barrel so I don't expect one until October. I hope by then my leave will be spent in Vt. Pray with me for it, will you.

...Speaking of Fig is all right but speaking to Fig is kind of difficult right now. He's gotten out of hand a little and I crossed him up yesterday. He has been running a great many errands during the last four months. He runs our movies and that includes getting the films as well as showing them. This means at least three trips a week. He tries to make it seven. On these trips he picks up stuff for

the office such as paper, cards, combs. That's all to the good. But he feels highly offended if there isn't transportation available for him. He forgets that there are 200 others who might want to go places. Yesterday he got mixed up. I told the driver of the truck he was going with to tell him that after that day I would have someone else pick up the Stars & Stripes. The driver garbled the message so that Fig was given to understand that I didn't want him to go at all. So he didn't go and I've been fixing up the Dog House for myself.

He's good natured when everything goes well but when he can't do what he wishes he takes personal offense against someone. The Colonel told me he was going to transfer him out. He said he is one of the worst soldiers we have. I defended Fig and talked the Colonel out of that. But he promised me that "The very first time I catch him at any unsoldierly conduct I'll put him to work digging a pit that'll take him a week." So, I can see that Fig's appetite is due for an increase soon. It's hard work digging a pit.

Well, my letter to the Stars & Stripes got published all right. I've taken a lot of good natured kidding about it but the nurses were very pleased. But I tremble every time I see a Wac. My good friend Lt. Balsley is over here somewhere, probably in Paris. I don't expect we shall be close enough together to see each other. I'd like to know what she thinks about it.

Hair Pulling?

Our nurses have done a fine job in the ETO. We have handled more than 11,000 medical and surgical cases since the first big push in November. These girls got pretty mad the other day when they went to the Army Sales Store to buy some clothes and were refused their request for pink skirts. "We're saving them for the Wacs," they were told. This incident and several others have created a store of resentment against the Wacs that will one day break out in something worse than hair pulling. Do you think something can be done to arrest the discrimination against the ANC in favor of the WAC?

—Gerald F. Miller, Chaplain, 111th Evac. Hosp, APO 339

Clipping of Gerald's letter in the *Stars and Stripes*

If every week is as busy as this one has been I shall not complain. It's hard to believe it's almost August. Next Tuesday will be our 13th anniversary. On Wednesday we plan a party to celebrate our first year overseas. I hope I don't see my second year over here. "I'd rather be home in our bed."

July 30, 1945

Dearest Doris:

Well, I'm going to Paris! Yesterday at an officers' meeting the Colonel said he had one pass to Paris. Who wanted to go? I raised my hand. So I'm going. My first vacation since we've been overseas. I leave by train from Karlsruhe on Saturday. I'll write you from Paris. Perhaps I can find something there I can buy you. I'm immensely pleased over this chance.

Yesterday I had a service at the 93rd Evac. On the way back we had to go through the local village. It was some kind of a religious holiday and about all the houses had flowers on the window sills and figures of saints or religious pictures. We happened through just as the service was letting out and a large procession was forming. Little children about three years old were first, then boys and girls, young women, old women and in the center the priests with banners and some religious relic. When the priests passed the people got down on their knees. I guess there were 2000 in the parade. The population of the village is 2400 so that was a good showing.

Now that our hospital has been in operation for a week we have had as many as 52 patients, mostly goldbricks. Things that lots of these fellows have wouldn't keep Kenneth home from school. But it gives us something to do.

...I've had quite a time with Fig lately, so bad, in fact, that I thought I would have to fire him. He's got into the habit of going off without either telling me where he is going or asking me if he may go. That's bad. People come in here and ask where he is and I have to say, "I don't know." It doesn't speak well for me as an officer. He took off on Sunday and made no arrangements at all for helping me with my service. Yesterday he was gone before breakfast and I didn't

see him until supper time. He studiously avoided me. I made up my mind we would have a show-down soon.

This morning his attitude has changed. I'm going to let things go until I get back from Paris. I'll be able to make up my mind after that what's best to do. I got his P.Ex. rations for him last night and that pleased him. When things go well he is very easy to get along with. If I wasn't afraid he would lose his rating I would have him transferred to the Special Service department. [Special Services did many things for service members' wellbeing, morale and entertainment.] *He does more work in that line than he does for me.*

We had ration day at the P.Ex. yesterday. We all received a basic ration of six Milky-Ways, a carton of cigarettes, an 8 oz. can of peanuts, an 18 oz. can of tomato juice and an 8 oz. box of oatmeal cookies. In addition we could choose one of some 15 different items like a flashlight, lighter fluid, talcum powder, shampoo liquid, towel, handkerchief, fingernail clipper, pocket knife, mirror, etc. I got a can of lighter fluid to give away by the lighter-full and for Fig I picked out a mirror. Besides I bought a cake of toilet soap & a cake [of] laundry soap apiece and a carton of gum. All this cost only $3.70.

Here Gerald mentions that my Aunt Virginia's brother, Garold Betters, was killed in battle. My cousin Allen has his first name as a middle name. I looked him up in the database at the WW2 Memorial in Washington, D.C., and he is indeed buried in one of the American cemeteries in Europe.

August 3, 1945

Dearest Doris:

I received a letter from you yesterday, the one sent on July 17. I was very glad to get it and it answered a few questions. I am very sorry to read in it that Virginia's brother was killed over here. If it will give her any comfort I will look up his grave and take a picture of it. I won't act, however, until I hear from you. Personally I don't think I would have any morbid curiosity about such a thing. Some people do, however, and there isn't a month that goes by that I don't have some request to tell where somebody is buried. So, if she's like these, I'll do all I can for her. I am also glad to know you received the helmet. Which boy has it? Or is it common property for all three? Fig says that the linen he sent home has arrived so it would seem that mine ought to be getting there by now.

...I've been absorbing information about Paris from those who have been there. I room with two of our youngest medical officers. Russell was there for about a month taking a course at a General hospital there. He has told me a lot about how to use my three days there. I have made [up] my mind on a few things I want to do. One is that I want to see the Arc de Triumph, the Eiffel Tower, the Cathedral of Notre Dame, the Palace of Versailles, the Opera and the Follies. I think I shall use one day for a Red Cross tour and the other two days for roaming around just to get the feel of the place. They say Paris is an easy city to get around in. And you know how easy it is for me to walk.

I have made up my mind not to buy anything at any French stores because everyone who has been there tells me that the Parisians just soak Americans at least ten times what anything is worth and with a sweet wife and three fine children to provide Christmas presents for I can't afford that. But I do understand that the P.Ex. in Paris has European things to sell at their approximate value. I have already in mind what I want to get Kenneth, but I shall have to plan very carefully for the rest. I fully expect to be home for Christmas so I can give the things to you all, but the Army has a way of disregarding people's plans, as you know. I really think that if I had to choose when I would rather be home I think I would say December first to January first. It may work out that way.

Note: read this to yourself first.

August 10, 1945

Dearest Doris:

Back from Paris. What a wonderful time! What a wonderful city! Everything about it was good except the train ride there and back. The train was very crowded and long. I guess two thousand took that train. It started from somewhere in Czecho-Slovakia, went through Munich, came up to Karlsruhe where we got on, went across the Rhine to Strasbourg and Sarrebourg in Lorraine. We went through the French Maginot Line in Lorraine. We saw some of the Voges Mountain range and came into France proper east of Luneville. We went through Nancy, a good sized city and other places like Bar-le-Deu, Chalons-sur-Marne, Epernay, Chateau-Therry, St. Denis, and finally Paris itself. We went in German coaches but I think our engines since leaving Strasbourg were French. The cars were the compartment kind with a narrow aisle down one side and a compartment holding six, in some cars, and eight in others taking up the rest of the space. The train had about 25 coaches besides a baggage car and a 40 and 8 freight car. The length of the trip in miles is about 325 miles but, when the train is on time it takes 16 hours. We were two hours late going to Paris so that made an 18 hour trip. We were 7½ hours late getting back so that trip took 23 hours. Quite a long time just to go 325 miles. This gives you an idea of the traveling conditions here.

We got into Paris at just about noon. I was in charge of seven enlisted men and I had to go to the Red Cross Headquarters in the city and get the billets for my men. While I was doing that the sergeant in the group was to make arrangements for the return trip. It took me two hours to get things all taken care of so it was two o'clock when I finally arrived at my hotel.

But what a fine hotel it was! Hotel Crillon, it was, and very famous because President Wilson stayed there while he was in Paris in 1919. It is an old hotel with six floors of rooms. Its dining room has beautiful chandeliers with hundreds of glass crystals on them. We had an orchestra to play for us and everything was high class but the food. I had a room all to myself and in it was a ¾ bed with inner-spring mattress, a large washbowl with hot and cold water, a closet with a huge full-length mirror on the door, in which I admired my appearance both clothed and unclothed. To get up out of bed and shave at that bowl while still in my pajamas was so delightfully easy that it was fun. Especially after shaving every morning in field conditions. There was a toilet a little way around the corner and, although I visited it at least three times a day while I was there, only once was it occupied. Just a little further was the bath room with a large tub. Toilet and bath are never combined in any place I've been on this continent. So I had two perfectly swell tub baths while I was there.

After shaving and eating some of my K ration I went out walking. I walked down the Rue de Rivoli past the Tuileries until I came to the Louvre. There I found a statue of Joan of Arc (Paris has dozens of them) in the Place des Pyramids. Our hotel was across from the Course de Concorde. I followed the Avenue d'Opera to the Square d'Opera where there are several booking offices for theatres. There I bought a ticket for the Casino de Paris for Monday night. Then I walked over to the Louvre, looked at the statues, mostly of unclothed women, saw the garden of the Tuileries, crossed the Seine and walked down the left bank of the river past the Institute of France to the island that has Palace of Justice and the Cathedral of Notre Dame. At Notre Dame I connected with a "personally conducted tour" group and went through the cathedral with them. We were told about its size (it is huge) its organ with 5 keyboards, the various saints depicted in statuary and admired. I'm glad I didn't follow the tour very far because it was so fast. The guide was not like Mark Twain's Furguson but a fast talking, wise-cracking Frenchman. He liked to tell little legends of the place and add a remark that spoiled the beauty of them. One saint in the statues out front had his head in his hand. The guide told the legend and added "That happened so long ago [a matter of about 1400 years] *that no witnesses are left." I went from there up the Seine and saw these little bookstalls where old books and pictures can be had by anyone who wants to buy. I bought a package of stamps there which I have already sent along to Kenneth. Then I went into the nearest Metro station (subway) and got on a train for the hotel.*

The Metro is a wonderful subway system which serves Paris in a very effective way. All persons in uniform ride free and everyone else pays 2 francs a ticket. There are 14 different routes with frequent intersections where changes are made. All I had to do was to get on a train that connected with the train that connected with the train that went where I wanted to go. All I had to be careful about was the direction. I got back to the hotel for supper, ate what was placed before me, listened to the music, joined in the conversation at the table and enjoyed everything but the coffee. Boy, how I hated that! What they make their coffee out of is a mystery. To get into the dining room I had to show my 3-day pass which the girl punched and gave me a ticket. The waiters collect the tickets very carefully.

After supper I decided I wanted to locate three things; the Seine Base P. Ex where I could get gifts, the Officers' Sales Store and the Casino de Paris. The P. Ex wasn't far away they said. I went down the Rue Royale to the Magdeline Cathedral, around that to the Boulevard Baussman until I located that. That was easy. Then I went by Metro to the Etoile, that great circle where the Arc de Triumph is standing, worked back until I found that. Then I headed for the spot on the map where the Casino was located. I walked two or three miles around the place called c-8 on the map but failed to find it. It got to be about ten o'clock and I started heading for home. I passed one of the many side walk café's and a couple of soldiers invited me to sit down and have a drink. Somehow all soldiers like chaplains better than any other kind of officers. I said, "Can you get anything soft here?" They said I could get orangeade but it wasn't good. So I stopped and talked with them awhile. Then I went down into a Metro station and headed for home. I went into the Red Cross do-nut bar and had a cup of coffee and two doughnuts and then went to bed after a nice tub bath.

The first thing I did on Monday morning was to hunt up Lt. Balsley, who was stationed in Paris. I knew she could show me Paris in a better way than I could see it without her. I found her, after going to two other American Com Z. headquarters first. She is in the I&E (intelligence and education) section and the building they used was the Shell Building in the Rue de Berri. She was real surprised to see me and glad, too. I asked her if she could get off on Tuesday and have an afternoon and evening with me. She said she could so we decided I was to meet her there at 12:30, she would take me to dinner and we would see Paris together. Then she went about the business of being Edyth Grace Balsley and I went about the business of being Jerry Miller.

My next move was to go to the Officers' Sales Store nearby where I bought a pair of green pants, a pair of pajamas, two suits of underwear, a G.I. belt, an O.D. shirt and had the pants altered to fit me. All this cost me $21.00. I got 200 Marks changed to francs (1000) and then it was time to head back to the hotel for chow. The chow line was long but I ate with the first batch and then set out for an afternoon of enjoyment.

I needed soap and I wanted candy so I headed for the P. Ex. I got what I wanted and then headed for up stairs where the gifts are sold. An M.P. told me I had to get my pass stamped before I could go up stairs. So I got it stamped "Gift Only" and went up. I looked around and discovered the collection of really useful items very slim. I bought a broach for Priscilla (don't tell her) and that's all. I could have bought a gaudy handbag for about $10 that looked like a Woolworth special 59¢. So I went away with my purchase. Prices in Paris stores are so high that it is a sheer waste of money to get anything in them. I know you aren't the kind who wishes me to spend $20 for a $2 article just because it comes from Paris.

At the P. Ex I met the sergeant of my group and found out he hadn't made any definite arrangements about our getting back. So I went to our station, Gar l'est and checked. Sure enough, we weren't on the list. So I had them put us on. Then I looked up the Casino and found it this time. Then I made my back to Notre Dame in search of a place one of my tent mates told me about where I could get something he wanted very much. It wasn't there so I looked up his directions again and found it was in another section of the city. I found it at last and went back for evening chow.

While in the station I looked into the inevitable bookstand and there I saw on display, along with various French magazines and papers a book by our old friend Jean de Brunhoff who writes the Barbar [sic] *stories. So I bought it for 90 francs and I'll bring it home with me. With the help of a French dictionary I think I can translate it and read it to the kids. It is called "Deux Barbar à un."* [This was a volume containing the stories published in English as *Babar and His Children* and *Babar and Father Christmas*. It was smaller than the American editions we had, and the pictures weren't in color, but even before I learned French I found it fascinating.]

Well, Monday night found me at the folies called "Charming Paris." I could have gone to the Folies Bergere but Russell, my tentmate has been to both and said that the Casino was better. So I decided on that. The Casino isn't so well known throughout the world, but the GI's in Paris know about it all right. The place was a sell-out. There were several women there including French Dames, American and English nurses and Wacs but the show catered to men who like to see girls in pretty costumes and like to see them take those costumes off. And that's just what they see.

I'd like to be in bed with you right now and demonstrate what I saw and heard there. The show started off with eight girls coming out in gaudy costumes and swished their trains to the cadence of the music. That lasted about five minutes. Then came a change in which there was a parade of girls with fancy costumes designed to display their breasts and backsides to great advantage. To a Puritan this was sinful but to a person without inhibitions on the subject of sex it was lovely for, as Mrs. Roosevelt wrote, nothing that is beautiful can be obscene. These girls paraded around to the music and went through their routine. Then they oozed off and a charming French girl came out and told what was coming next. That was a scene supposed to represent a noble maiden of about 600 years ago going to bed. There was the big bed, the maids in waiting to undress her and to tuck her in. Which they did. They took off her dress and petticoats and exposed her down to just a g string which covered you-know-what. Then they put on her a nightie of black lace that hid just enough to make her seem --- well, I'll tell you all *about it when I get home. The show cost 170 Fr. the program 20 more, the usher expected a tip of at least 10 fr for showing each person to his seat. I'll bet those girls pick up thirty dollars a night just showing us around. My trip to the Folies cost me about $6.*

On Tuesday morning I went to the Eiffel Tower. What a huge thing it is. Stretching from its wide base under which the U.S. Air Force has a display of planes to the sky about 1000 feet up in the heavens. I went up to the first landing in the elevator and walked up to the second landing. What a climb! Even that didn't take me more than half way up. All Paris could be seen from there. The people down below looked pretty small. There were souvenirs sold up there and I bought a book called "Paris for You." It told about the interesting places there. That took up the morning.

I went to dinner with Lt. Balsley and she stays with the other Wac. officers in the Hotel Celtic on Rue de Balzac. We had typical French service and mostly American food. The redeeming feature about the meal was that we were served tea instead of the terrible French coffee. Then we started on our tour.

We had quite a day and I don't believe I got in much more walking in a day of mowing cemeteries than I did that afternoon. We visited the Arc de Triumph again, the Pantheon, walked by buildings of the Sorbonne, France's famous university, through narrow streets, peeked into courtyards, noticed fancy railings and then went to Notre Dame again. We walked on the little park on the tip of the island of the Seine, saw several Frenchmen fishing but never a fish and walked by the Palace of Justice where Pétain is being tried until we came to the Louvre. We went in and saw hundreds of famous paintings, which meant more to her than to me and famous statues, too. It is a wonderful treat and her comments brought out the interesting and remarkable features of each significant display.

From there we went to the Cathedral of the Sacred Heart in the notorious Montmartre district of Paris. [i.e. Sacré-Cœur, which for all its grandeur is a parish church, not a cathedral.] *This Cathedral is built of white stone and has five domes. Its location on a high hill gives it a view of most of the city. It's a splendid edifice with countless altars, mosaics of great beauty and an atmosphere of extravagance amid surroundings of squalor so characteristic of Catholic religion. Leaving the place we walked down the tortuous street of that area until we came to the Boulevard Rochechouart and thence to a Metro station where we headed for St. Augustine Square where she thought we could have supper at the St. Augustine Club for Officers. I inquired and was told that I couldn't eat there unless I had an officer on orders to take me in as guest. She had her orders, so that filled the bill.*

In the evening we went to the Bois de Boulogne where the famous race courses are, walked along the little lake there, sat down until the mosquitoes bothered her and then called it a day. She told of what a hard time she had in Paris keeping the men at arm's length. U.S. officers seemed to think every U.S. girl there is willing to indulge in a little loving after a few hours of acquaintance. She likes to dance but that's the only situation in which she'll tolerate any man closer than a foot away. Once she made that point I kept my distance.

On Wednesday I joined a Red Cross tour to Versailles. Along the way our guide pointed out famous places and told us about them. We passed a replica of our Statue of Liberty on the tip of a little island in the Seine and said it was facing America. We passed the bombed-out Renault Automobile works, the famous porcelain factory and arrived at the famous palace just as the gates were opened. He took us through the place, showed us the famous Hall of Mirrors (the mirrors needed cleaning), through the various bedrooms of the kings and queens and showed us the paintings and statues of the famous genius of each period. The outstanding thing was the gardens, tailor-made and trimmed as far as one could see. History books show them but one has to see them to really appreciate the possibilities latent in the landscape gardeners' trade. I've never seen a woman's dress that was more elaborate than they.

That about winded up my sight-seeing. In the afternoon I went to the gardens at the Parc Monceau where there was a little pond and ducks in it. I sat the afternoon out with Lt. Balsley and we just talked and enjoyed the setting. The trip back was long and hard. But we finally made it. We got into Karlsruhe at midnight, called up the 111th and were finally brought home at 4 o'clock. We were greeted with the news that we are now Class IV. [I think he means Category IV, which designated a unit to be disbanded and sent home. Category I meant part of the occupying force to remain in Germany, II was for units to be sent to fight in the Pacific Theater, and category III units were to be reclassified as I or II after reorganization and retraining. ("Demobilization of United States armed forces after World War II," Wikipedia, referencing Earl F. Ziemke, *The U.S. Army in the Occupation of Germany 1944–1946,* Washington, DC: GPO, p. 328. https://en.wikipedia.org/wiki/Demobilization_of_United_States_armed_forces_after_World_War_II, accessed March 30, 2022.]

On Friday the Colonel showed me a pretty little electric train set made in Germany which I can buy for $12.70. I ordered one for Bruce. I think I'll bring it home with me. It is smaller than Kenneth's so there need be no jealousy. I think it is the only thing in the whole exhibit of toys that is worth taking home. The Colonel said he considered the set worth at least $50. I don't know about that but the whole thing looks mighty good to me.

[As the letter of August 22 tells, Dad ended up getting a different train set for Bruce. It was German made, HO gauge with three-rail track. Kenneth already had an American Flyer O gauge train. (Later American Flyer trains were S gauge with two-rail track.) Years later, Dad bought me a Marx O gauge set from Sears mail order, and Bruce figured out how to combine Kenneth's track with mine for a complex layout.]

My whole trip to Paris cost only $42. The E.M. [enlisted men] *that went with me all spent over $100. The sergeant bought a blouse for his wife and spent $100 for that. One of the boys bought a pen for $7, the Woolworth 59¢ kind. I am in debt to Fig $30. That is all. Unless other leaves come up I ought to be able to pay him back in 2 months.*

We are all pondering the meaning of this good news about the end of the war with Japan. The Colonel thinks we'll be home by Christmas. I certainly hope so.

I guess this brief note will have to do for now.

Yours with all my love.
Write soon and often.
Jerry

August 13, 1945

Dearest Doris:

How did you survive my long letter of two days ago? It is now Monday morning and I have survived another Sunday. Sundays are more or less a pain to me because so few come out to church. There was a party on Saturday night. Excuse—the new chief nurse had a birthday. After a party the officers never come to church so yesterday our attendance consisted of five nurses, five patients, five enlisted men & me. The Colonel doesn't give me any support but pretends to be very interested. He's like the Jersey cow your Grandfather told Mr. Kent about.

I went in on Friday morning to thank him for my trip to Paris and he told me I was responsible for getting him into trouble with 7th Army Hqs. I knew what was coming but looked innocent. It was about the jeep I was supposed to have but which everybody used except me. He pretended he didn't know what the situation was but he did. The result was that he had the adjutant type out an order that said jeep was mine and was not to be used by anyone without written permission from me. The jeep in question remains in the motor pool with the front wheels off. I'm interested to see whether it gets fixed before it is time for me to send in another monthly report.

...Everyone is anxious about the news now. It so happens that just when I'd like it most, my radio doesn't work because there is no electricity in my tent. We had a wind and rain storm on Friday that blew down the wires and they haven't yet fixed mine up again.

[Picture postcard showing Empire State Building, addressed to *Mrs. Gerald Miller, E. Arlington, Vermont, c/o Max Grout.*]

Mother:

We are going to Macy's soon and then to the zoo

Much love
Kenneth
Priscilla

Aug. 19, 1945

Dearest Doris:

Another rainy day. And how it rains! Being out in tents isn't so much fun when the rain comes down steadily all day long. There isn't any heat to be had anywhere except in the mess tents. So we do appreciate the sun.

I suppose you are now (as I write this) enjoying a change of scene in Arlington, Troy or New York. I imagine that you are enjoying a renewal of acquaintances that is good to see....

The mail situation has been bad here, not only for me, but everyone. I guess everybody back home was fooled like you were about the Ninth Army coming home. [The Ninth Army Headquarters had sailed from Le Havre on July 28 and landed in New York August 6. (*The Conquering Ninth*, p.224.)] *So they've stopped writing. The only letters I have received in two weeks has been one from you, one from Edna and a request from the father of one of our boys to get that boy to write. Not much mail for two weeks.*

Edna wrote that she is anticipating with pleasure a visit from our two older children. I'll bet they'll brighten the apartment in Islip considerably and have more to tell about their adventures in Long Island and Manhattan than I'll have to tell about mine in Europe. I'd sure like to be walking down a street and run into them.

...We had beans for dinner today and I said, "I'll be glad when I can be where they really know how to bake beans." "Who's that, your mother?" I was asked. "No, my wife," I said with

emphasis. When at last it is home there are going to be a great many things I shall enjoy.

...I can imagine Anthony is a very interesting character with his garrulous speech and his propensities toward forsaking the horizontal for the vertical. I expect I shall have a good time helping him increase his vocabulary. And it won't be long before he'll be saying, "Daddy, fool with me." Where have I heard that before? [Dad loved to play with little children. I remember visits to Aunt Edna and Uncle Al, years later when they had children, where Dad would sit in an easy chair, feet on a stool, and let my little cousins crawl all over him. They loved it, and so did he.]

Now, let me orient myself. Kenneth will be twelve on December fourth and will enter the seventh grade this fall. Right? Priscilla is now nine and will enter the Fourth grade this fall. Right? Bruce is six and will enter the first grade this fall. Right? And Anthony is now 16 months, 9 days old and will enter childhood this fall. Or is he still an infant "mewing and puking in his mother's arms"? How did I come out in that review?

...One of my greatest problems here is to find things with which to pay my laundry bill. Money's no good to these people because there is hardly anything for sale. So, when I send out my laundry I put in a couple of candy bars, two packages of gum, a box of matches, a package of cigarettes, half a cake of laundry soap and, if I have it, some toilet soap. This, to me, represents an investment of about 30¢ but to the German family it represents a great deal more, probably 4 or 5 dollars on the Black Market. There is a boy who comes for the laundry and brings it back after two days. The person who does it does fine work. She irons everything except the socks, mends all holes and sews on buttons. As long as I can keep ahead a supply of negotiable stuff I am all right.

I preached a sermon yesterday (it is now Monday) on being anxious. I mentioned various things people were anxious about such as going home, their jobs, a future depression and especially the thought that their children would not know them. I told them that, judging from my past experience, a child under six would very probably forget his father if the father was away more than a year. After that I began to wonder if my children would forget me, especially Bruce. Suppose I should meet Bruce on the street in Burlington, do you think he would notice me? How about Priscilla? And Kenneth? Well, I'm not going to be anxious about it.

Aug. 22, 1945

Dearest Doris:

Another letter from you arrived two days ago, the one about the Old Choir Sunday [at the Enosburg Center church].... *I certainly wish I could have been there. Perhaps I shall be on hand for the Christmas celebration.*

I did get a train after all. A patient of ours who gets around pretty well found a place where he could get two trains, transformer included, so he brought them back. As I have three boys, more than anyone else in the outfit, he decided I should have it. $9.94 is cost. I'm going to send it to you. Please don't let anyone open it until Christmas, when I hope to be on hand to open it myself. I think the .22 German rifle will be Kenneth's present. Priscilla will have the brooch and so I have only you and Anthony to think of. Talk about doing your Christmas shopping early!! With 101 shopping days before Christmas. Not bad!

Homeward Bound

August 27, 1945

...I had my second overseas wedding on Saturday. We had a staff sergeant who was in love with one of our nurses. The nurse was twice as much in love with him. It was because she used to come to my office to see him in Heerlen that I got into my only trouble with Colonel O'Brian. They finally decided to get married so, on Saturday I married them after they had been married by the Burgermeister.

I heard from our ex-chief nurse, who is the other person I married while over here. She wrote me from Rheims, France, that she expected to fly home the next week. As her letter was written on July 22nd I expect she is safely back in the U.S. by now. She is going to be discharged because she is going to have a baby. It seems that all any nurse has to do to get discharged is just that. Convenient, isn't it? Those that want to take this way out and who have husbands in the E.T.O. that are willing to accommodate have done so. Some who don't have husbands manage to get someone else to co-operate in this way....

I'm glad you finally got started on your trip. I think you'll have a much better time in East Arlington than you would have with my relatives anyway. I sincerely echo your sentiments. To heck with them! I'm sorry your dad had his accident and I hope he's better soon.

Yours with love,
Jerry

Sept. 1, 1945

...The 111th is sailing for home in September but only a few are going with it. Officers with 95 points, nurses with 55 points,

enlisted men with 75 points. I'm not in the lucky group so next week or later I shall be assigned to another unit for a while until they get ready to take home Chaplains with 83 points. When I discover where I'm going I will send a V-mail letter with my new address on it. Write no more letters, or rather don't send any letters to me until you get my new address. We are all separating soon. I went to Army Hqs. to see where I was going and they couldn't tell me. The Army Chaplain said Chaplains with 85 points are going home now. The assistant Army Chaplain said I'd be going in about three months. Doris, my dearest, if you want me home for Christmas please do some earnest and regular praying about it! I want to be with you so much!

I saw the movie "Junior Miss" this week. What a swell picture. If you have a chance be sure to see it.

Yours with love,
Jerry

Sept. 12, 1945

...Our unit is going to pieces pretty fast. Yesterday my two tent mates, Russell and Spalding, and two other medical officers from the next tent, Allison and Axinn left us. Today we lost all but nine of our nurses. Four more medical officers left us and this afternoon we shall lose more. Tomorrow all our officers will be gone except me. In the meantime we have been getting more and more new people. By Saturday we shall have our new personnel and only about ten of the men, seven of the nurses and I will remain of the 111th that started operating ten months ago. It's kind of sad saying good-bye to these people I have worked with so long, but the hope of being on our way home soon is ample compensation.

[V-mail, postmarked September 20, 1945]
Dearest Doris:

We have a new C.O. now, a Lt. Col. Berry. He asked me yesterday what was my chance of going home with the 111th. I told him what Col. Anderson said, i.e. officers who had less than 95 points would be transferred out. Co. B. said, “You’d better go to Army Hqs. and see. I think you’ll be going with us.” So I went to 7th Army Hqs. this morning and saw the Army Chaplain and he asked me, “What do you want to do?” “I want to go home,” I said. “Then you can.” So, unless he is wrong I’ll be sailing with the Unit before many weeks. Perhaps I’ll be home for Thanksgiving or before. Have you been doing some heavy praying?

...Now I expect you have three children in school, each one of them a twelve-point rascal. I hope Bruce likes school as well as the other children did and do. Maybe, before snow flies, I’ll have a chance to visit school with all three.

I sent home the German rifle after all. I heard we wouldn’t be allowed to take it with us, so it is on the way. I won’t bother you about it like I did the other things I sent because I hope to beat it to the States.

Sept. 25, 1945

...Yesterday they checked our records and I discovered that I have an efficiency rating of excellent. Col. Oglesby of the 85th Chemical Battalion gave me a rating of Superior, which is the highest possible. Colonel gave me a Superior once and contented himself with an excellent the other times.... I found out, by looking at my record for the first time that Colonel O’Brian applied for a Catholic Chaplain to replace me because there were 122 Catholics to 88 Protestants in the outfit at that time. But General Barthoff of the 5th Hqs. said it couldn’t be done and said that a chaplain wasn’t expected to minister only to men of his own faith but to everyone in the unit. The chaplain was doing his duty if he provided opportunities for men of other faiths to worship elsewhere. I guess Col. O’Brian was satisfied after six months because he got me

promoted. Someday, if you won't be bored we'll go over the army record together and I can tell you lots of interesting things.

September 26

Dear Mother Leach:

[On the long way home at last] *...We passed through St. Avold, the place where a U.S. Military Cemetery has been founded to take care of all who were buried in Germany and have been exhumed and reburied there. Garold Betters* [Virginia Leach's brother] *occupies a grave there in Plot A, Row 5 Grave 60. We didn't go by the Cemetery for it is on another road.*

...When we pulled out of the parking area on Thursday morning, drove through town and on to N-3 westbound we found that our convoy was part of one huge string of U.S. Army vehicles that were heading for Reims. I expect that this large stream of trucks and jeeps was thirty or forty miles long. As far as we could see either way were trucks all going our direction....

This is a tent city. There are a few wooden buildings for P.Ex. and administrative purposes but the movies, Service clubs, Red Cross, theatres, chapel, mess rooms are all tents. There are tents for perhaps ten thousand but only about 2000 of us are here.

We stay here about two weeks. I expect we shall pull out by train next Monday or Tuesday. Our hardest job is filling in the time....

When they get ready for us they'll load us into Quartermaster trucks and take us to the railhead. Then we'll be loaded on a French train for the 4-day trip to Marseille... and by Hallowe'en I ought to be a common preacher again looking for a church.

But if I don't get a church until February it will be all right. I hope to be able to accept the invitation (if given one) to attend the Leach Thanksgiving Dinner. Won't that be something!

Calas Staging Area

Oct. 7, 1945

Dear Doris:

I guess it is a week or more since I have written to you. After two whole weeks at Camp San Antonio we left there at 11 o'clock last Thursday night. We were loaded into these huge half-trailer trucks that are used for hauling supplies. In this we rode to the railroad, about twelve miles away until we were chilled pretty well. I enjoyed the ride because it was a clear, crisp night and the stars were bright. I amused myself by finding the familiar constellations and keeping track of our direction by close scrutiny of the Big Dipper. Several meteors raced across the sky during the trip and some left a trail of fire behind them like small comets.

We arrived at the railhead, as they call it in the Army, and loaded into third-class German coaches. These cars consist of six compartments each entered by doors on each side of the car. For a short ride a compartment can accommodate eight, but on a 45 hour ride to put that many on those two wooden benches is too much. There were five in our compartment and the postures we took to induce sleep during the hours of darkness were something Norman Rockwell would enjoy. The slimmest, a chief warrant officer named Harris, climbed up into the baggage rack and slept there. Captains Reinke and Dufour sprawled out, one on the bench I sat on and the other on the floor. Warrant officer Maurer, a 215 pound bohonk tried to rest his hind end on my alter kit and his feet on my bench and his head and shoulders on the bench across. I just sat erect and slept as well as I could, which was surprisingly well. We didn't get started until three o'clock. Once we did get started we didn't go very fast. We didn't mind that very much while we were sleeping, but during the daytime it became very tedious. The trip was about 550 miles and with ordinary U.S. connections we could have made it in about 20 hours. But this isn't the U.S. Just about everything passed us and we waited and waited at stations. But we finally made it. We arrived at the end of the line some dozen or so miles from Marseilles at 12 o'clock on Saturday night. We waited there for an hour standing in the dark until chow was ready. We ate a hot meal and then waited until about four for our trailer-trucks to come. We loaded into them 65 to the truck and waited for them to start. At about 4:30 we started off and drove to this place called Calas. We unloaded, got into winterized tents and hit the sack at about 5:30 Sunday a.m.

The trip down by rail took us [by] Dijon, a city as old as the Roman occupation, Langres, north of it, where we had breakfast, Beaune, where we ate again, Macon where we stopped a long time. There we saw a train pull in and unload lots of children who were cared for by a few French Red Cross workers. The men began to throw the kids candy and gum and the children would come out onto the tracks for it. This wouldn't do and the Red Cross girl in charge had some time trying to keep those kids on the platform. Soon the men on our train caught on and threw the stuff far enough. Sometimes a G.I. would go over with his hands full of gum and the children would entirely engulf him. One was smart enough to give his donation to the Red Cross girl herself and she took care of it. I expect it was her intention to hand it out to the less aggressive kids who got nothing but a good trampling in the scramble. Finally their train pulled in and they got on. Even then the G.I.s threw gum and candy into the windows. When the train pulled out they waved at us and threw us many kisses and smiles. What a time.

Our route took us steadily south through Lyon...at about supper time we pulled into Avignon. Here we must have stayed for two hours and a very interesting episode in our journey was acted out. A train pulled up on the track right next to us and our officers began to trade with the French on that train, especially the girls. The French franc is supposed to be worth 2¢ to us and we are paid on that basis. But to the French it is worth a trifle under a cent and they act accordingly. So our officers began to bring out what they had to spare. Cigarettes went for 50 francs a pack, gum for 20 a package, candy bars for 20 each and one officer sold his field coat for 3000. Maurer sold his combat jacket for 500. One of the officers took off his O.D. shirt, but it didn't sell. Another had a German blanket which sold for 1000. Gee, what fun. Right across from us a couple of parents with two small children tried to buy something but the market was too turbulent for sedate middle-age people. However, Reinke gave the kids some gum and they were satisfied. When their train finally pulled out our men were richer by thousands of francs. It won't amount to anything though. Money has so little value over here.

This is a large camp with accommodations for about 40,000 homeward bound soldiers, I would estimate. Most of us live in tents that are winterized. That means there are floors and sides on the tents, the sides being about three feet high. These are much more comfortable than the tents at Camp San Antonio, but our tents here have neither light nor heat except whatever amounts of each the sun is able to donate to us. There are several buildings here made out of cement building blocks. These are used for PEx., mess halls, and wash rooms. We have wooden buildings used for administrative purposes. We have three open air theatres here, several beer gardens and three closed-in theatres. There are two Red Cross Snack bars for the E.M. [enlisted men] *and two for the officers. This place is located about twenty miles or so east of Marseille and a dozen or so miles from the Mediterranean...*

...if our stay here is average we shall probably pull out on the 16th. Give us a day to get loaded and then our time on the oceans will be determined by the type of ship we sail on. If we go by Army Transport we'll be ten days. If we go by Victory Ship it will be two weeks. If by Liberty ship it'll be eighteen days...this leaves the time of my being with you as somewhere between November first at the earliest and November 21st at the latest. I'll call you when I get to Devens [Fort Devens, Mass.] *and I'll let you know by telegram as to when I shall be arriving at Burlington. This is taking much longer than I thought it would but there is nothing I can do about it except be glad I am on my way and keep praying that I shall soon be with you.*

I hope you are not working too hard. I expect to be able to help you a great deal when I come home. I don't want this to mean I don't expect you to employ help if you can get it. Just that I shall be very glad to be with you and make life more enjoyable for you in every way, and for the kids too, the 12 point rascals and the newly evolved biped.

October 22, 1945

Dearest Doris:

We are now starting our third week here and we are starting our second month "down the pipe-line" that leads to home. However, indications are that we may load on a ship toward the end of this week or the beginning of next. We are losing our nurses and getting in 18 officers. This means they can now put us on any kind of a boat.

I preached to about 400 yesterday and I'm to preach again tonight. We have our services on Sunday with two or three chaplains taking part. There is a small chapel on the post where there are services every evening of the week but Saturday. I go there on Sunday evening and Friday. On Friday they do nothing but sing and as there are about 50 men they sing well. It feels good to go there and sing the songs I used to like so well when I was growing up, songs I haven't sung since my C.E. [Christian Endeavor] *days in Bangor.*

I wonder how Priscilla is developing as a singer. I hope she likes to sing and I hope she still takes piano lessons. We can have a lot of fun with music when I get home again.

October 26, 1945

Dear Doris:

I expect we load onto a Liberty Ship tomorrow and probably start on our journey homeward on Sunday [Oct. 28]. *This ship will take eighteen days. We sail for Boston. Expect your telephone to ring sometime after six o'clock and before ten any evening after*

November 14. There's a good chance I might get home for Thanksgiving.

Yours with love,
Jerry

The reunited family: Kenneth and Gerald standing behind Bruce, Priscilla, Anthony, and Doris

Epilogue

Dad made it home, apparently in time for Thanksgiving with the family, though Priscilla doesn't remember for sure. We all posed for our picture in a photographer's studio. I'm the toddler on Mother's lap; Kenneth stands beside Dad and behind Bruce and Priscilla. Lieutenant Edyth Grace Balsley took a lasting interest in the family and stayed in touch for years. She sent a party dress for Priscilla she still remembers. Every year in time for Christmas, we got a box of pears from Harry and David's Orchard in Oregon, courtesy of Lt. Balsley.

After leaving Army service, Dad served these parishes:

North Waterford, Maine	1946-1949
Scarboro, Maine	1949-1952
Mont Vernon, NH	1952-1953
Haverhill, NH	1953-1958
Hinsdale, NH	1958-1966
Milton, NH	1966-1970

He was in the Army Reserve with the rank of Major, and I remember his serving on active duty for a few weeks at Fort Devens, Mass. He was promoted to Lieutenant Colonel just before his reserve commitment was up, which he called being "kicked upstairs." Except in Milton, he always ministered to two churches at once: one of one to two hundred members, which provided a parsonage for the family to live in, and a smaller church a few miles away. He conducted worship at the smaller church at 8:30 or 9:00 am, and then drove to the larger church for the 11:00 service. He used to say the early congregation got his sermon "fresh," and the later group heard it "polished."

Uncle Charles's wife, Florence, died a few years after the war; I have no memory of her, nor of Dad's oldest sister, Caroline, who had been a missionary in Africa. We visited back and forth with Aunt Gladys's family all through my childhood. Uncle Percy Craven managed the family finances himself, even doing the grocery shopping. When Sally was old enough to drive, Percy bought her a car and paid for her driving lessons, but Gladys never drove. When Percy died, Gladys found she was well provided for, but until then

she had no idea of their financial position.
My uncle Carroll Jr. ran the farm after Grandpa Leach died; his son Allen, Allen's son Billy, and their wives run it now. The land has now been in the family for two centuries. Aunt Edna worked as a physical therapist and also taught school for some years. Her husband, Alphonse Paré, worked as a civilian electronics technician during and after the war at the Portsmouth (NH) Naval Yard, and had an electronics repair business on the side. I went to his 90th birthday celebration at a lobster restaurant on the Maine coast.
After Dad retired from the ministry, he and Mother moved from Milton, NH, to a mobile home they bought and set up permanently on Priscilla's husband's property in Barre, Vt. Priscilla lives in that mobile home today. Dad died of prostate cancer in 1975, six weeks after my marriage to Anne Marie Thompson. He made it to the wedding and talked with many friends and relatives, who could enjoy seeing him without the shadow of knowing it would be the last time. Mother remarried three years later to Jim Willis, a wonderful man they had known in one of Dad's earliest parishes, when both couples were young parents. Jim lost his wife unexpectedly, and after a suitable period he contacted Mother. Jim had five grown children by his first wife, so including grandchildren, the combined family was quite a brood. Over forty people attended a family reunion at their house in Beckett, Mass. They had almost ten years together, and then Mother died after a week in hospital. Jim lived well past his 90th birthday.

Sources

Chaplain Gerald Miller's original letters have been donated to the Veterans History Project at the Library of Congress. I kept photocopies, some 900 pages.

The New York Times Complete World War II: the coverage from the battlefields to the home front. New York, Black Dog & Leventhal Publishers, 2016. Useful for relating progress of the war in general to the events in Gerald's letters.

Prefer, Nathan N. *The Conquering Ninth: the Ninth U.S. Army in World War II.* Philadelphia, Casemate Publications, c2020. Confirms and coordinates the actions of units supported by the 111th Evacuation Hospital in Europe.

About the Author

Anthony Gerald Miller was born in 1944, shortly before his father, Reverend Gerald Miller, shipped to Europe as a chaplain in the U.S. Army. After the war, the family moved around Maine and New Hampshire each time Gerald was called to a new parish. His parents and three older siblings were the constants in his life as he had to make a new set of school friends every few years. After twelve years as the "baby" of the family, he became big brother to the fifth sibling, Paul. Anthony attended several different public school systems and won admission as a high-school junior to Mount Hermon School, a private boys' boarding school founded by evangelist Dwight L. Moody. He served as an Army translator in Viet Nam, then studied music at Harvard and library science at Columbia University.

After finishing his Master of Arts in Library Service degree in 1973, Anthony was hired as a music librarian in the New York Public Library's performing arts branch at Lincoln Center. He also cataloged music recordings in the Music Library of the State University of New York at Buffalo before landing in 1978 at the Atlanta Public Library's Central Library as Music Subject Specialist. He worked there through several administrations and reorganizations, retiring in 2013.

In 2004, at his brother Bruce's suggestion, Anthony excerpted, typed up, printed and handed out a compilation of their father's letters from World War II at a family reunion that summer. Now he has added extensive notes, giving context and relating Gerald's experiences to the war's general progress.

Anthony and his wife, Anne Marie Miller, have three children and seven grandchildren, and live near Athens, Georgia, with a large black cat who adopted them.